Table of Contents

Math Manipulatives

Below are suggested materials to support the activities in this book and help you create a stimulating math environment in your home. Most of these can be purchased at a teacher store.

paper
two-pocket folders
Unifix cubes
pattern blocks
number line
hundred chart
place value mat
base-ten blocks
geoboard and
   rubber bands
calendar
analog clock
digital clock
"play" clock

pencils
resealable plastic bags
envelopes
play money (or real)
money chart
ice-cream sticks
buttons
sea shells
marbles
uncooked pasta
beans
paper clips
collections of other
   small objects

markers
crayons
playground chalk
double-sided counters
flash cards
attribute blocks
tangrams
calculator
game pieces
dice
spinners

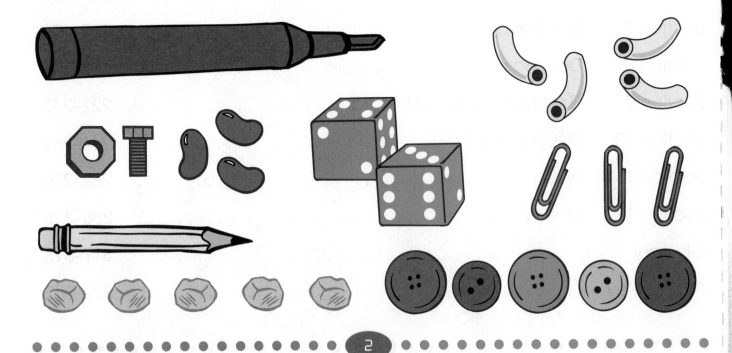

Section 1

Place Value

Name _____

Outstanding Elephant Math

Connect the dots in order from least to greatest.

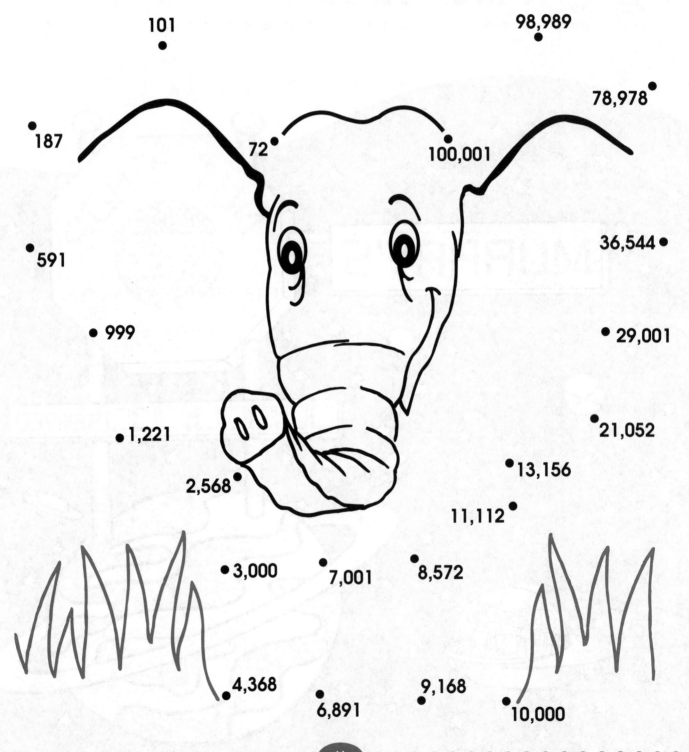

Name _____

Place Value Riddles

Using the clues below, choose the number each riddle describes. As you read, draw an **X** on all the numbers that do not fit the clue. After you have read all the clues for each riddle, there should be only one number left.

| 305 | 3005 | 35 | 3050 | 3500 | | 769 | 6,379 | 973 | 3,796 | 3,691 |

1. I am greater than 300.
2. I have a 5 in the ones place.
3. I have a zero in the hundreds place.
4. Circle the number.

1. I have a number greater than 6 in the tens place.
2. I am between 3,000 and 4,000.
3. I have a 6 in the hundreds place.
4. Circle the number.

| 423 | 4023 | 324 | 3,412 | 2,143 | | 4058 | 584 | 845 | 5048 | 8540 |

1. I have a 2 in the tens place.
2. I am less than 1,000.
3. I have a 4 in the ones place.
4. Circle the number.

1. I have a 4 in the tens place.
2. I am greater than 5,000.
3. I have a 0 in the hundreds place.
4. Circle the number.

Now, fold a blank sheet of paper in half three times to create eight boxes. Create eight of these place value riddles. You may want to use words like these when writing your clues:

ones, tens, hundreds, thousands place
greater than
less than
have a ___ somewhere

4-3-2-1-Blast Off!

Color these spaces red:

- three thousand five
- 1,000 less than 3,128
- six thousand eight hundred eighty-nine
- 100 more than 618,665
- 10 less than 2,981
- fifty-nine thousand two

Color these spaces blue:

- 10 less than 4,786
- eight thousand six hundred two
- 1,000 less than 638,961
- two thousand four hundred fifty-one
- 100 more than 81,136
- 10,000 less than 48,472

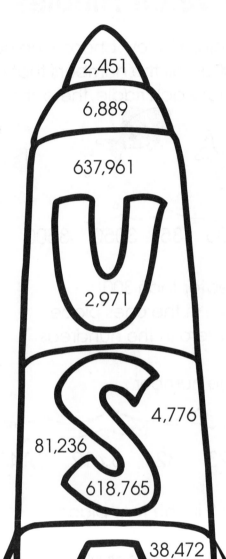

Name _Sammy_

Place Value Puzzles

Complete the puzzle.

ACROSS

A. 3 thousand 5 hundred 9
C. 100 less than 8,754
E. one hundred sixty-two
G. seven hundred eighty-two
I. 100, 150, 200, ___
J. 1, 2, 3, 4, 5 mixed up
L. two
M. 100 less than 9,704
O. three zeros
P. eight
Q. 10,000 more than 56,480
R. one
S. 1 ten, 1 one

DOWN

A. 10 more than 3,769
B. ninety-one
C. 28 backwards
D. 5 hundreds, 8 tens, 5 ones
F. 100 less than 773
H. 5, 10, 15, 20, ___
I. ten less than 24,684
K. 2 tens, 9 ones
L. two thousand one
N. 1000, 2000, 3000, _____
P. eight hundreds, 6 tens, 1 one

Name _____

Write That Number

Write the numeral form for each number.

 342

Example: three hundred forty-two = 342

1. six hundred fifty thousand, two hundred twenty-five _____

2. nine hundred ninety-nine thousand, nine hundred ninety-nine _____

3. one hundred six thousand, four hundred thirty-seven _____

4. three hundred fifty-six thousand, two hundred two _____

5. Write the number that is two more than 356,909. _____

6. Write the number that is five less than 448,394. _____

7. Write the number that is ten more than 285,634. _____

8. Write the number that is ten less than 395,025. _____

Write the following numbers in word form.

9. 3,208 _____

10. 13,656 _____

Name _____

Place Value

$$1\,,2\,3\,4\,,5\,6\,7$$

millions · hundred thousands · ten thousands · thousands · hundreds · tens · ones

Write each numeral in its correct place.

1. The number 8,672,019 has:

_____ thousands   _____ ten   _____ hundred thousands

_____ millions   _____ ones   _____ ten thousands

_____ hundreds

2. What number has:

6 ones   3 millions   9 tens

7 hundreds   4 ten thousands   8 thousands

5 hundred thousands

The number is _____ .

3. The number 6,792,510 has:

_____ ten thousands   _____ millions   _____ hundreds

_____ ones   _____ thousands   _____ ten

_____ hundred thousands

4. What number has:

5 millions   3 tens   6 thousands

1 hundred   8 ten thousands   4 ones

0 hundred thousands

The number is _____ .

Place Value

Name _____

Big Numbers Game

Preparation: Cut out the spinners, number cards and gameboard pattern on the next page. Glue the spinners and gameboard onto cardboard and let them dry. Cut them out. Attach a large paper clip or safety pin to the spinner base with a brad or paper fastener. The paper clip (or safety pin) should spin freely.

Give each player one set of ten cards. Also, each player will need a marker and a copy of the gameboard.

Rules: This game involves 2–6 players. The first player is the one who has the most letters in his/her last name. Play goes in a clockwise direction.

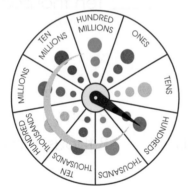 

Directions: Player One spins the place value spinner first. Then, he/she spins the numerical spinner. Player One then puts the number marker on the place indicated by the spinner. (For example, if Player One spins hundreds on the place value spinner and 8 on the numerical spinner, he/she should put an 8 number marker in the hundreds place on the gameboard.) If the number shown on either spinner is already filled on the board, Player One loses his/her turn. The first player who fills all the spaces on his/her board and is able to read the number aloud is the winner.

HUNDRED MILLIONS	TEN MILLIONS	MILLIONS	HUNDRED THOUSANDS	TEN THOUSANDS	THOUSANDS	HUNDREDS	TENS	ONES
						8		

Game Parts for Big Numbers Game

ONES	
TENS	
HUNDREDS	
THOUSANDS	
TEN THOUSANDS	
HUNDRED THOUSANDS	
MILLIONS	
TEN MILLIONS	
HUNDRED MILLIONS	

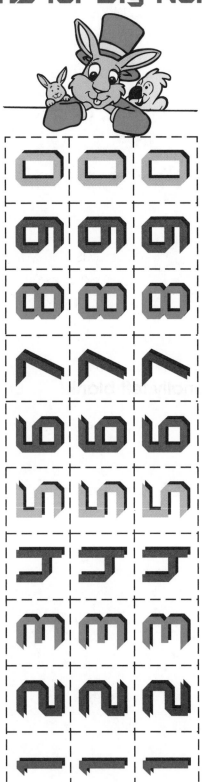

Numeral Spinner

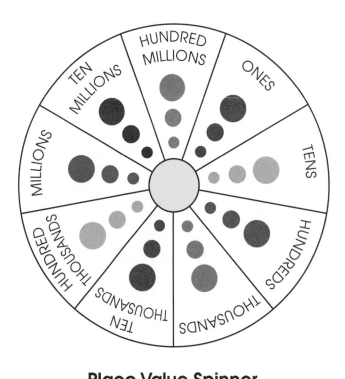

Place Value Spinner

This page intentionally left blank.

Estimate by Rounding Numbers

Estimate by rounding numbers to different place values. Use these rules.

Example: Round 283 to the nearest hundred.

- Find the digit in the place to be rounded.

   2̣83

- Now, look at the digit to its right.

   2̣83

- If the digit to the right is less than 5, the
digit being rounded remains the same.

- If the digit to the right is 5 or more, the digit being
rounded is increased by 1.

   2̣83   Rounds to 300

- Digits to the right of the place to be rounded
become 0's. Digits to the left remain the same.

Examples: Round 4,385 . . .

to the nearest thousand	to the nearest hundred	to the nearest ten
4,385	4,385	4,385
3 is less than 5.	8 is more than 5.	5 = 5.
The 4 stays the same.	The 3 is rounded up to 4.	The 8 is rounded up to 9.
4,000	4,400	4,390

Complete the table.

NUMBERS TO BE ROUNDED	ROUND TO THE NEAREST THOUSAND	NEAREST HUNDRED	NEAREST TEN
2,725			
10,942			
6,816			
2,309			
7,237			
959			

Round, Round, Round You Go

Round each number to the nearest ten.

45 _____   72 _____   61 _____   255 _____

27 _____   184 _____   43 _____   97 _____

Round each number to the nearest hundred.

562 _____   1,246 _____   761 _____   4,593 _____

347 _____   859 _____   238 _____   76 _____

Round each number to the nearest thousand.

6,543 _____   83,246 _____   3,741 _____   66,357 _____

7,219 _____   9,814 _____   2,166 _____   8,344 _____

Round each number to the nearest ten thousand.

32,467 _____   871,362 _____   334,212 _____

57,891 _____   45,621 _____   79,356 _____

Round each number to the nearest hundred thousand.

116,349 _____   946,477 _____   732,166 _____

762,887 _____   365,851 _____   225,631 _____

Round each number to the nearest million.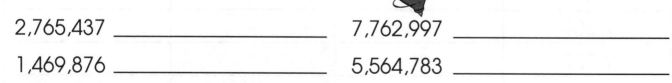

2,765,437 _____   7,762,997 _____

1,469,876 _____   5,564,783 _____

14,537,123 _____   4,117,655 _____

Name _____

The First State

What state is known as the first state? Follow the directions below to find out.

1. If 31,842 rounded to the nearest thousand is 31,000, put an **A** above number 2.

2. If 62 rounded to the nearest ten is 60, put an **E** above number 2 .

3. If 4,234 rounded to the nearest hundred is 4,200, put an **R** above number 7.

4. If 677 rounded to the nearest hundred is 600, put an **L** above number 3.

5. If 344 rounded to the nearest ten is 350, put an **E** above number 5.

6. If 5,599 rounded to the nearest thousand is 6,000, put an **A** above number 4.

7. If 1,549 rounded to the nearest hundred is 1,500, put an **A** above number 6.

8. If 885 rounded to the nearest hundred is 800, put a **W** above number 2.

9. If 521 rounded to the nearest ten is 520, put an **E** above number 8.

10. If 74 rounded to the nearest ten is 80, put an **R** above number 6.

11. If 3,291 rounded to the nearest thousand is 3,000, put an **L** above number 3.

12. If 248 rounded to the nearest hundred is 300, put an **R** above number 4.

13. If 615 rounded to the nearest ten is 620, put a **D** above number 1.

14. If 188 rounded to the nearest ten is 200, put a **W** above number 1.

15. If 6,817 rounded to the nearest thousand is 7,000, put a **W** above number 5.

**Peach Blossom
State Flower**

**Blue Hen Chicken
State Bird**

**Fort Christina—site of the first
state's first permanent settlement.
Built by the Swedes and Finns.**

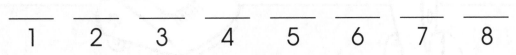

___ ___ ___ ___ ___ ___ ___ ___
 1   2   3   4   5   6   7   8

Section 2

Addition

Dial-A-Word

Use the phone pad to calculate the "value" of the words.

Example: PHONE = 74663

PHONE = 7 + 4 + 6 + 6 + 3 = 26

(your name) = _____ = _____

CALCULATOR = _____ = _____

DICTIONARY = _____ = _____

PET TRICKS = _____ = _____

BASEBALL GAME = _____ = _____

COMPUTERS = _____ = _____

TENNIS SHOES = _____ = _____

ADDITION = _____ = _____

MENTAL MATH = _____ = _____

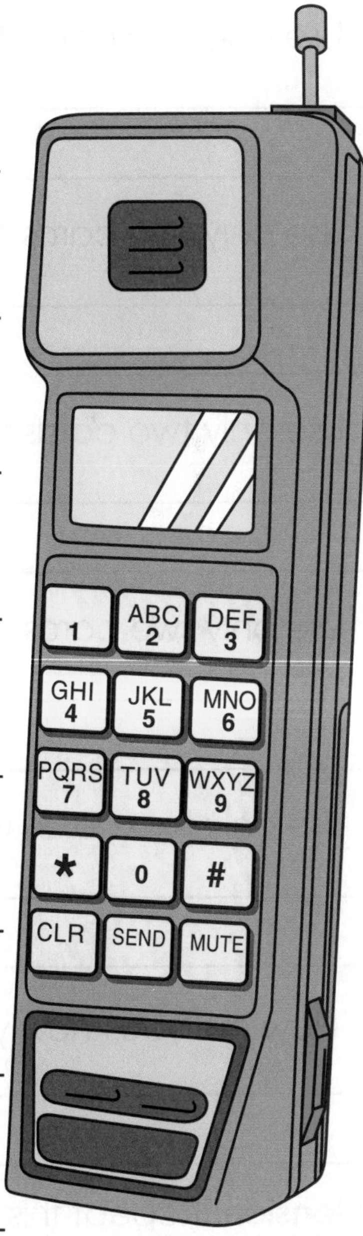

Using Number Concepts 2 7 5 4 8

Cut out the set of cards on the next page. Use them to form number sentences that answer the questions below.

1. Use only two cards to list all the ways you can make the sum of 10.

_____

_____

2. Use only two cards to list all the ways you can make the sum of 13.

_____

_____

3. Use only two cards to list all the ways you can make the sum of 16.

_____

_____

4. Use only two cards to list all the ways you can make the sum of 12.

_____

_____

5. Use only two cards to list all the ways you can make the sum of 15.

_____

_____

6. Use only two cards to list all the ways you can make the sum of 17.

_____

_____

7. How did you know you found all the ways?

_____

_____

Extension: Repeat this exercise using three cards to make each sum.

 Addition

Using Number Concepts

0	1	2	3
4	5	6	
7	8	9	10
	11	12	13
14	15	16	17
+	+	=	

This page intentionally left blank.

Mushrooming Addition

Follow the arrows to **add**.

Example: 52 + 28 = 80
28 + 91 = 119
119 + 80 = ?

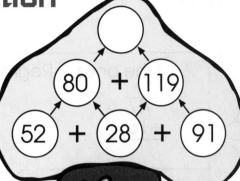

80 + 119
52 + 28 + 91

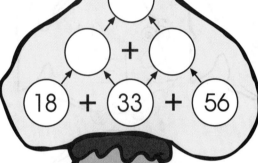

○ + ○
18 + 33 + 56

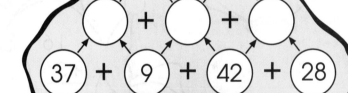

○ + ○
○ + ○ + ○
37 + 9 + 42 + 28

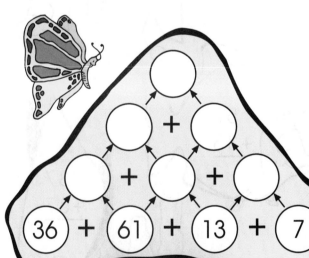

○ + ○
○ + ○ + ○
36 + 61 + 13 + 7

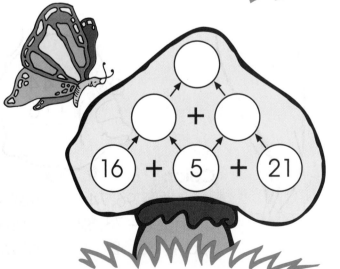

○ + ○
16 + 5 + 21

Name _____

Fishy Addition

28
+54

Add the ones.	Regroup, if needed.	Add the tens.
47 +18	47 +18 ___ 5	¹ 47 +18 ___ 65

26
+25

59
+18

34
+39

16
+36

13
+36

42
+24

67
+29

44
+16

57
+35

37
+37

27
+ 8

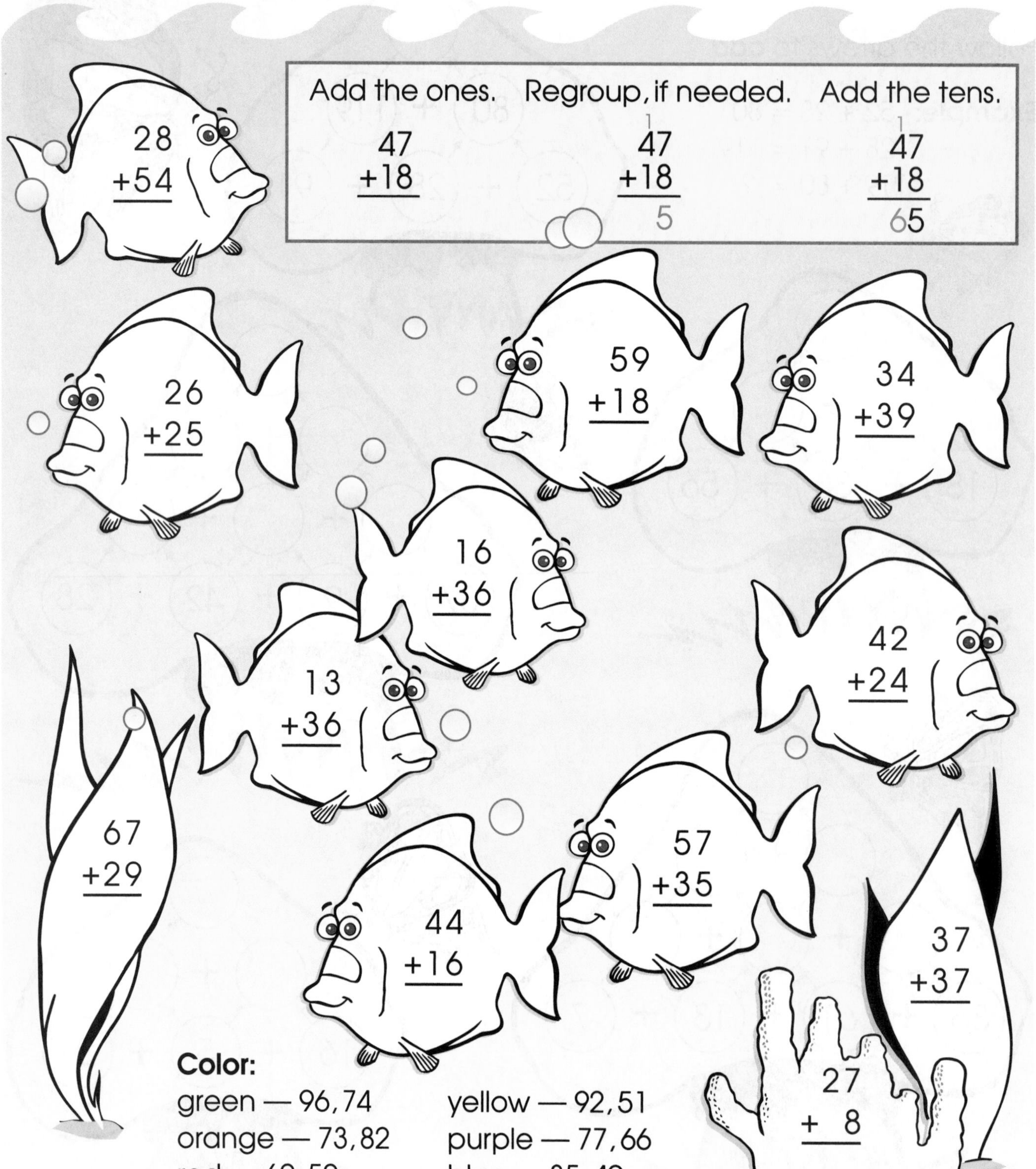

Color:

green — 96, 74
orange — 73, 82
red — 60, 52

yellow — 92, 51
purple — 77, 66
blue — 35, 49

Make the Windows Shine!

Add.

476 +319 795	248 +629 877	327 +544 871
572 +318 890	815 +177 992	527 +144 671

429 +343 772	462 +319 781	462 +529 991	648 +238 886
756 +127 883	563 +208 771	646 +248 894	924 + 66 990
628 +259 887	526 +347 873	927 + 46 973	765 +218 983

Addition Ace

Add. **Color** the ribbon according to the code below.

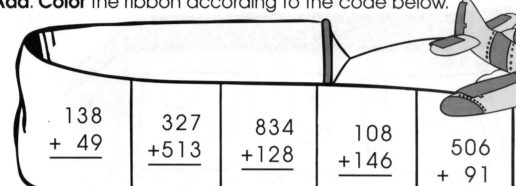

| 138
+ 49 | 327
+513 | 834
+128 | 108
+146 | 506
+ 91 | 249
+128 |

If the sum is in the:

100's — green	400's — blue	700's — pink
200's — yellow	500's — purple	800's — gold
300's — red	600's — orange	900's — silver

| 367
+424 | 724
+ 39 | 704
+283 | 691
+205 | 265
+319 |

| 432
+249 | 528
+349 | 924
+ 56 | 306
+248 | 226
+165 |

| 826
+164 | 328
+145 | 426
+261 | 747
+143 |

Space Shuttle Addition

Add the ones.	Regroup.	Add the tens and regroup.	Add the hundreds.
362 +439	¹ 362 +439 1	¹ ¹ 362 +439 01	¹ ¹ 362 +439 801

Add.

371 +439	629 +184	146 +587	264 +483	438 +290

347 +328	362 +459	528 +391	382 +249	327 +649

283 +346	409 +292		465 +193	566 +283

283 +519	423 +392

625 +246	498 +123

Underwater Addition

Add.

```
  446        476        509        251
+ 489      + 527      + 375      + 368
```

```
             708        438        334
           + 507      + 419      + 278
```

```
  464        589        288        811        609
+ 456      + 322      + 377      + 386      + 475
```

```
             531        810
           + 249      + 428
```

```
  831        445        211        230        319
+ 438      + 476      + 396      + 284      + 287
```

```
             714        767        911
           + 185      + 246      + 427
```

Let's Climb to the Top!

Add.

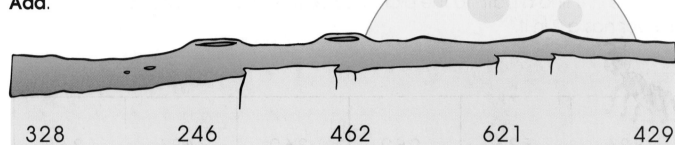

328 +449	246 +492	462 +781	621 +489	429 +636
	409 +736	921 + 87	562 +614	824 +597
	982 +220	207 +913		826 + 95
	547 +782	284 +493		506 +214
200 +489	684 +519	425 +594	536 +184	623 +192

Name _____

Picnic Problems

Help the ant find a path to the picnic. **Solve** the problems. **Shade** the box if an answer has a 9 in it.

836 + 90	536 +248	952 + 8	362 + 47	486 +293	368 +529
789 526 +214	2,846 +6,478	932 +365	374 +299	835 +552	956 874 + 65
4,768 +2,894	38 456 +3,894	4,507 +2,743	404 +289	1,843 +6,752	4,367 +3,574
639 + 77	587 342 +679	5,379 1,865 +2,348	450 +145	594 +278	459 +367
29 875 +2,341	387 29 +5,614	462 379 +248			

Grand Prix Addition

Solve each problem. Beginning at 7,000, run through this racetrack to find the path the race car took. When you reach 7,023, you're ready to exit and gas up for the next race.

3,536 +3,482 = 7,018	1,792 +5,225 = 7,021	3,838 +3,178 = 7,016	3,767 +3,248 = 7,015	1,874 +5,140 = 7,014	4,809 +2,204 = 7,013
3,561 +3,458 = 7,019	4,162 +2,858 = 7,020	3,771 +4,213 = 7,084	4,123 +2,887 = 7,010	5,879 +1,132 = 7,011	1,725 +5,287 = 7,012
3,544 +3,478 = 7,022	1,273 +5,748 = 7,021	2,435 +5,214 = 7,649	4,853 +2,156 = 7,009	3,589 +3,419 = 7,008	5,218 +1,789 = 7,007
5,997 +1,026 = 7,023	5,289 +1,713 = 7,002	3,698 +3,305 = 7,003	4,756 +2,248 = 7,004	4,248 +2,757 = 7,005	4,658 +2,348 = 7,006
4,853 +2,147 = 7,000	2,216 +4,785 = 7,001	1,157 +6,412 = 7,569	3,720 +3,698 = 7,418	3,612 +3,552 = 7,164	1,687 +5,662 = 7,359

Name _____

Gearing Up

Add the ones. Regroup.	Add the tens. Regroup.	Add the hundreds. Regroup.	Add the thousands. Regroup.
1 7,465 +4,978 ――― 3	1 1 7,465 +4,978 ――― 43	1 1 1 7,465 +4,978 ――― 443	1 1 1 7,465 +4,978 ――― 12,443

Solve the problems. **Color** each answer containing a **3**—blue, **4**—red and **5**—yellow.

1 1 1
2,549
+9,577
――――
13,126

1 1
6,456
+4,948
――――
10,404

1 1 1
3,849
+7,261
――――
11,110

1 1 1
6,843
+7,568
――――
14,411

1 1 1
7,767
+4,948
――――
12,715

1 1 1
5,678
+6,984
――――
12,662

1 1 1
2,698
+8,499
――――
11,197

1 1 1
9,224
+7,878
――――
17,102

1 1 1
9,764
+7,459
――――
17,223

1 1 1
8,796
+8,975
――――
17,771

1 1 1
6,591
+5,569
――――
12,160

1 1 1
9,653
+1,568
――――
11,221

1 1 1
9,853
+8,798
――――
18,651

Bubble Math

Add to solve the problems.

2,647
+3,281
5,928

3,426
+2,841
6,207

5,642
+1,819
7,461

4,629
+1,258
5,687

3,690
+2,434
6,124

6,241
+2,363
8,604

5,942
+1,829
7,771

4,625
+1,817
6,442

6,843
+2,391
9,234

4,826
+2,098
6,924

5,642
+2,919
8,561

2,641
+6,259
8,900

2,648
+1,923
3,571

8,465
+1,386
9,851

3,142
+2,639
5,781

9,124
+1,348
10,472

7,205
+1,839
9,044

2,643
+7,427
10,070

Bubble Blaster 2000

Name _____

Cotton Pickin' Math

Solve the problems.

```
  1 1                2                  2                                    1 1
 7,215            4,621              6,117             2,481              3,204
    62               35                 24             2,514                182
   141            1,318                315                 2                 23
+2,015            +    9            +2,136            +   43              +    5
───────          ───────           ───────           ───────            ───────
 9,433            5,983              8,592                                3,414
```

```
                                                                          3 2
 8,143               35             7,006               521                496
    60              242                242             3,134              8,172
   235                6                  9                64                 83
+1,423           +1,203            +   31             +  243             +  199
───────          ───────           ───────           ───────            ───────
                                                                         8,930
```

```
 6,201            5,242             4,162             6,425
   325              342               328                41
    41                8                41               324
+2,136           +   51            +  503             +    3
───────          ───────           ───────           ───────
```

```
 4,205            2,516             5,426
    81              310               310
     3               82               512
+  414           +    3            +    4
───────          ───────           ───────
```

Palindrome Sums

A **number palindrome** is similar to a word palindrome in that it reads the same backward or forward.

Examples:
75,457
1,689,861

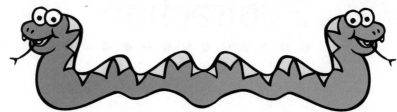

Create number palindromes using addition.

Your Number

To do this, choose any number:

652

_____

Then, **reverse** that number's digits:

256

_____

and **add** the two numbers together:

652 + 256 = 908

_____

If the sum is not a palindrome, **reverse** the digits in that sum and add as you did in the first step:

908 + 809 = 1717

_____

Continue in this manner until the sum is a palindrome.

1717 + 7171 = 8888

_____

_____

_____

_____

The example required three steps to produce a palindrome.
How many steps did it take for you to create a number palindrome?_____

Subtraction

20 - 16 =

8 - 5 = 3

8 - 1 = 7

Mountaintop Getaway

Solve the problems. **Find** a path to the cabin by shading in all answers that have a 3 in them.

			98 −52	46 −12	68 −17
	79 −53	65 −23	63 −31	86 −32	
59 −45	75 −64	67 −24	87 −54	55 −43	
87 −65	44 −32	57 −24	88 −25	75 −61	48 −26
69 −25	95 −24	48 −13	58 −16	35 −13	39 −17

SECRET PATHS

Name _____

Stay on Track

Add or **subtract**. **Write** each answer in the puzzle.

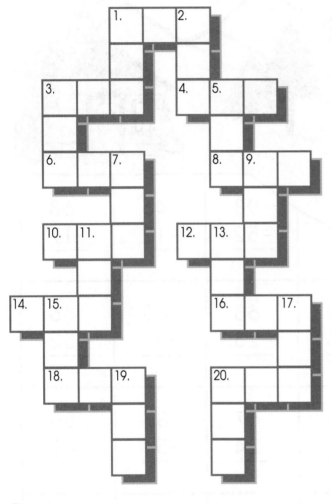

Across

1. 413
  +312

3. 102
  +415

4. 223
  +103

6. 131
  +253

8. 324
  +321

10. 207
   +222

12. 105
   +214

14. 315
   +400

16. 121
   +503

18. 451
   +421

20. 312
   +281

Down

1. 859
  −112

2. 985
  −402

3. 887
  −344

5. 789
  −583

7. 699
  −240

9. 589
  −100

11. 767
   −512

13. 497
   −321

15. 259
   −151

17. 974
   −511

19. 689
   −450

20. 797
   −236

Subtracting Two-Digit Numbers
With Regrouping

Step 1: Decide whether to regroup. In the ones column, 3 is less than 9 so,
regroup 4 tens 3 ones to 3 tens 13 ones.

$$\begin{array}{r} \overset{3}{\cancel{4}}\,13 \\ -\ 1\ 9 \\ \hline \end{array}$$

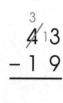

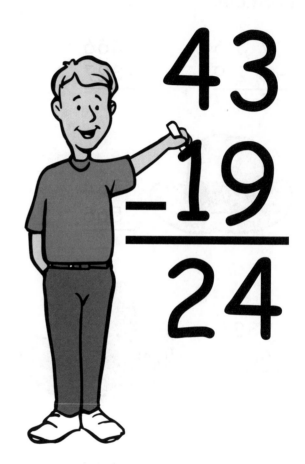

Step 2: Subtract the ones.

$$\begin{array}{r} \overset{3}{\cancel{4}}\,13 \\ -\ 1\ 9 \\ \hline 4 \end{array}$$

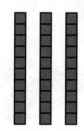 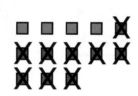

Step 3: Subtract the tens.

$$\begin{array}{r} \overset{3}{\cancel{4}}\,13 \\ -\ 1\ 9 \\ \hline 2\ 4 \end{array}$$

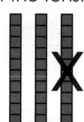 

Subtract to find the difference. **Regroup**, if needed.

67 −34	85 −12	86 −47	91 −48	44 −27	61 −34
32 −14	97 −36	60 −45	52 −22	71 −19	83 −15

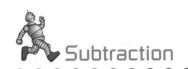

Name _____

Hats, Hats, Hats

Subtract to find the difference. If the bottom number is larger than the top number in a column, you will need to regroup from the column to the left.

Example:

$$\begin{array}{r} 7\ \overset{2}{\cancel{3}}{}^{16} \\ -\ 6\ 2\ 9 \\ \hline 1\ 0\ 7 \end{array}$$

$$\begin{array}{r} 466 \\ -327 \\ \hline \end{array}$$

$$\begin{array}{r} 837 \\ -529 \\ \hline \end{array}$$

$$\begin{array}{r} 742 \\ -428 \\ \hline \end{array}$$

$$\begin{array}{r} 784 \\ -565 \\ \hline \end{array}$$

$$\begin{array}{r} 673 \\ -458 \\ \hline \end{array}$$

$$\begin{array}{r} 648 \\ -426 \\ \hline \end{array}$$

$$\begin{array}{r} 982 \\ -665 \\ \hline \end{array}$$

$$\begin{array}{r} 947 \\ -729 \\ \hline \end{array}$$

$$\begin{array}{r} 543 \\ -426 \\ \hline \end{array}$$

$$\begin{array}{r} 928 \\ -619 \\ \hline \end{array}$$

$$\begin{array}{r} 847 \\ -628 \\ \hline \end{array}$$

$$\begin{array}{r} 427 \\ -318 \\ \hline \end{array}$$

$$\begin{array}{r} 524 \\ -318 \\ \hline \end{array}$$

$$\begin{array}{r} 245 \\ -126 \\ \hline \end{array}$$

$$\begin{array}{r} 852 \\ -328 \\ \hline \end{array}$$

$$\begin{array}{r} 545 \\ -221 \\ \hline \end{array}$$

Subtraction

Soaring to the Stars

Connect the dots in order and form two stars. Begin one star with the subtraction problem whose difference is 100 and end with the problem whose difference is 109. Begin the other star with 110 and end with 120. Then, **color** the pictures.

953
−839

774
−658

493
−378

364
−247

751
−638

844
−726

839
−728

570
−458

446
−327

384
−279

383
−273

696
−576

590
−487

575
−471

653
−547

493
−386

359
−257

862
−754

190
− 89

359
−259

585
−476

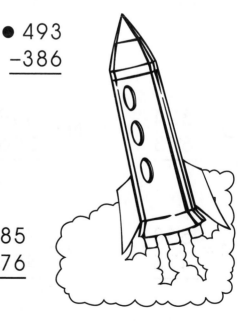

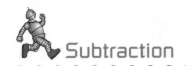

Name _____

Dino-Code

How is a T-Rex like an explosion?
To find out, **solve** the following problems and **write** the matching letter above each answer on the blanks.

He's . . . $\overline{\hspace{1em}}_{195}$ $\overline{\hspace{1em}}_{185}$ $\overline{\hspace{1em}}_{92}$ $\overline{\hspace{1em}}_{92}$ $\overline{\hspace{1em}}_{171}$ $\overline{\hspace{1em}}_{195}$

$\overline{\hspace{1em}}_{265}$ $\overline{\hspace{1em}}_{74}$ $\overline{\hspace{1em}}_{183}$ $\overline{\hspace{1em}}_{171}$ — $\overline{\hspace{1em}}_{93}$ $\overline{\hspace{1em}}_{74}$ $\overline{\hspace{1em}}_{45}$ $\overline{\hspace{1em}}_{181}$ $\overline{\hspace{1em}}_{191}$!

Remember to regroup when the bottom number is larger than the top number in a column.

$$F = \begin{array}{r} 348 \\ -153 \\ \hline \end{array}$$

$$L = \begin{array}{r} 765 \\ -673 \\ \hline \end{array}$$

$$G = \begin{array}{r} 427 \\ -382 \\ \hline \end{array}$$

$$T = \begin{array}{r} 637 \\ -446 \\ \hline \end{array}$$

$$H = \begin{array}{r} 878 \\ -697 \\ \hline \end{array}$$

$$U = \begin{array}{r} 548 \\ -363 \\ \hline \end{array}$$

$$O = \begin{array}{r} 824 \\ -653 \\ \hline \end{array}$$

$$N = \begin{array}{r} 439 \\ -256 \\ \hline \end{array}$$

$$I = \begin{array}{r} 447 \\ -373 \\ \hline \end{array}$$

$$M = \begin{array}{r} 568 \\ -475 \\ \hline \end{array}$$

$$D = \begin{array}{r} 748 \\ -483 \\ \hline \end{array}$$

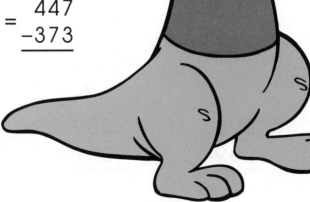

Name _____

Paint by Number

Solve each problem. **Color** each shape according to the key below.

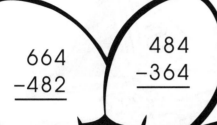

664
−482

484
−364

548
−283

614
−453

904
−392

629
−583

563
−382

732
−561

926
−564

642
−462

705
−493

529
−364

635
−573

439
−275

529
−373

853
−522

513
−321

328
−182

896
−145

626
−394

843
−392

If the difference in
the tens column is:

1 — blue
2 — blue
3 — orange
4 — yellow
5 — orange
6 — red
7 — yellow
8 — blue
9 — orange

Name _____

Sailing Through Subtraction

Subtract, regrouping when needed.

Example:

```
    7 14
  8 5 12
 -4 6 4
 ------
  3 8 8
```

542 −383	638 −453	836 −478	737 −448
243 −154	567 −384	984 −643	468 −399
524 −342	674 −495	374 −185	246 −158
	736 −557	642 −557	435 −286

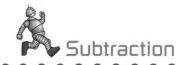
Gobble, Gobble

Solve each problem. **Color** the picture according to the key below. If the answer has a **3** in it, color it orange, **4**—red, **5**—purple, **6**—brown, **7**—yellow, **8**—blue and **9**—green. Remember to regroup when needed.

$$\begin{array}{r} 721 \\ -539 \\ \hline \end{array}$$

$$\begin{array}{r} 631 \\ -299 \\ \hline \end{array}$$

$$\begin{array}{r} 563 \\ -375 \\ \hline \end{array}$$

$$\begin{array}{r} 912 \\ -195 \\ \hline \end{array}$$

$$\begin{array}{r} 441 \\ -269 \\ \hline \end{array}$$

$$\begin{array}{r} 512 \\ -387 \\ \hline \end{array}$$

$$\begin{array}{r} 724 \\ -199 \\ \hline \end{array}$$

$$\begin{array}{r} 921 \\ -497 \\ \hline \end{array}$$

$$\begin{array}{r} 603 \\ -487 \\ \hline \end{array}$$

$$\begin{array}{r} 632 \\ -491 \\ \hline \end{array}$$

$$\begin{array}{r} 728 \\ -429 \\ \hline \end{array}$$

$$\begin{array}{r} 818 \\ -689 \\ \hline \end{array}$$

Round and Round She Goes

When regrouping with zeros follow these steps:

1. 7 is larger than 0. Go to the tens
   column to regroup. Since there is a
   0 in that column, you can't regroup.
   Go to the hundreds column.

```
    2
    3̸ 0 0
  - 1 4 7
```

2. Take one hundred away. Move it to
   the tens column.

```
    2
    3̸ 10 0
  - 1 4 7
```

3. Regroup the tens column by
   subtracting one ten and adding
   that ten to the ones column.

```
    2  9
    3̸ 1̸0 10
  - 1 4  7
```

4. Now, subtract, starting at the ones
   column.

```
    2  9
    3̸ 1̸0 10
  - 1 4  7
  ───────────
    1 5  3
```

800 −736	400 −243	900 −623
200 − 82	700 −543	800 −746
400 −278	600 −432	900 −824
500 −248	400 −365	300 −284

Name _____

 Subtraction

Jungle Math

Solve these problems.

Across

2. 517
  −228

7. 535
  −248

9. 561
  −247

3. 428
  −249

8. 857
  −389

5. 824
  −247

4. 562
  −274

Down

1. 421
  −342

6. 921
  −346

2. 627
  −348

7. 926
  −718

5. 924
  −348

3. 362
  −194

8. 721
  −240

6. 923
  −346

4. 582
  −346

10. 768
  −292

Name _____

Timely Zeros

Subtract.

```
  300        803        504
 -189       -324       -362
 _____      _____      _____
```

```
  900        800        702
 -648       -724       -561
 _____      _____      _____
```

```
  200        600        500        807        406
 -149       -476       -362       -298       -328
 _____      _____      _____      _____      _____
```

```
  300        600        700        308        500
 -243       -421       -348       -189       -384
 _____      _____      _____      _____      _____
```

```
             302        600        400
            -195       -247       -108
            _____      _____      _____
```

```
             205                   308
            -148                  -189
            _____                 _____
```

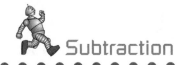

Name _____

Subtraction Maze

Solve the problems. Remember to regroup, when needed.

4,172	6,723	547	834	562	7,146
−1,536	−2,586	−259	−463	−325	−3,498

9,427	8,149	5,389	421	7,456	818
−6,648	−5,372	−1,652	−275	−3,724	−639

772	6,529	5,379	6,275	5,612	8,355
−586	−4,538	−2,835	−3,761	−1,505	−5,366

Shade in the answers from above to find the path.

	2,514	288	186	3,732	2,989
	2,779	156	1,901	2,414	4,137
3,748	3,337	2,777	371	179	1,991
3,048	3,737	146	2,717		
679	237	374	4,107		
886	2,636	2,544	3,648		

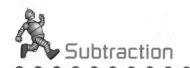

Name _____

High Class Math

Solve these problems.

	3,270 −1,529	8,248 −1,513	

| 7,648
−3,291 | 4,321
−1,809 | 8,241
−3,516 | 3,002
−1,231 | 9,200
−3,146 |

| 5,017
−2,408 | 8,254
−3,187 | 7,265
−2,134 | 3,846
−1,359 | 8,006
−3,084 |

| 3,084
−1,926 | 6,265
−4,189 | 4,824
−1,913 | 6,205
−1,054 | 5,253
−4,428 |

| 9,205
−3,187 | 5,809
−3,913 | 5,642
−2,408 |

Name _____

Kite Craze!

Subtract.

8,794 −6,428	9,643 −8,825

8,825 −7,436	5,648 −3,929

7,005 −6,223	8,416 −3,509	4,162 −2,840	6,514 −3,282

5,436 −2,924	9,246 −8,518	4,862 −3,946	9,486 −6,294

9,085 −6,241	8,462 −6,391

7,643 −6,521	6,430 −4,252

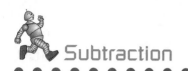
Subtraction on Stage!

Subtract.

5,648 −2,425	2,148 − 825

7,641 −5,246	7,648 −3,289	5,408 −1,291	8,209 −4,182

8,419 −2,182	6,249 −1,526	6,428 −4,159	4,287 −2,492

7,645 −2,826	2,016 −1,021	8,247 −6,459	9,047 −6,152

5,231
−1,642

7,689
−2,845

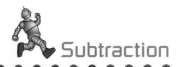

Subtraction Search

Solve each problem. **Find** the answer in the chart and **circle** it. The answers may go in any direction.

2	1	6	3	2	7	5
6	3	3	2	1	0	8
2	2	1	6	3	3	4
0	2	2	6	5	0	6
8	5	4	2	0	8	7
8	9	0	6	1	5	6
3	2	8	4	4	2	1
8	3	4	8	8	5	0
8	1	9	8	7	2	9
3	4	5	8	5	6	7
8	1	3	7	0	4	2
9	3	2	1	7	0	2

6,003 −2,737	5,040 −3,338	9,000 −5,725
7,200 −4,356	3,406 −1,298	5,602 −3,138
7,006 −5,429	3,006 −2,798	3,605 −2,718
5,904 −3,917	5,039 −1,954	8,704 −2,496

4,081 −3,594	6,508 − 399	5,039 −2,467	9,006 − 575	5,001 −2,351
	8,002 −5,686	6,058 −2,175	9,504 −7,368	7,290 −1,801

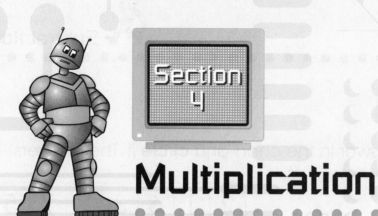

Section 4

Multiplication

Name _____

Skipping Through the Tens

Skip count by tens. Begin with the number on the first line. **Write** each number that follows.

0, 10 , 20 , 30 , 40 50 , 60 , 70 , 80 , 90 , 100

3, 13 , 23 33 , 43 , 53 , 63 , 73 , 83 , 93 , 103

1, 11 , 21 , 31 , 41 , 51 , 61 , 71 , 81 , 91 , 101

8, 18 , 28 38 , 48 , 58 , 68 , 78 , 88 , 98 , 108

6, 16 , 26 , 36 , 46 , 56 , 66 , 76 , 86 , 96 , 106

4, 14 , 24 34 , 44 54 , 64 , 74 , 84 , 94 , 104

2, 12 , 22 32 , 42 52 62 , 72 , 82 , 92 , 102

5, 15 , 25 35 , 45 , 55 , 65 , 75 , 85 , 95 , 105

7, 17 , 27 , 37 , 47 , 57 67 , 77 , 87 , 97 , 107

9, 19 , 29 , 39 , 49 59 , 69 , 79 , 89 , 99 , 109

What is ten more than . . . ?

26	36	29	39
44	54	77	87
53	63	91	101
24	34	49	59
66	76	35	45
54	64	82	92

Name _____

Counting to 100

Skip count to 100.

By twos:

2	4	6	8	10	12	14	16	18	20	22	24	26	28
30	32	34	36	38	40	42	44	46	48	50	52	54	56
58	60	62	64	66	68	70	72	74	76	78	80	82	84
86	88	90	92	94	96	98	100						

By threes:

3	6				21						39	
			57						75			
	90			102								

By fours:

4	8							40				
60						88			100			

On another sheet of paper, count by fives to 100. Then, count by sixes.

Count the Legs!

Multiplication is a quick way to add. For example, count the legs of the horses below. They each have 4 legs. You could add 4 + 4 + 4. But it is quicker to say that there are 3 groups of 4 legs. In multiplication, that is 3 x 4.
Multiply to find the number of legs. **Write** each problem twice.

__3__ horses x __12__ legs = __36__

__3__ x __12__ = __36__

__3__ ostriches x __6__ legs = __16__

__3__ x __6__ = __16__

_____ insects x _____ legs = _____

_____ x _____ = _____

_____ stools x _____ legs = _____

_____ x _____ = _____

_____ cows x _____ legs = _____

_____ x _____ = _____

_____ birds x _____ legs = _____

_____ x _____ = _____

Name _____

Fact Snacks

Directions: Ask an adult for a paper plate and a couple of snacks, such as popcorn, pretzels, candy corn or chocolate-covered candies. Arrange the snacks into sets, such as five sets of 5 or nine sets of 3.

Now, **add** the sets together. **Write** the related fact. Use the snack manipulatives to **answer** the following multiplication problems. Group the snacks into sets with the number shown in each set.

$4 \times 2 =$ 4 sets with 2 in each set = 8

1. 3 $\times 2$	2. 5 $\times 3$	3. 1 $\times 7$	4. 2 $\times 9$	5. 6 $\times 6$
6. 7 $\times 4$	7. 8 $\times 5$	8. 3 $\times 4$	9. 6 $\times 7$	10. 10 $\times 2$
11. 1 $\times 3$	12. 4 $\times 8$	13. 9 $\times 2$	14. 3 $\times 3$	15. 5 $\times 7$

After you **answer** and **check** the problems, enjoy the tasty fact snacks.

Name _____

Multiplying

Numbers to be multiplied together are called **factors**. The answer is the **product**.
Example: 3 x 6

1. The first factor tells how many groups there are.
   There are 3 groups.
2. The second factor tells how many are in each group. There are 6 in each group.

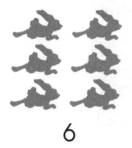  

3 groups of 6 equal 18.
3 x 6 = 18

$$6 \quad + \quad 6 \quad + \quad 6 \quad = 18$$

Some helpful hints to remember when multiplying:

- When you multiply by 0, the product is always 0. **Example:** 0 x 7 = 0
- When you multiply by 1, the product is always the factor being multiplied. **Example:** 1 x 12 = 12
- When multiplying by 2, double the factor other than 2. **Example:** 2 x 4 = 8
- The order doesn't matter when multiplying. **Example:** 5 x 3 = 15, 3 x 5 = 15
- When you multiply by 9, the digits in the product add up to 9 (until 9 x 11).
  Example: 7 x 9 = 63, 6 + 3 = 9
- When you multiply by 10, multiply by 1 and add 0 to the product. **Example:** 10 x 3 = 30
- When you multiply by 11, write the factor you are multiplying by twice (until 10).
  Example: 11 x 8 = 88

Multiply.

2	3	4	2	5	10	7	11	9
x9	x8	x9	x11	x9	x 5	x6	x 4	x7

8	7	8	10	4	5	8	3	7
x6	x12	x5	x10	x8	x5	x8	x6	x8

Name _____

Factor Fun

When you change the order of the factors, you have the same product.

Multiply.

7	3	6	5	2	3
x 3	x 7	x 5	x 6	x 3	x 2

4	6	2	9	8	4
x 6	x 4	x 9	x 2	x 4	x 8

7	2	3	6	9	4
x 2	x 7	x 6	x 3	x 4	x 9

8	3	5	2	9	3
x 3	x 8	x 2	x 5	x 3	x 9

Racing to the Finish

Multiply.

5 x 3	2 x 8	4 x 6	9 x 3	7 x 5	3 x 9
4 x 2	6 x 2	4 x 4	0 x 6	3 x 2	7 x 2
6 x 5	3 x 4	8 x 3	4 x 5	5 x 2	7 x 4
6 x 3	4 x 8	2 x 2	8 x 5	3 x 7	5 x 5
5 x 9	9 x 2	4 x 6	9 x 4		

Name _____

Climbing Granite Boulders!

Multiply.

9	6	3
x1	x1	x9

$3 \times 3 =$ _____

$4 \times 4 =$ _____

2	8	7	8
x9	x9	x8	x7

6	2
x7	x6

$9 \times 9 =$ _____

$6 \times 6 =$ _____

7	5
x7	x9

$9 \times 0 =$ _____

8
x8

5
x7

$8 \times 6 =$ _____ $3 \times 5 =$ _____

$4 \times 8 =$ _____ $2 \times 8 =$ _____

$7 \times 2 =$ _____ $3 \times 7 =$ _____

$3 \times 6 =$ _____

$6 \times 6 =$ _____

$5 \times 6 =$ _____ $4 \times 7 =$ _____

$2 \times 2 =$ _____ $4 \times 6 =$ _____

$2 \times 3 =$ _____ $0 \times 4 =$ _____

$6 \times 9 =$ _____ $7 \times 9 =$ _____

$5 \times 5 =$ _____

On the Right Track

Preparation: Glue the gameboard on page 63 onto poster board. Make a spinner, using the pattern below. Use a brass fastener to attach a paper clip to the center of the spinner so the clip spins freely.

Directions: This game involves two players. Players spin the spinner. The player with the highest number goes first. Players start at the station. Player One spins and moves his/her marker to the first space on the track that has a multiple of the number he/she spun. A multiple is the product or answer you would get when you multiply the number on the spinner by another number. If no multiple remains, Player One loses his/her turn. If a player puts his/her marker on a wrong multiple or skips a multiple, he/she must go back to the station. The first player to reach the end of the line is the winner.

This page intentionally left blank.

On the Right Track Gameboard

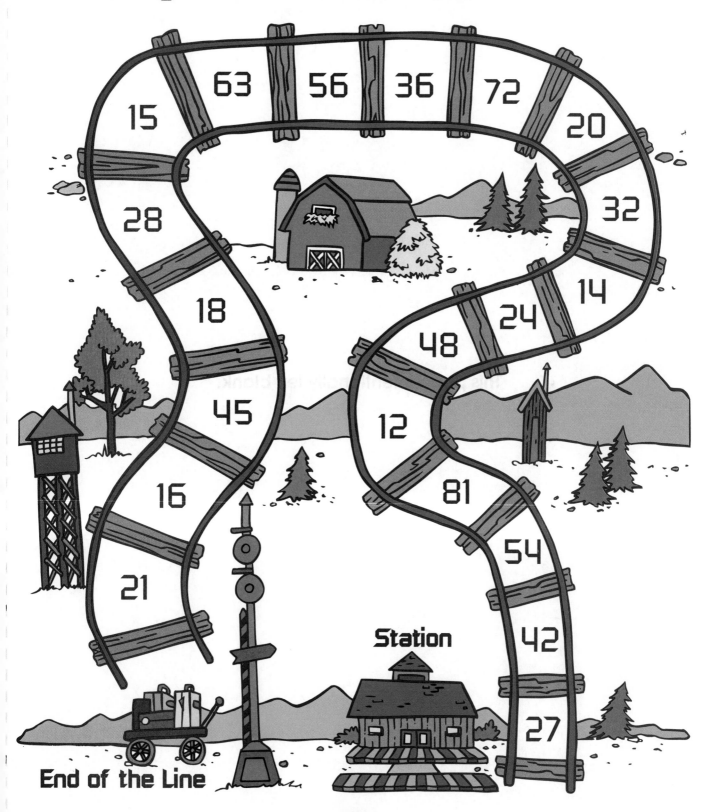

This page intentionally left blank.

Time To Multiply

Complete the table. Try to do it in less than 3 minutes.

X	0	1	2	3	4	5	6	7	8	9
0	0									
1										
2			4							
3										
4										
5						25				
6										
7										
8										
9										

Name _____

Double Trouble

Solve each multiplication problem. Below each answer, **write** the letter from the code that matches the answer. **Read** the coded question and **write** the answer in the space provided.

1	4	9	16	25	36	49	64	81	100	121	144
E	G	H	I	N	O	S	T	U	W	X	Y

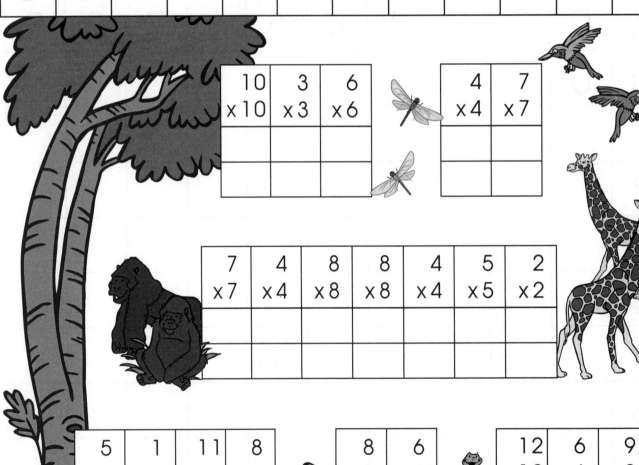

10 x10	3 x3	6 x6

4 x4	7 x7

7 x7	4 x4	8 x8	8 x8	4 x4	5 x5	2 x2

5 x5	1 x1	11 x11	8 x8

8 x8	6 x6

12 x12	6 x6	9 x9

?

Answer: _____

Crossnumber Fun

Write the word form of each product in the puzzle.

Across

3. 9 x 4 = _36_

8. 10 x 5 = _____

9. 2 x 9 = _____

10. 3 x 12 = _____

12. 7 x 11= _____

14. 4 x 10 = _____

15. 6 x 5 = _____

16. 0 x 7 = _____

Down

1. 7 x 8 = _____

2. 6 x 1 = _____

4. 2 x 5 = _____

5. 11 x 3 = _____

6. 5 x 1 = _____

7. 5 x 4 = _____

11. 12 x 8 = _____

13. 3 x 8 = _____

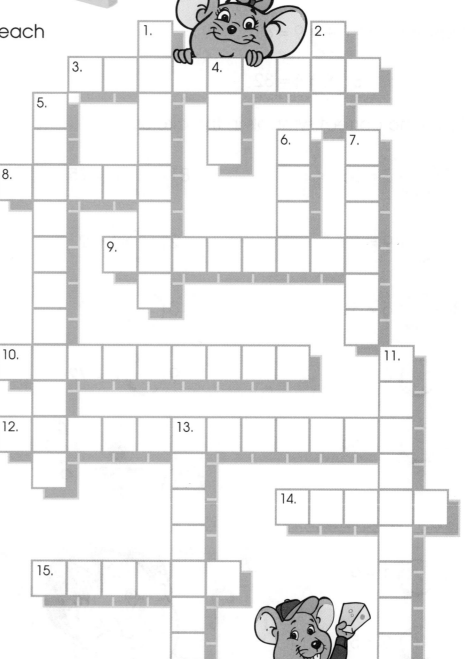

Hmm, What Should I Do?

Example: 52 (+) 9 = 61

8 (X) 4 = 32

Write the correct symbols in the circles.

7 ◯ 8 = 56   81 ◯ 6 = 75   55 ◯ 3 = 52

54 ◯ 9 = 6   2 ◯ 1 = 2   40 ◯ 2 = 38

36 ◯ 5 = 31   0 ◯ 2 = 2   8 ◯ 8 = 64

12 ◯ 6 = 18   9 ◯ 8 = 72   18 ◯ 5 = 23

72 ◯ 7 = 65   32 ◯ 5 = 37

0 ◯ 1 = 0   48 ◯ 6 = 8

9 ◯ 1 = 9   32 ◯ 4 = 8

45 ◯ 9 = 5   6 ◯ 7 = 42

Name _____

Wacky Waldo's Snow Show

Wacky Waldo's Snow Show is an exciting and fantastic sight. Waldo has trained whales and bears to skate together on the ice. There is a hockey game between a team of sharks and a pack of wolves. Elephants ride sleds down steep hills. Horses and buffaloes ski swiftly down mountains.

Write each problem and its answer.

 1 Wacky Waldo has 4 ice-skating whales. He has 4 times as many bears who ice skate. How many bears can ice skate?

_____ X _____ = _____

2 Waldo's Snow Show has 4 shows on Thursday, but it has 6 times as many on Saturday. How many shows are there on Saturday?

_____ X _____ = _____

3 The Sharks' hockey team has 3 great white sharks. It has 6 times as many tiger sharks. How many tiger sharks does it have?

_____ X _____ = _____

 4 The Wolves' hockey team has 4 gray wolves. It has 8 times as many red wolves. How many red wolves does it have?

_____ X _____ = _____

 5 Waldo taught 6 buffaloes to ski. He was able to teach 5 times as many horses to ski. How many horses did he teach?

_____ X _____ = _____

6 Buff, a skiing buffalo, took 7 nasty spills when he was learning to ski. His friend Harry Horse fell down 8 times as often. How many times did Harry fall?

_____ X _____ = _____

Name _____

Space Race

Complete the products. Begin by multiplying the ones place first, then the tens place. See the shading in the examples.

Example:

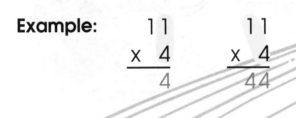

```
  11        11
x  4      x  4
-----     -----
   4        44
```

```
  22        23        43        58        34        31        21
x  3      x  3      x  2      x  1      x  2      x  3      x  4
-----     -----     -----     -----     -----     -----     -----
```

```
  10        44        11        22        89        11        32
x  5      x  2      x  6      x  4      x  1      x  8      x  3
-----     -----     -----     -----     -----     -----     -----
```

```
  42        57        11        78        11        22        64
x  2      x  1      x  5      x  1      x  9      x  4      x  1
-----     -----     -----     -----     -----     -----     -----
```

```
  10        23        33        33        10        11        21
x  7      x  2      x  2      x  3      x  4      x  5      x  3
-----     -----     -----     -----     -----     -----     -----
```

```
  22        24        41        49        10        12        87
x  3      x  2      x  2      x  1      x  9      x  4      x  1
-----     -----     -----     -----     -----     -----     -----
```

Name _____

Multiplying and Regrouping

| 1. Multiply 3 x 8 in the ones column. Ask: Do I need to regroup? | 2. Multiply 3 x 3 in the tens column. Add the 2 you carried over from the ones column. Ask: Do I need to regroup? |

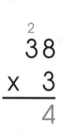

$$\begin{array}{r} 2 \\ 38 \\ \times\ 3 \\ \hline 4 \end{array}$$

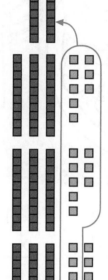

24 ones =
2 tens
4 ones

$$\begin{array}{r} 2 \\ 38 \\ \times\ 3 \\ \hline 114 \end{array}$$

11 tens =
1 hundred
1 ten

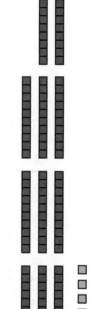

$$\begin{array}{r} 38 \\ \times\ 3 \\ \hline \end{array}$$

is the
same as

$$\begin{array}{r} 38 \\ 38 \\ +\ 38 \\ \hline \end{array}$$

Multiply.

$$\begin{array}{r} 29 \\ \times\ 3 \\ \hline \end{array}$$

$$\begin{array}{r} 62 \\ \times\ 4 \\ \hline \end{array}$$

$$\begin{array}{r} 39 \\ \times\ 4 \\ \hline \end{array}$$

$$\begin{array}{r} 86 \\ \times\ 7 \\ \hline \end{array}$$

$$\begin{array}{r} 43 \\ \times\ 6 \\ \hline \end{array}$$

$$\begin{array}{r} 28 \\ \times\ 6 \\ \hline \end{array}$$

$$\begin{array}{r} 48 \\ \times\ 2 \\ \hline \end{array}$$

$$\begin{array}{r} 31 \\ \times\ 9 \\ \hline \end{array}$$

$$\begin{array}{r} 25 \\ \times\ 5 \\ \hline \end{array}$$

$$\begin{array}{r} 55 \\ \times\ 5 \\ \hline \end{array}$$

Name _____

Multiplying Points

Multiply.

12 x 9	22 x 8	32 x 5	19 x 9
22 x 7	33 x 4	27 x 2	14 x 6
38 x 2	25 x 3	15 x 4	16 x 5

28 x 3	18 x 5	14 x 7	13 x 5	24 x 4	13 x 6	29 x 2
17 x 4	36 x 2	29 x 3	14 x 5	18 x 4	19 x 3	28 x 2
17 x 5	19 x 4	37 x 2	27 x 3	12 x 8	26 x 3	35 x 5

48
x 2

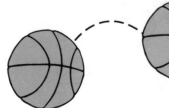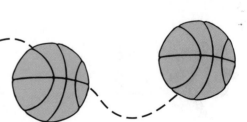

27
x 4

Under the Big Top!

Complete this
crossnumber puzzle.

43	x	4	=	172
x				
2	x	58	=	116
=		x		
86	x	7	=	
		=		
		71		

65	x	4	=	
x		x		
5	x	77	=	
=		=		

Name _____

Wacky Ones

Directions: In card games, aces are often considered as ones. Tear out the gameboard on page 75. Have it laminated, if possible. Use a deck of cards with the face cards and the tens removed. Any number of people can play.

Player One chooses a random card from the deck and places that card in any one of the boxes. Repeat this two or more times. After a number is placed, it may not be changed. Then, he/she will solve the problem. Check the product using a calculator and award points. The next player continues play the same way.

Award points using the following rules:
1. If the product is incorrect, the score is zero.
2. If the product is correct, the score is five points.
3. Bonus—If the product contains a wacky one, the following bonus points are scored: 1 point—ones place, 2 points—tens place, 3 points—hundreds place.

Wacky Ones Gameboard

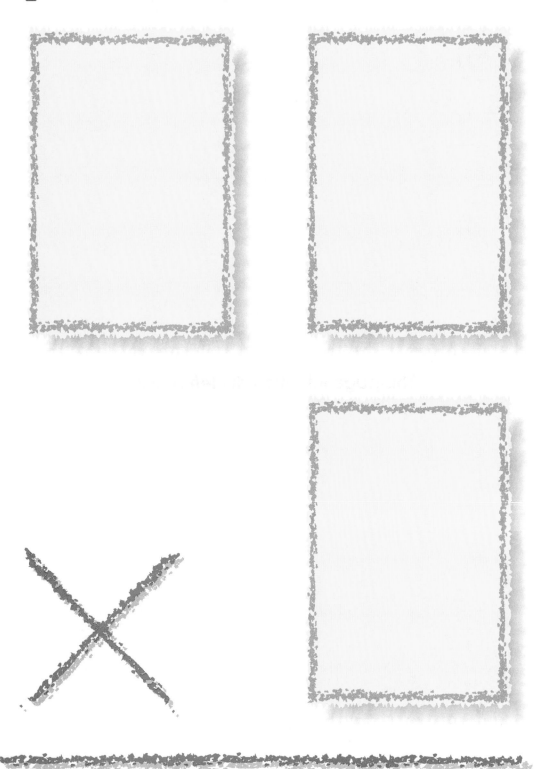

This page intentionally left blank.

More Multiplication

Write the numbers given in the correct boxes to get the given answer.

4 7 5
[5] [4]
x   [7]
3 7 8

7 7 9
☐ ☐
x ☐
6 7 9

8 7 9
☐ ☐
x ☐
6 3 2

4 8 7
☐ ☐
x ☐
5 8 8

7 6 3
☐ ☐
x ☐
4 3 8

6 9 4
☐ ☐
x ☐
5 6 4

7 3 9
☐ ☐
x ☐
3 3 3

5 2 9
☐ ☐
x ☐
4 6 0

9 5 6
☐ ☐
x ☐
3 4 5

2 7 5
☐ ☐
x ☐
1 7 5

4 5 6
☐ ☐
x ☐
2 2 4

5 7 6
☐ ☐
x ☐
3 8 0

3 6 9
☐ ☐
x ☐
2 3 4

4 8 7
☐ ☐
x ☐
3 3 6

6 6 7
☐ ☐
x ☐
4 0 2

5 5 4
☐ ☐
x ☐
2 7 0

2 3 3
☐ ☐
x ☐
9 6

7 8 4
☐ ☐
x ☐
5 9 2

6 5 7
☐ ☐
x ☐
3 8 0

9 4 2
☐ ☐
x ☐
9 8

Multiplying With Molly

Write the problem and the answer for each question.

1 Molly is the toughest football player in her school. She ran for 23 yards on one play and went 3 times as far on the next play. How far did she run the second time?

2 Molly keeps a rock collection. She has 31 rocks in one sack. She has 7 times as many under her bed. How many rocks are under her bed?

3 Molly had 42 marbles when she came to school. She went home with 4 times as many. How many did she go home with?

4 Molly stuffed 21 sticks of gum in her bag in the morning. In the afternoon, she crammed 9 times as many sticks into her bag. How many sticks did she have in her bag?

5 Molly did 51 multiplication problems in math last week. This week, she did 8 times as many. How many did she do this week?

6 Molly did 21 science experiments last year. This year, she did 7 times as many. How many experiments did she do this year?

Multiplication

Name _____

Three-Digit Regrouping

> 1. Multiply the ones column.
>   Ask: Do I need to regroup?

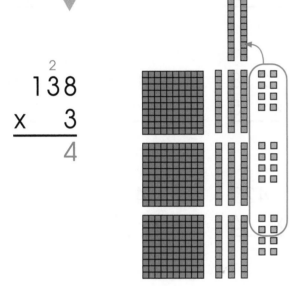

$$
\begin{array}{r}
\overset{2}{1}38 \\
\times\ \ \ 3 \\
\hline
4
\end{array}
$$

> 2. Multiply the tens column.
>   Ask: Do I need to regroup?

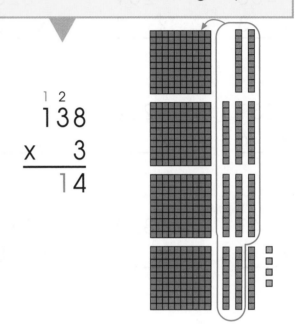

$$
\begin{array}{r}
\overset{1\ 2}{1}38 \\
\times\ \ \ 3 \\
\hline
14
\end{array}
$$

> 3. Multiply the hundreds column.
>   Ask: Do I need to regroup?

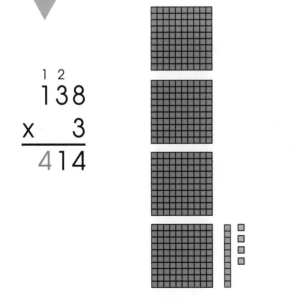

$$
\begin{array}{r}
\overset{1\ 2}{1}38 \\
\times\ \ \ 3 \\
\hline
414
\end{array}
$$

Multiply.

$$
\begin{array}{r}
129 \\
\times\ \ 3 \\
\hline
\end{array}
\qquad
\begin{array}{r}
547 \\
\times\ \ 2 \\
\hline
\end{array}
\qquad
\begin{array}{r}
214 \\
\times\ \ 6 \\
\hline
\end{array}
$$

$$
\begin{array}{r}
306 \\
\times\ \ 8 \\
\hline
\end{array}
\qquad
\begin{array}{r}
536 \\
\times\ \ 2 \\
\hline
\end{array}
\qquad
\begin{array}{r}
629 \\
\times\ \ 3 \\
\hline
\end{array}
$$

$$
\begin{array}{r}
264 \\
\times\ \ 4 \\
\hline
\end{array}
\qquad
\begin{array}{r}
814 \\
\times\ \ 5 \\
\hline
\end{array}
\qquad
\begin{array}{r}
128 \\
\times\ \ 7 \\
\hline
\end{array}
$$

Name _____

Space Math

Complete this mission.

406	281	326	923	817	204
x 3	x 4	x 5	x 2	x 6	x 8

231	262	214	218	126	306
x 6	x 7	x 2	x 5	x 9	x 7

241	329	310	421	431	814
x 8	x 6	x 5	x 6	x 3	x 9

231	624	896	742	525	606
x 4	x 7	x 1	x 8	x 4	x 7

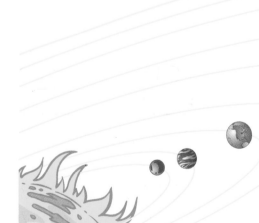
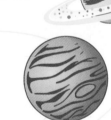

Solve It!

What set of ridges and loops are different on every person?
To find out, **solve** the following problems and **write** the matching letter above each answer at the bottom of the page.

I. 303
x 3
9

303
x 3
09

303
x 3
909

R. 214
x 2

N. 413
x 2

N. 142
x 2

R. 211
x 4

F. 104
x 2

T. 131
x 2

P. 232
x 3

E. 301
x 2

I. 134
x 1

G. 244
x 2

S. 334
x 2

___ ___ ___ ___ ___ ___ ___ ___ ___ ___ ___ ___
208 909 826 488 602 844 696 428 134 284 262 668

Name _____

Four-Digit Regrouping

1. Multiply the ones column. Ask: Do I need to regroup?	2. Multiply the tens column. Ask: Do I need to regroup?

$$\begin{array}{r} \overset{1}{6,2}14 \\ \times\ \ \ \ 3 \\ \hline 2 \end{array}$$

12 ones =
1 ten 2 ones

$$\begin{array}{r} \overset{1}{6,2}14 \\ \times\ \ \ \ 3 \\ \hline 42 \end{array}$$

3. Multiply the hundreds column. Ask: Do I need to regroup?	4. Multiply the thousands column. Ask: Do I need to regroup?

$$\begin{array}{r} \overset{1}{6,2}14 \\ \times\ \ \ \ 3 \\ \hline 642 \end{array}$$

$$\begin{array}{r} \overset{1}{6,2}14 \\ \times\ \ \ \ 3 \\ \hline 18,642 \end{array}$$

Multiply.

$$\begin{array}{r} 4,121 \\ \times\ \ \ \ 6 \\ \hline \end{array} \qquad \begin{array}{r} 7,216 \\ \times\ \ \ \ 3 \\ \hline \end{array} \qquad \begin{array}{r} 2,318 \\ \times\ \ \ \ 4 \\ \hline \end{array} \qquad \begin{array}{r} 4,326 \\ \times\ \ \ \ 8 \\ \hline \end{array} \qquad \begin{array}{r} 2,463 \\ \times\ \ \ \ 9 \\ \hline \end{array}$$

$$\begin{array}{r} 6,425 \\ \times\ \ \ \ 5 \\ \hline \end{array} \qquad \begin{array}{r} 7,195 \\ \times\ \ \ \ 5 \\ \hline \end{array} \qquad \begin{array}{r} 8,083 \\ \times\ \ \ \ 7 \\ \hline \end{array} \qquad \begin{array}{r} 5,993 \\ \times\ \ \ \ 7 \\ \hline \end{array} \qquad \begin{array}{r} 6,218 \\ \times\ \ \ \ 4 \\ \hline \end{array}$$

Amazing Arms

What will happen to a starfish that loses an arm? To find out, **solve** the following problems and **write** the matching letter above the answer at the bottom of the page.

O. 2,893
x   4

W. 1,763
x   3

W. 7,665
x   5

A. 1,935
x   6

W. 3,097
x   3

E. 2,929
x   4

G. 6,366
x   5

T. 7,821
x   8

L. 6,283
x   7

I. 5,257
x   3

R. 3,019
x   6

N. 2,908
x   7

I. 6,507
x   8

N. 5,527
x   2

L. 6,626
x   3

O. 7,219
x   9

E. 3,406
x   6

___ ___
52,056   62,568

___ ___ ___ ___   ___ ___ ___ ___
5,289   15,771   43,981   19,878   31,830   18,114   64,971   9,291

___   ___ ___ ___   ___ ___ ___!
11,610   20,356   20,436   38,325   11,572   11,054   11,716

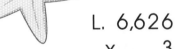

Multiplying by a Two-Digit Number

Multiply.

1. Multiply by the ones place.
$3 \times 2 = 6$
Ignore the 1 in the tens place.

$$\begin{array}{r} 43 \\ \times 12 \\ \hline 6 \end{array}$$

$$\begin{array}{r} 19 \\ \times 11 \\ \hline \end{array}$$

$$\begin{array}{r} 32 \\ \times 31 \\ \hline \end{array}$$

2. Multiply by the ones place.
$4 \times 2 = 8$

$$\begin{array}{r} 43 \\ \times 12 \\ \hline 86 \end{array}$$

$$\begin{array}{r} 54 \\ \times 20 \\ \hline \end{array}$$

$$\begin{array}{r} 68 \\ \times 10 \\ \hline \end{array}$$

3. Multiply by the tens. Place a zero in the ones column.
$3 \times 1 = 3$

$$\begin{array}{r} 43 \\ \times 12 \\ \hline 86 \\ 30 \end{array}$$

$$\begin{array}{r} 83 \\ \times 32 \\ \hline \end{array}$$

$$\begin{array}{r} 42 \\ \times 24 \\ \hline \end{array}$$

4. Multiply by the tens place.
$4 \times 1 = 4$

$$\begin{array}{r} 43 \\ \times 12 \\ \hline 86 \\ 430 \end{array}$$

$$\begin{array}{r} 73 \\ \times 23 \\ \hline \end{array}$$

$$\begin{array}{r} 62 \\ \times 43 \\ \hline \end{array}$$

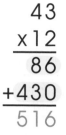

5. Add.
$86 + 430 = 516$

$$\begin{array}{r} 43 \\ \times 12 \\ \hline 86 \\ +430 \\ \hline 516 \end{array}$$

Now, **check** your answers with a calculator.

Multiplying by a Two-Digit Number
With Regrouping

Multiply.

1. Multiply by the ones.
   8 x 7 = 56 (Carry the 5.)

   $$\begin{array}{r} {}^{5} \\ 67 \\ \times 38 \\ \hline 6 \end{array}$$

   $$\begin{array}{r} 37 \\ \times 24 \\ \hline \end{array}$$

   $$\begin{array}{r} 77 \\ \times 21 \\ \hline \end{array}$$

2. Multiply by the ones.
   8 x 6 = 48 + 5 = 53
   (When they are completed, cross out all carried digits.)

   $$\begin{array}{r} \cancel{5} \\ 67 \\ \times 38 \\ \hline 536 \end{array}$$

   $$\begin{array}{r} 23 \\ \times 45 \\ \hline \end{array}$$

   $$\begin{array}{r} 54 \\ \times 38 \\ \hline \end{array}$$

3. Multiply by the tens. Place a zero in the ones column.
   3 x 7 = 21 (Carry the 2.)

   $$\begin{array}{r} {}^{2}\,\cancel{5} \\ 67 \\ \times 38 \\ \hline 536 \\ 10 \end{array}$$

   $$\begin{array}{r} 48 \\ \times 62 \\ \hline \end{array}$$

   $$\begin{array}{r} 67 \\ \times 29 \\ \hline \end{array}$$

4. Multiply by the tens.
   3 x 6 = 18 + 2 = 20

   $$\begin{array}{r} \cancel{2}\,\cancel{5} \\ 67 \\ \times 38 \\ \hline 536 \\ 2010 \end{array}$$

5. Add.
   536 + 2010 = 2,546

   $$\begin{array}{r} \cancel{2}\,\cancel{5} \\ 67 \\ \times 38 \\ \hline 536 \\ +2010 \\ \hline 2,546 \end{array}$$

Now, **check** your answers with a calculator.

Multiplication

Name _____

Multiplying by a Two-Digit Number

1. Multiply by the ones.
   6 x 3 = 18 (Carry the 1.)

$$\begin{array}{r} ^1 43 \\ \times 26 \\ \hline 8 \end{array}$$

Multiply.

$$\begin{array}{r} 21 \\ \times 54 \\ \hline \end{array}$$

$$\begin{array}{r} 52 \\ \times 34 \\ \hline \end{array}$$

2. Multiply by the ones.
   6 x 4 = 24 + 1 = 25
   (When they are completed, cross out all carried digits.)

$$\begin{array}{r} \cancel{} 43 \\ \times 26 \\ \hline 258 \end{array}$$

$$\begin{array}{r} 56 \\ \times 14 \\ \hline \end{array}$$

$$\begin{array}{r} 24 \\ \times 60 \\ \hline \end{array}$$

3. Multiply by the tens. Place a zero in the ones column.
   2 x 3 = 6

$$\begin{array}{r} \cancel{} 43 \\ \times 26 \\ \hline 258 \\ 60 \end{array}$$

$$\begin{array}{r} 23 \\ \times 32 \\ \hline \end{array}$$

$$\begin{array}{r} 69 \\ \times 19 \\ \hline \end{array}$$

4. Multiply by the tens.
   2 x 4 = 8

$$\begin{array}{r} \cancel{} 43 \\ \times 26 \\ \hline 258 \\ 860 \end{array}$$

5. Add.
   258 + 860 = 1,118

$$\begin{array}{r} \cancel{} 43 \\ \times 26 \\ \hline 258 \\ +860 \\ \hline 1,118 \end{array}$$

Now, **check** your answers with a calculator.

Name _____

Name _____

Elephant Escapades

Multiply.

56 x43	13 x24	24 x56	20 x93

23 x54	28 x43	21 x64	25 x34

13 x64	13 x82	34 x21	32 x55	42 x23	62 x31	51 x43

21 x64	10 x84	35 x24	24 x30	24 x53	81 x46	32 x27

Name _____

Multiplication Drill

Multiply. Color the picture below by matching each number with its paint brush.

| 134 | 48 | 876 | 432 |
| x 22 | x66 | x 13 | x 64 |

| 68 | 5,478 | 248 | 6,897 |
| x11 | x 8 | x 61 | x 6 |

| 82 | 6,798 | 79 | 694 |
| x 4 | x 5 | x86 | x 38 |

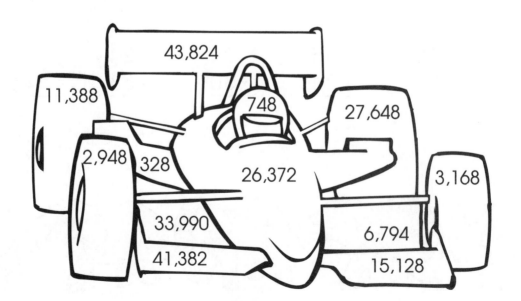

Name _____

Step by Step

Read the problems below. **Write** each answer in the space provided.

Work space

1. One battalion of ants marches with 25 ants in a row. There are 35 rows of ants in each battalion. How many ants are in one battalion?

   _____

2. The Ant Army finds a picnic! Now, they need to figure out how many ants should carry each piece of food. A team of 137 ants moves a celery stick. They need 150 ants to carry a carrot stick. A troop of 121 ants carries a very large radish. How many ants in all are needed to move the vegetables?

   _____

3. Now, the real work begins—the big pieces of food that would feed their whole colony. It takes 1,259 ants to haul a peanut butter and jelly sandwich. It takes a whole battalion of 2,067 ants to lug the lemonade back, and it takes 1,099 ants to steal the pickle jar. How many soldiers carry these big items?

   _____

4. Look-outs are posted all around the picnic blanket. It takes 53 soldiers to watch in front of the picnic basket. Another group of 69 ants watch out by the grill. Three groups of 77 watch the different trails in the park. How many ant-soldiers are on the look-out?

   _____

Name _____

Equally Alike

Label six shoe boxes with one of these numbers: 12, 18, 20, 24, 36 and 48. **Fill** each box with the number of objects on its label. For example, 12 game pieces may be in one box and 18 marbles in another.

Directions:
1. **Count** the number of objects in each box.
2. **Divide** the number of objects into different sets of equal numbers. **Write** all possible multiplication sentences for each one. Try to **write** the related division sentences as well.
3. **Complete** the activity chart below.

Box #	Number in set	Multiplication problem	Related division problem
12			
18			
20			
24			
36			
48			

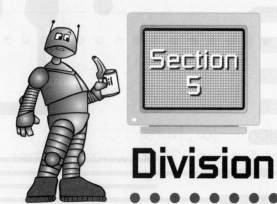

Section 5

Division

Name _____

Backward Multiplication

Division problems are like multiplication problems—just turned around.
As you solve $8 \div 4$, think, "how many groups of 4 make 8?" or "what number 'times' 4 is eight?"

2 x 4 = 8, so 8 ÷ 4 = **2**.

Use the pictures to help you **solve** these division problems.

9 ÷ 3 =

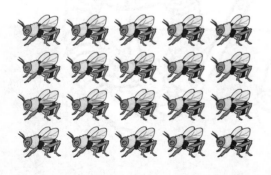

6 ÷ 2 =

16 ÷ 4 =

10 ÷ 5 =

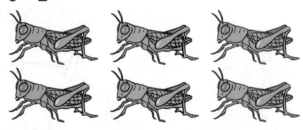

20 ÷ 1 =

18 ÷ 3 =

What Exactly Is Division?

In division, you begin with an amount of something (the dividend), separate it into small groups (the divisor), then find out how many groups are created (the quotient).

Dividend Divisor Quotient
$$15 \div 3 = 5 \text{ sets}$$
in   in
all   each
          set

$$\overset{5 \text{ sets}}{3\overline{)15}} \text{ in all}$$
in
each
set

Solve these division problems.

$21 \div 3 =$ _____ $3\overline{)21}$

$18 \div 3 =$ _____ $3\overline{)18}$

$20 \div 5 =$ _____ $5\overline{)20}$

$16 \div 4 =$ _____ $4\overline{)16}$

$14 \div 7 =$ _____ $7\overline{)14}$

$12 \div 2 =$ _____ $2\overline{)12}$

$18 \div 2 =$ _____ $2\overline{)18}$

$24 \div 6 =$ _____ $6\overline{)24}$

Name _____

Sandwich Cookie

Oops! This recipe below makes 24 dozen or 288 cookies.
Reduce the ingredients to make four dozen or 48 cookies. Then, follow the
directions to bake the cookies. (We divided 24 dozen by 6 to get 4 dozen.
Divide the rest of the ingredients by 6 also.)

Ingredients:

6 cups butter

6 eggs

3 teaspoons salt (think 6 half teaspoonsfull)

6 cups sugar

18 cups flour, sifted

strawberry jam

powdered sugar

Ingredients:

____ cups butter

____ eggs

____ teaspoons salt

____ cups sugar

____ cups flour, sifted

strawberry jam

powdered sugar

Directions: In a mixing bowl, cream the butter with the sugar until they are light and fluffy. Beat in the eggs. Sift the flour and salt into the butter/egg mixture. Mix until well blended. Refrigerate for 1 hour. Divide the dough in half and keep one-half in the refrigerator until needed. Preheat oven to 375°.

Bottom Cookie: Roll out the first half of the dough to 1/8" thickness on a lightly floured surface. Cut out the dough using a 2"–3" round cookie cutter. Place the dough shapes on a cookie sheet. Bake for 10 to 12 minutes.

Top Cookie: Roll out the other half of the dough. Cut the dough using the same cookie cutter, but after it is cut, use a very small cookie cutter or a small bottle cap, floured, to cut a hole in the center of each dough shape. Place the shapes on a cookie sheet and bake them for 10 to 12 minutes. While they are cooling, sprinkle them lightly with powdered sugar.

When both sets of cookies are cool, spread jam on the bottom cookie. Cover it with the top cookie.

Make It Fair

While your cookies are baking, practice fair sharing by completing these problems. **Circle** the objects and **write** two division problems to go with each picture.

There are six children. **Circle** the number of cookies each child will get if the cookies are divided equally.

_____ ÷ _____

_____ ÷ _____

There are four dogs. **Circle** the dog bones each dog will get if the dog bones are divided equally.

_____ ÷ _____

_____ ÷ _____

Divide the pepperoni so that five pizzas will have the same amount.

_____ ÷ _____

_____ ÷ _____

Divide the books so that there will be the same number of books on three shelves.

_____ ÷ _____

_____ ÷ _____

Division

Name _____

Blastoff!

Divide.

1⟌6   20⟌0

2⟌12   2⟌14

2⟌16 9⟌0 6⟌0 2⟌8 15⟌0

1⟌19 2⟌18 7⟌0 2⟌10 1⟌35

1⟌23 1⟌17 1⟌7 2⟌4 12⟌0

        2⟌6 1⟌11 1⟌5

Name _____

Carrier Math Messengers

Divide.

$3\overline{)12}$ $8\overline{)48}$ $2\overline{)18}$

$9\overline{)72}$

$5\overline{)25}$ $9\overline{)72}$ $4\overline{)24}$

$6\overline{)42}$ $8\overline{)40}$ $2\overline{)4}$ $7\overline{)56}$ $9\overline{)63}$

$9\overline{)45}$ $7\overline{)7}$ $3\overline{)15}$ $2\overline{)8}$ $7\overline{)63}$

$8\overline{)48}$

$3\overline{)24}$ $6\overline{)30}$ $9\overline{)54}$

$9\overline{)81}$ $7\overline{)28}$ $4\overline{)32}$

Name _____

Bath Math!

Divide.

8)32

6)36   7)7

7)56

8)40   9)72

6)12   9)36

6)42   6)48   7)21

7)28

8)24

8)16   9)81

6)54   6)18

8)8   6)24   7)35

9)18   8)48

9)45

9)63   9)27

Division Tic-Tac-Toe

Solve the problems. **Draw** an **X** on the odd (9, 7, 5, 3) answers. **Draw** an **O** on the even (8, 6, 4, 2) answers.

$4\overline{)36}$	$4\overline{)24}$	$10 \div 5$
$5\overline{)40}$	$32 \div 4$	$25 \div 5$
$35 \div 5$	$20 \div 4$	$12 \div 4$

$4\overline{)32}$	$12 \div 4$	$5\overline{)30}$
$4\overline{)28}$	$4\overline{)20}$	$20 \div 4$
$20 \div 5$	$10 \div 5$	$15 \div 5$

$24 \div 4$	$5\overline{)45}$	$28 \div 4$
$5\overline{)45}$	$5\overline{)20}$	$8 \div 4$
$4\overline{)16}$	$5\overline{)15}$	$30 \div 5$

$25 \div 5$	$4\overline{)8}$	$16 \div 4$
$32 \div 4$	$5\overline{)20}$	$5\overline{)35}$
$40 \div 5$	$4\overline{)12}$	$15 \div 5$

$5\overline{)10}$	$4\overline{)8}$	$24 \div 4$
$4\overline{)36}$	$5\overline{)35}$	$4\overline{)32}$
$45 \div 5$	$5\overline{)30}$	$4\overline{)12}$

$8 \div 4$	$45 \div 5$	$4\overline{)16}$
$5\overline{)25}$	$36 \div 4$	$4\overline{)24}$
$5\overline{)10}$	$25 \div 5$	$4\overline{)36}$

$4\overline{)12}$	$5\overline{)10}$	$5\overline{)45}$
$30 \div 5$	$5\overline{)25}$	$35 \div 5$
$4\overline{)32}$	$8 \div 4$	$5\overline{)20}$

$36 \div 4$	$4\overline{)28}$	$16 \div 4$
$24 \div 4$	$5\overline{)35}$	$5\overline{)40}$
$5\overline{)25}$	$8 \div 4$	$36 \div 4$

$28 \div 4$	$5\overline{)30}$	$45 \div 5$
$16 \div 4$	$32 \div 4$	$15 \div 5$
$4\overline{)20}$	$4\overline{)12}$	$4\overline{)8}$

Name _____

Jersey Division

Write the numbers in the correct footballs to get the given answer.

 712

21 ÷ 7 = 3

 423

⬭ ÷ ⬭ = 8

 972

⬭ ÷ ⬭ = 3

 848

⬭ ÷ ⬭ = 6

 819

⬭ ÷ ⬭ = 2

 554

⬭ ÷ ⬭ = 9

 274

⬭ ÷ ⬭ = 6

 658

⬭ ÷ ⬭ = 7

 794

⬭ ÷ ⬭ = 7

 376

⬭ ÷ ⬭ = 9

 663

⬭ ÷ ⬭ = 6

 804

⬭ ÷ ⬭ = 5

Name _____

Lizzy the Lizard Bags Her Bugs

Lizzy the Lizard separates her bugs into separate bags so that her lunch is ready for the week. Help her decide how to divide the bugs.

1 Lizzy caught 45 cockroaches. She put 5 into each bag. How many bags did she use?

_____ ÷ _____ = _____

2 Lizzy found 32 termites. She put 4 into each bag. How many bags did she need?

_____ ÷ _____ = _____

3 Lizzy captured 49 stinkbugs. She put them into 7 bags. How many stinkbugs were in each bag?

_____ ÷ _____ = _____

4 Lizzy bagged 27 horn beetles. She used 3 bags. How many beetles went into each bag?

_____ ÷ _____ = _____

5 Lizzy lassoed 36 butterflies. She put 9 into each bag. How many bags did she need?

_____ ÷ _____ = _____

6 Lizzy went fishing and caught 48 water beetles. She used 6 bags for her catch. How many beetles went into each bag?

_____ ÷ _____ = _____

Name _____

Two-Digit Quotients

Steps:

Divide.

1. Ask: Is the tens digit large enough to divide into? (Yes.) Divide. Multiply the partial quotient (2) by the divisor (4) and subtract from the partial dividend (8).

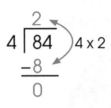

$$3\overline{)63} \qquad 2\overline{)72}$$

8 tens divided into 4 groups. How many are in each group? (2)

$$4\overline{)48} \qquad 2\overline{)56}$$

2. Carry down the 4 in the ones column. Ask: How many groups of 4 are there in 4? (1) Divide. Multiply the partial quotient (1) by the divisor (4) and subtract from the partial dividend (4).

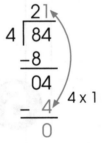

$$3\overline{)96} \qquad 2\overline{)82}$$

3. When 84 things are divided into 4 groups, there will be 21 in each group.

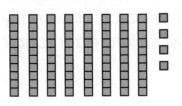 =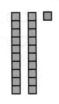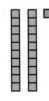

$$\begin{array}{r} 21 \\ 4\overline{)84} \\ -8 \\ \hline 04 \\ -4 \\ \hline 0 \end{array}$$

84 ÷ 4 = 21 + 21 + 21 + 21

Name _____

Snowball Bash

Divide this mound of giant snowballs!

$7\overline{)84}$ $5\overline{)75}$

$3\overline{)45}$ $9\overline{)99}$ $4\overline{)88}$ $5\overline{)80}$

$4\overline{)64}$ $3\overline{)57}$ $3\overline{)78}$ $3\overline{)72}$ $8\overline{)96}$

$2\overline{)86}$ $2\overline{)38}$ $6\overline{)66}$ $5\overline{)65}$ $4\overline{)52}$

$4\overline{)68}$ $6\overline{)78}$ $7\overline{)91}$ $2\overline{)42}$ $6\overline{)72}$

Name _____

Three-Digit Quotients

Steps:

Divide.

1. Ask: Is the hundreds digit large enough to divide into? (Yes.) Divide. Multiply the partial quotient by the divisor and subtract from the partial dividend.

```
      1
7 | 9 3 8
   -7
    2
```

```
6 | 8 8 8
```

```
2 | 5 4 2
```

2. Ask: Can I divide the remaining 2 by 7? (No.) Bring down the 3 tens.

```
      1
7 | 9 3 8
   -7
    2 3
```
2 hundreds
+ 3 tens
= 23 tens

```
3 | 6 9 3
```

```
4 | 5 4 4
```

3. Divide the 23 tens by 7. Multiply the partial quotient by the divisor and subtract.

```
      1 3
7 | 9 3 8
   -7
    2 3
   -2 1
      2
```

4. Ask: Can I divide the remaining 2 by 7? (No.) Bring down 8 ones.

```
      1 3
7 | 9 3 8
   -7
    2 3
   -2 1
      2 8
```
2 tens
+ 8 ones
= 28 ones

```
7 | 8 9 6
```

```
5 | 6 3 5
```

5. Divide the 28 ones by 7. Multiply the partial quotient by the divisor and subtract.

```
      1 3 4
7 | 9 3 8
   -7
    2 3
   -2 1
      2 8
    - 2 8
        0
```

Name _____

On-Stage Division

Divide.

6)888   2)956   2)712   4)860      5)845

6)750   9)999   8)968   3)774   5)735   8)920

8)984   4)500   2)846   4)712

Name _____

Name _____

Bargain Bonanza at Pat's Pet Place

Pat is having a gigantic sale.
Help him divide his animals
into groups for the sale.

SALE

1 Pat has 84 rabbits. He is putting 4 rabbits in each cage. How many cages does he need?

2 Pat sells guppies in plastic bags with 5 guppies in each bag. He has 195 guppies. How many plastic bags does he need?

3 Pat has 392 white mice. They are kept in cages of 7 mice each. How many cages does Pat need?

4 Pat has 324 goldfish. If he puts 6 goldfish in each bag, how many plastic bags will he need?

5 Pat received 116 hamsters. He keeps them in cages of 4 each. How many cages does he need for his hamsters?

6 Pat has 120 parrots. They live in bird cages with 3 to each cage. How many bird cages does Pat need?

Zeros in the Quotient

Steps:

1. Decide where to place the first digit in the quotient.
- 3 can go into 4.

$480 \div 3$

2. Divide. Then, multiply.
- $4 \div 3 = 1$
- $3 \times 1 = 3$

$3\overline{)480}$

3. Subtract and compare.
- $4 - 3 = 1$
- Is 1 less than 3? (Yes.)

$$3\overline{)480}$$
$$\begin{array}{r} 1 \\ 3\overline{)480} \\ -3 \\ \hline 1 \end{array}$$

4. Bring down. Repeat the steps.
- Bring down 8.
- $18 \div 3 = 6$
- $6 \times 3 = 18$
- $18 - 18 = 0$
- Bring down 0.
- 3 cannot go into 0.
- $0 \times 3 = 0$

$$\begin{array}{r} 160 \\ 3\overline{)480} \\ -3 \\ \hline 18 \\ -18 \\ \hline 00 \\ -0 \\ \hline 0 \end{array}$$

Steps:

1. Decide where to place the first digit in the quotient.
- 3 can go into 3.

$327 \div 3$

2. Divide. Then, multiply.
- $3 \div 3 = 1$
- $3 \times 1 = 3$

$3\overline{)327}$

3. Subtract and compare.
- $3 - 3 = 0$
- Is 0 less than 3? (Yes.)

$$\begin{array}{r} 1 \\ 3\overline{)327} \\ -3 \\ \hline 0 \end{array}$$

4. Bring down. Repeat the steps.
- Bring down the 2.
- 3 cannot go into 2.
- $0 \times 3 = 0$
- $2 - 0 = 2$
- Bring down the 7.
- $27 \div 3 = 9$
- $9 \times 3 = 27$
- $27 - 27 = 0$

$$\begin{array}{r} 109 \\ 3\overline{)327} \\ -3 \\ \hline 02 \\ -0 \\ \hline 27 \\ -27 \\ \hline 0 \end{array}$$

Divide.

$3\overline{)624}$ $4\overline{)680}$ $2\overline{)722}$ $6\overline{)648}$ $2\overline{)814}$ $3\overline{)912}$

Name _____

Marty's Mania

Help Marty Mouse eat all the cheese by traveling the route.

$3\overline{)963}$

$6\overline{)612}$

$6\overline{)654}$

$8\overline{)816}$

$2\overline{)816}$

$3\overline{)540}$

$2\overline{)722}$

$4\overline{)836}$

$4\overline{)724}$

$7\overline{)763}$

$4\overline{)836}$

$5\overline{)705}$

$3\overline{)618}$

$6\overline{)840}$

$2\overline{)806}$

$5\overline{)515}$

$3\overline{)618}$

$2\overline{)780}$

$4\overline{)640}$

$5\overline{)550}$

Name

Name _____

Yum! Yum!

What edible fungus is occasionally found on pizzas or in omelets? To find out, **solve** the following problems and **write** the matching letter above the answer at the bottom of the page.

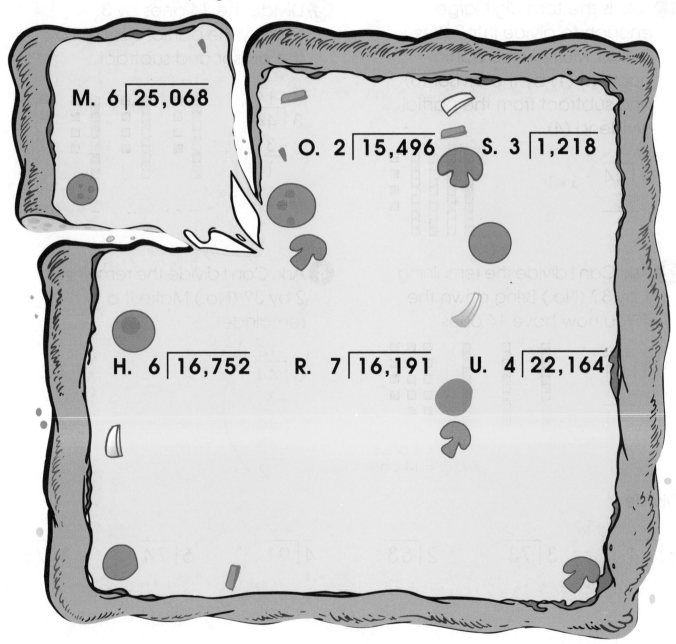

M. 6) 25,068

O. 2) 15,496   S. 3) 1,218

H. 6) 16,752   R. 7) 16,191   U. 4) 22,164

| 4,178 | 5,541 | 406 | 2,792 | 2,313 | 7,748 | 7,748 | 4,178 | 406 |

Two-Digit Quotients
With Remainders

Steps:

1. Ask: Is the tens digit large enough to divide into? (Yes.) Divide. Multiply the partial quotient (1) by the divisor (3) and subtract from the partial dividend (4)

 3⟌44) 3 x 1
  −3
   1

2. Ask: Can I divide the remaining 1 by 3? (No.) Bring down the 4. You now have 14 ones.

     1
3⟌44
  −3
   14

1 ten
+ 4 ones
= 14 ones

3. Divide the 14 ones by 3. Multiply the partial quotient by the divisor and subtract.

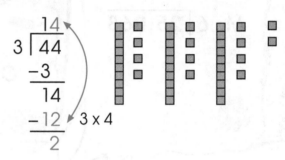
    14
3⟌44
  −3
   14
  −12 3 x 4
    2

4. Ask: Can I divide the remaining 2 by 3? (No.) Make it a remainder.

    14 R 2
3⟌44
  −3
   14
  −12
    2

Divide.

 5⟌64   3⟌73   2⟌53   4⟌91   6⟌74   3⟌76

Mr. R Means Business

Solve the division problems below. **Write** the quotient and the remainder.

Use me when a problem doesn't come out even.

No Remainder	Remainder
$\begin{array}{r} 6 \\ 4\overline{)22} \\ -24 \end{array}$	$\begin{array}{r} 5\ R\ 2 \\ 4\overline{)22} \\ -20 \\ \hline 2 \end{array}$

$\begin{array}{r} 5\ R\ 3 \\ 5\overline{)28} \\ -25 \\ \hline 3 \end{array}$

$\begin{array}{r} 4\ R \\ 4\overline{)19} \end{array}$

$\begin{array}{r} 3\ R \\ 8\overline{)26} \end{array}$

$\begin{array}{r} 6\ R \\ 7\overline{)45} \end{array}$

$\begin{array}{r} R \\ 3\overline{)26} \end{array}$

$\begin{array}{r} R \\ 2\overline{)19} \end{array}$

$\begin{array}{r} R \\ 6\overline{)51} \end{array}$

$\begin{array}{r} R \\ 9\overline{)65} \end{array}$

$\begin{array}{r} R \\ 8\overline{)43} \end{array}$

$\begin{array}{r} R \\ 9\overline{)59} \end{array}$

$\begin{array}{r} R \\ 7\overline{)33} \end{array}$

$\begin{array}{r} R \\ 4\overline{)27} \end{array}$

Name _____

Division Checklist

Solve the division problems. **Draw** a line from the division problem to the matching checking problem. **Solve** the checking problem to be sure you divided correctly.

How to check division:
  Quotient
x Divisor
_____

+ Remainder
Dividend

```
   18 R2         2
3│56           18
  -3          x  3
 ___          ____
  26            54
 -24          +  2
 ___          ____
   2            56
```

```
3│127          59          3│178          21          3│175
             x  3                      x  3

             +  1                      +  1
```

```
  42         3│236          10          3│32           58
x  3                      x  3                       x  3

+  1                      +  2                       +  1
```

```
  28         3│86           78          3│247          82
x  3                      x  3                       x  3

+  2                      +  2                       +  1
```

Name _____

Looking to the Stars

Solve the problems. To find the path to the top, your answers should match the problem number. **Color** the path.

27. 3⎡63	28. 3⎡84	29. 4⎡97	30. 6⎡74	
22. 4⎡74	23. 2⎡46	24. 2⎡48	25. 3⎡75	26. 6⎡96

15. 5⎡92	16. 3⎡41	17. 3⎡57	18. 4⎡84	19. 4⎡76	20. 7⎡86	21. 5⎡72
8. 5⎡57	9. 3⎡65	10. 2⎡87	11. 5⎡55	12. 7⎡84	13. 3⎡87	14. 7⎡93
1. 3⎡96	2. 6⎡94	3. 5⎡93	4. 9⎡36	5. 2⎡97	6. 6⎡84	7. 3⎡68

Name _____

Three-Digit Quotients
With Remainders

Steps:

1. Ask: Is the hundreds digit large enough to divide into? (Yes.) Divide. Multiply the partial quotient by the divisor and subtract from the partial dividend.

```
     2
4 | 854
   -8
    0
```

4. Divide the 14 ones by 4. Multiply the partial quotient by the divisor and subtract.

```
    213
4 | 854
   -8
    05
   - 4
    14
   - 12
     2
```

2. Bring down the 5 tens. Ask: Can I divide 5 by 4? (Yes.) Multiply the partial quotient by the divisor and subtract.

```
    21
4 | 854
   -8
    05
   - 4
     1
```

5. Ask: Is the remaining difference of 2 less than the divisor? (Yes.) Make 2 a remainder.

```
    213 R2
4 | 854
   -8
    05
   - 4
    14
   - 12
     2
```

3. Ask: Is the difference of 1 less than the divisor 4? (Yes.) Bring down the 4 ones.

1 ten + 4 ones = 14 ones

```
    21
4 | 854
   -8
    05
   - 4
    14
```

Divide.

2 | 631   6 | 945   3 | 860   5 | 914   4 | 927   8 | 972

Name _____

Puzzling Problems

Solve the following problems. **Write** the answers in the puzzle.

Across

2. 2$\overline{)917}$ **4.** 6$\overline{)830}$

7. 4$\overline{)975}$ **8.** 2$\overline{)859}$

12. 2$\overline{)779}$ **14.** 3$\overline{)475}$

16. 3$\overline{)680}$ **17.** 8$\overline{)988}$

18. 3$\overline{)971}$ **19.** 5$\overline{)927}$

Down

1. 3$\overline{)776}$ **3.** 7$\overline{)948}$ **5.** 3$\overline{)740}$

6. 7$\overline{)897}$ **9.** 4$\overline{)751}$ **10.** 5$\overline{)714}$

11. 4$\overline{)639}$ **13.** 6$\overline{)749}$ **15.** 5$\overline{)634}$

Four-Digit Quotients
With Remainders

Steps:

$14,648 \div 6$

Divide.

1. Decide where to place the
first digit in the quotient.

$6\overline{)14,648}$

- 6 cannot go into 1.
- 6 can go into 14.

$$5\overline{)22,464}$$

$$6\overline{)23,445}$$

2. Divide. Then, multiply.
- $14 \div 6 = 2$
- $6 \times 2 = 12$

$$6\overline{)\begin{array}{r}2 \\ 14,648 \\ -12 \\ \hline 2\end{array}}$$

3. Subtract and compare.
- $14 - 12 = 2$
- Is 2 less than 6? (Yes.)

4. Bring down. Repeat
the steps.
- Bring down the 6.
- $26 \div 6 = 4$
- $6 \times 4 = 24$
- $26 - 24 = 2$
- Is 2 less than 6? (Yes.)
- Bring down the 4.
- $24 \div 6 = 4$
- $6 \times 4 = 24$
- $24 - 24 = 0$
- Is 0 less than 6? (Yes.)
- Bring down the 8.
- $8 \div 6 = 1$
- $6 \times 1 = 6$
- $8 - 6 = 2$
- Is 2 less than 6? (Yes.)
- No more numbers, so 2 is
the remainder.

$$6\overline{)\begin{array}{r}2,441 \text{ R2} \\ 14,648 \\ -12 \\ \hline 26 \\ -24 \\ \hline 24 \\ -24 \\ \hline 08 \\ -6 \\ \hline 2\end{array}}$$

$$3\overline{)14,458}$$

$$8\overline{)50,469}$$

$$3\overline{)23,767}$$

$$4\overline{)23,303}$$

Name _____

To Catch a Butterfly

Solve the problems. **Draw** a line to connect each net to the butterfly with the correct answer.

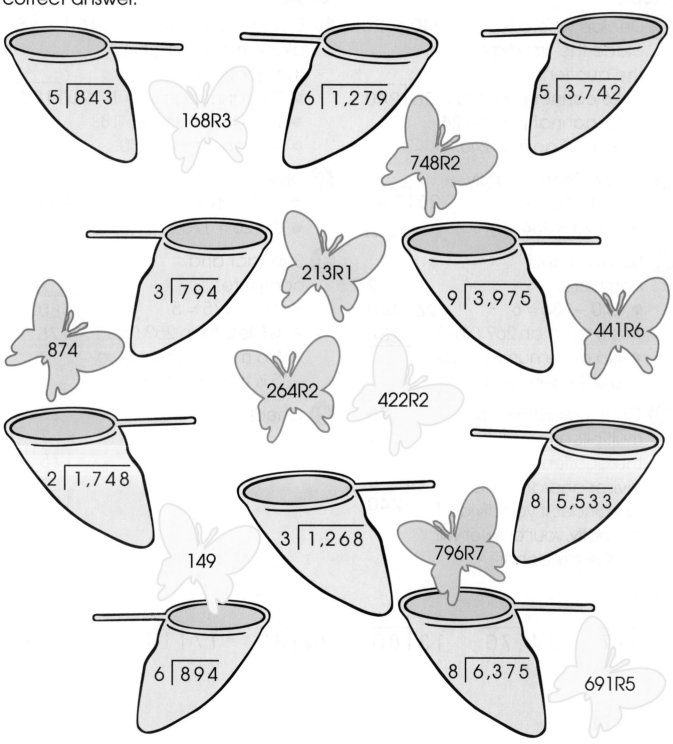

Two-Digit Divisors
With Remainders

Steps:

1. Decide where to place the first digit in the quotient. $240 \div 26$
   - 26 cannot go into 2.   26$\overline{)240}$
   - 26 cannot go into 24.
   - 26 can go into 240.

2. Divide. Then, multiply.
   - $240 \div 26 = 9$
   - $9 \times 26 = 234$

   $$26\overline{)240} \quad \begin{array}{r} 9 \\ \end{array}$$
   $$-234$$

3. Subtract and compare.
   - $240 - 234 = 6$
   - Is 6 less than 26? (Yes.)
   - No more numbers, so 6 is the remainder.

   $$26\overline{)240} \quad \begin{array}{r} 9 \ \text{R6} \\ \end{array}$$
   $$-234$$
   $$6$$

4. Check division with multiplication. Multiply the quotient by the divisor and add the remainder. If you divided correctly, your answer will be the dividend!

   $$\begin{array}{r} 26 \\ \times\ 9 \\ \hline 234 \\ +\ 6 \\ \hline 240 \end{array}$$

Steps:

1. Decide where to place the first digit in the quotient. $180 \div 25$
   - 25 cannot go into 1.   25$\overline{)180}$
   - 25 cannot go into 18.
   - 25 can go into 180.

2. Divide. Then, multiply.
   - $180 \div 25 = 7$
   - $7 \times 25 = 175$

   $$25\overline{)180} \quad \begin{array}{r} 7 \\ \end{array}$$
   $$-175$$

3. Subtract and compare.
   - $180 - 175 = 5$
   - Is 5 less than 25? (Yes.)
   - No more numbers, so 5 is the remainder.

   $$25\overline{)180} \quad \begin{array}{r} 7 \ \text{R5} \\ \end{array}$$
   $$-175$$
   $$5$$

4. Check.

   $$\begin{array}{r} 25 \\ \times\ 7 \\ \hline 175 \\ +\ 5 \\ \hline 180 \end{array}$$

Divide.

14$\overline{)77}$ 34$\overline{)70}$ 13$\overline{)80}$ 24$\overline{)82}$ 17$\overline{)140}$ 47$\overline{)290}$

Name _____

Hoppin' Division

Solve these division problems.

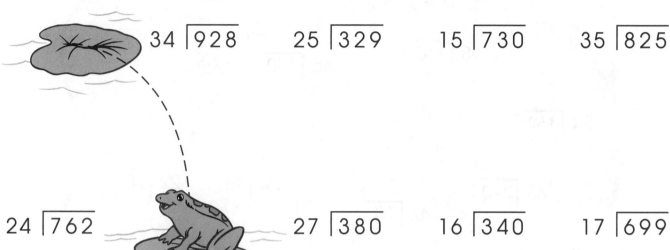

$34\overline{)928}$ $25\overline{)329}$ $15\overline{)730}$ $35\overline{)825}$

$24\overline{)762}$ $27\overline{)380}$ $16\overline{)340}$ $17\overline{)699}$

$33\overline{)864}$ $22\overline{)290}$ $32\overline{)876}$ $18\overline{)766}$

$23\overline{)375}$ $13\overline{)678}$ $26\overline{)607}$ $14\overline{)884}$

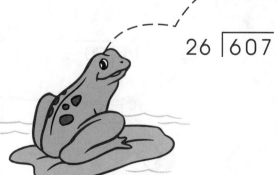

Name _____

China's Dragon Kite

Solve the problems in this incredible dragon kite!

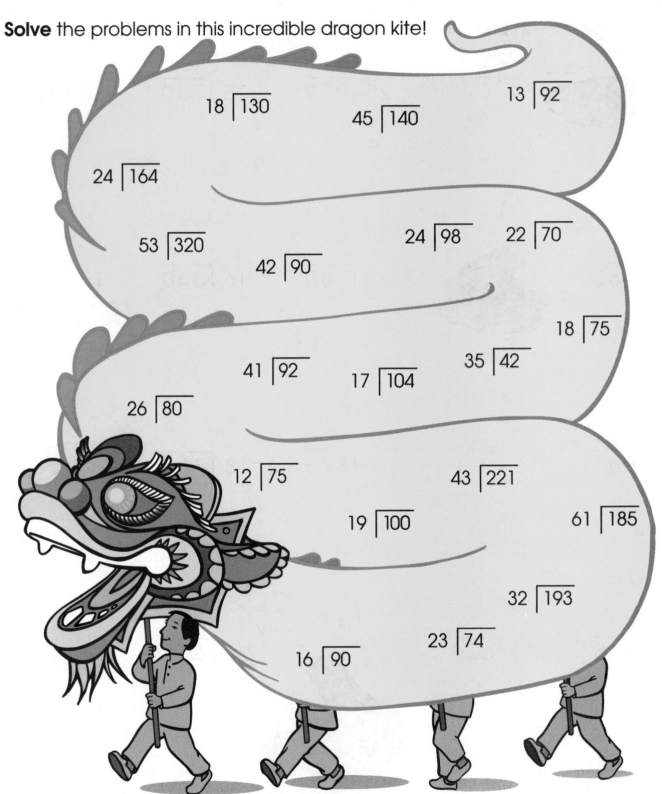

$18\overline{)130}$

$45\overline{)140}$

$13\overline{)92}$

$24\overline{)164}$

$53\overline{)320}$

$42\overline{)90}$

$24\overline{)98}$

$22\overline{)70}$

$18\overline{)75}$

$41\overline{)92}$

$17\overline{)104}$

$35\overline{)42}$

$26\overline{)80}$

$12\overline{)75}$

$43\overline{)221}$

$19\overline{)100}$

$61\overline{)185}$

$32\overline{)193}$

$23\overline{)74}$

$16\overline{)90}$

Number Puzzles

Solve these number puzzles.

1

Write your age.	_____
Multiply it by 3.	_____
Add 18.	_____
Multiply by 2.	_____
Subtract 36.	_____
Divide by 6. (your age)	_____

2

Write any number.	_____
Double that number.	_____
Add 15.	_____
Double again.	_____
Subtract 30.	_____
Divide by 2.	_____
Divide by 2 again.	_____

3

Write any 2-digit number.	_____
Double that number.	_____
Add 43.	_____
Subtract 18.	_____
Add 11.	_____
Divide by 2.	_____
Subtract 18.	_____

4

Write the number of children in your neighborhood.	_____
Double that number.	_____
Add 15.	_____
Double it again.	_____
Subtract 30.	_____
Divide by 4.	_____

Name _____

Identifying Operations

Write the correct sign in each circle.

5 ◯ 5 = 10

9 ◯ 9 = 81

56 ◯ 8 = 48

91 ◯ 16 = 75

54 ◯ 6 = 9

28 ◯ 17 = 11

25 ◯ 5 = 5

72 ◯ 9 = 63

64 ◯ 8 = 56

36 ◯ 4 = 9

45 ◯ 5 = 40

14 ◯ 59 = 73

56 ◯ 17 = 73

40 ◯ 5 = 8

9 ◯ 3 = 27

29 ◯ 37 = 66

6 ◯ 5 = 30

36 ◯ 5 = 31

56 ◯ 8 = 7

7 ◯ 1 = 7

57 ◯ 9 = 48

7 ◯ 6 = 42

21 ◯ 9 = 30

64 ◯ 8 = 8

7 ◯ 8 = 56

76 ◯ 19 = 57

43 ◯ 7 = 50

4 ◯ 9 = 36

48 ◯ 8 = 6

9 ◯ 1 = 9

45 ◯ 5 = 9

36 ◯ 27 = 63

48 ◯ 6 = 42

9 ◯ 8 = 72

8 ◯ 8 = 64

82 ◯ 9 = 91

36 ◯ 63 = 99

6 ◯ 9 = 54

33 ◯ 57 = 90

27 ◯ 3 = 9

63 ◯ 9 = 54

8 ◯ 38 = 46

2 ◯ 9 = 18

55 ◯ 37 = 92

81 ◯ 9 = 9

80 ◯ 17 = 63

32 ◯ 4 = 8

71 ◯ 15 = 86

Which Problem Is Correct?

Circle the equation on the left you should use to solve the problem. Then, **solve** the problem. Remember the decimal point in money questions.

1.
$$
\begin{array}{r} 56 \\ +17 \\ \hline \end{array}
\qquad
\begin{array}{r} 56 \\ -17 \\ \hline \end{array}
$$
Bill and his friends collect baseball cards. Bill has 17 fewer cards than Mack. Bill has 56 cards. How many baseball cards does Mack have?

2.
$$
\begin{array}{r} 54 \\ \times\ 3 \\ \hline \end{array}
\qquad
3\overline{)54}
$$
Amos bought 54 baseball cards. He already had 3 times as many. How many baseball cards did Amos have before his latest purchase?

3.
$$
\begin{array}{r} 3.80 \\ +3.50 \\ \hline \end{array}
\qquad
\begin{array}{r} 3.80 \\ -3.50 \\ \hline \end{array}
$$
Joe paid $3.50 for a Mickey Mantle baseball card. Ted Williams cost him $3.80. How much more did he pay for Ted Williams than for Mickey Mantle?

4.
$$
\begin{array}{r} 3.60 \\ \times\ 9 \\ \hline \end{array}
\qquad
9\overline{)3.60}
$$
Will bought 9 baseball cards for $3.60. How much did he pay per (for each) card?

5.
$$
\begin{array}{r} 8.00 \\ +\ .50 \\ \hline \end{array}
\qquad
\begin{array}{r} 8.00 \\ -\ .50 \\ \hline \end{array}
$$
Babe Ruth baseball cards were selling for $8.00. Herb Score baseball cards sold for 50 cents. Herb Score cards sold for how much less than Babe Ruth cards?

6.
$$
\begin{array}{r} 0.75 \\ \times\ 8 \\ \hline \end{array}
\qquad
8\overline{)0.75}
$$
Andy bought 8 baseball cards at 75 cents each. How much did Andy pay in all?

Name _____

Emery Prepares for His Party

Read each story problem carefully. What is the question? What information is given that will help with the answer? Will drawing a picture help? Remember that solving story problems takes time.

Write each problem and its answer.

1. If Emery needed 329 knives, 329 forks and 329 spoons, how many pieces of silverware did Emery need altogether?

_____

2. Emery cooked 329 eggs for his guests. How many dozen eggs did he need to buy?

_____

3. Emery baked tarts for dessert. The recipe he followed yielded 8 tarts. How many batches of tarts would he have to make to get 329 tarts?

_____

4. If each recipe called for 2 eggs, how many eggs would Emery need to make the tarts? To solve this problem, you will need the information from problem 3.

_____

5. The guests sat at 54 tables. Each table had 2 vases. Emery put 5 flowers in each vase. How many flowers did he have to pick?

_____

The Lion Dance

The Lion Dance, which started in China, became a Japanese folk dance. In this dance, many people line up under a long piece of colorful cloth. The person in front wears a mask of a lion's head. As a group, the line of people dances in the streets around the town.

In this Lion Dance, the children lined up in this order: 2 boys, 2 girls, 2 boys, 2 girls. The order remained the same through the entire line.

- Masato, a Japanese boy, stood behind the fifth boy. Find and circle his left foot.

- Koko, a Japanese girl, stood in front of the seventh boy. Put a box around her left foot.

- If every two children needed a 4-foot section of the cloth and the lion's head was 4 feet long, how many feet long is the entire costume?

  _____ feet

Challenge!
How many yards long is the entire lion costume?

_____ yards

Name _____

On the Average . . .

Division is good for finding averages. An **average** is a number that tells about how something is normally.

The children on the 6-on-6 basketball team made the following number of baskets:

April	1	Beth	3
Colton	3	Ryan	1
Jen	2	J.J.	2

The school paper wants to write about the game, but they don't have room for such a long list. Instead the reporter will find the average by following the steps below.

Steps:

1. **Add** all the team members' baskets together.

_____ + _____ + _____ + _____ + _____ + _____ = _____

2. **Count** to find out how many team members there were.

_____

3. **Divide** your answer for step 1 by the number in step 2.

_____ ÷ _____ = _____

The paper will report that each team member normally makes an average of 2 baskets each. Remember—add, count, divide.

Find the average for the following problem:
In their last 3 games, the Longlegs scored 24 points, 16 points and 20 points.
  1) Add.   2) Count.   3) Divide.

What was their average? _____

Work It Out

The **average** is the result of dividing the **sum** of addends by the **number** of addends. **Match** the problem with its answer.

Add. 62
  79 } **Count.**
  +87
  ‾‾‾‾
  228

Divide. 76
  3) 228

1. 80 + 100 + 90 + 95 + 100   ◯   A. 53

2. 52 + 56 + 51   ◯   B. 190

3. 85 + 80 + 95 + 95 + 100   ◯   C. 410

4. 782 + 276 + 172   ◯   D. 91

5. 125 + 248 + 214 + 173   ◯   E. 93

6. 81 + 82 + 91 + 78   ◯   F. 55

7. 40 + 60 + 75 + 45   ◯   G. 83

8. 278 + 246   ◯   H. 33

9. 75 + 100 + 100 + 70 + 100   ◯   I. 3

10. 0 + 0 + 0 + 0 + 15   ◯   J. 262

11. 21 + 34 + 44   ◯   K. 89

12. 437 + 509 + 864 + 274   ◯   L. 94

13. 80 + 80 + 100 + 95 + 95   ◯   M. 8

14. 4 + 6 + 7 + 12 + 11   ◯   N. 90

15. 75 + 100 + 100 + 100 + 95   ◯   O. 521

Name _____

Story Problems

Solve the following problems.

Work Space

1. The daily temperatures for one week in May were 49°F, 51°F, 52°F, 69°F, 76°F, 77°F and 81°F. What was the average daily temperature for the entire week?

   _____

2. Over a 5-day period, 255 cold lunches were brought to school. What was the average daily number of cold lunches brought to school over the 5-day period?

   _____

3. Kayla scored 86%, 96%, 92%, 98%, 86% and 100% on her last six spelling tests. Based on these percentages, what is her average score?

   _____

4. Jonah practices basketball every night, and his goal is to practice an average of 60 minutes a night. He practiced 50 minutes on Monday, 68 minutes on Tuesday, 40 minutes on Wednesday, 40 minutes on Thursday and 72 minutes on Friday. What is the average amount of minutes per day Jonah

   practiced this past week? _____

   Did Jonah reach his goal? _____

5. During the past soccer season, the Newhall Rovers had an average of 5 goals per game. If they play 25 games this coming season and score a total of 150 goals, will they achieve the same average number of goals?

   _____

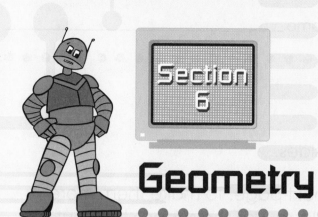

Section 6

Geometry

Geometry Match-Ups

A **polygon** is a closed shape with straight sides.

Directions: Cut out each polygon on the next page. To make them more durable, glue them onto cardboard or oaktag. Use the shapes to fill out the table below. (Keep the shapes for other activities as well.)

Game: Play this game with a partner. Put the shapes in a bag or cover them with a sheet of paper. Player One pulls out a shape and tells how many sides and angles it has. Without showing the shape, he/she puts the polygon back. Player Two should name the shape. Then, Player Two puts his/her hand in the bag and, without looking, tries to find the polygon from the description. Then, switch roles. Continue the game until all the polygons have been identified.

When you finish playing, **complete** the chart below.

Drawing of the shape (or polygon)	Shape name	Number of sides	Number of angles (or corners)
	triangle		
	square		
	pentagon		
	rectangle		
	hexagon		

Shapes

hexagon

pentagon

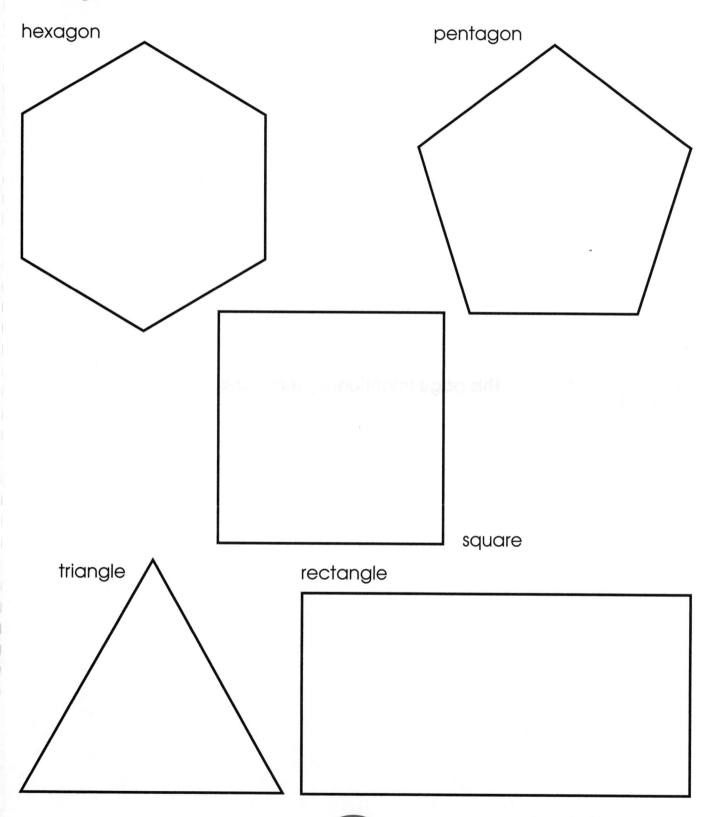

square

triangle

rectangle

This page intentionally left blank.

Triangle Puzzle

Directions: Using the triangle pattern below, cut out 37 triangles using the same color of construction paper. If you want, glue the gameboards and the triangles to tagboard for added strength. Next, arrange the triangles to make the shapes on the gameboards on pages 135 and 137. You have the exact number of triangles needed to complete all the shapes. The triangles may not be folded or cut in any way. To make this a game, you could have someone time you to see how long it takes. Keep the puzzle pieces in an envelope to use alone or with someone.

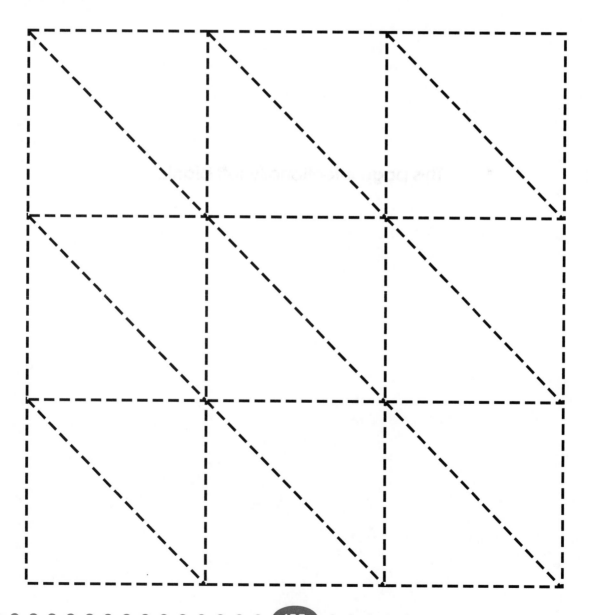

This page intentionally left blank.

Triangle Puzzle

parallelogram

square

triangle

rectangle

triangle

square

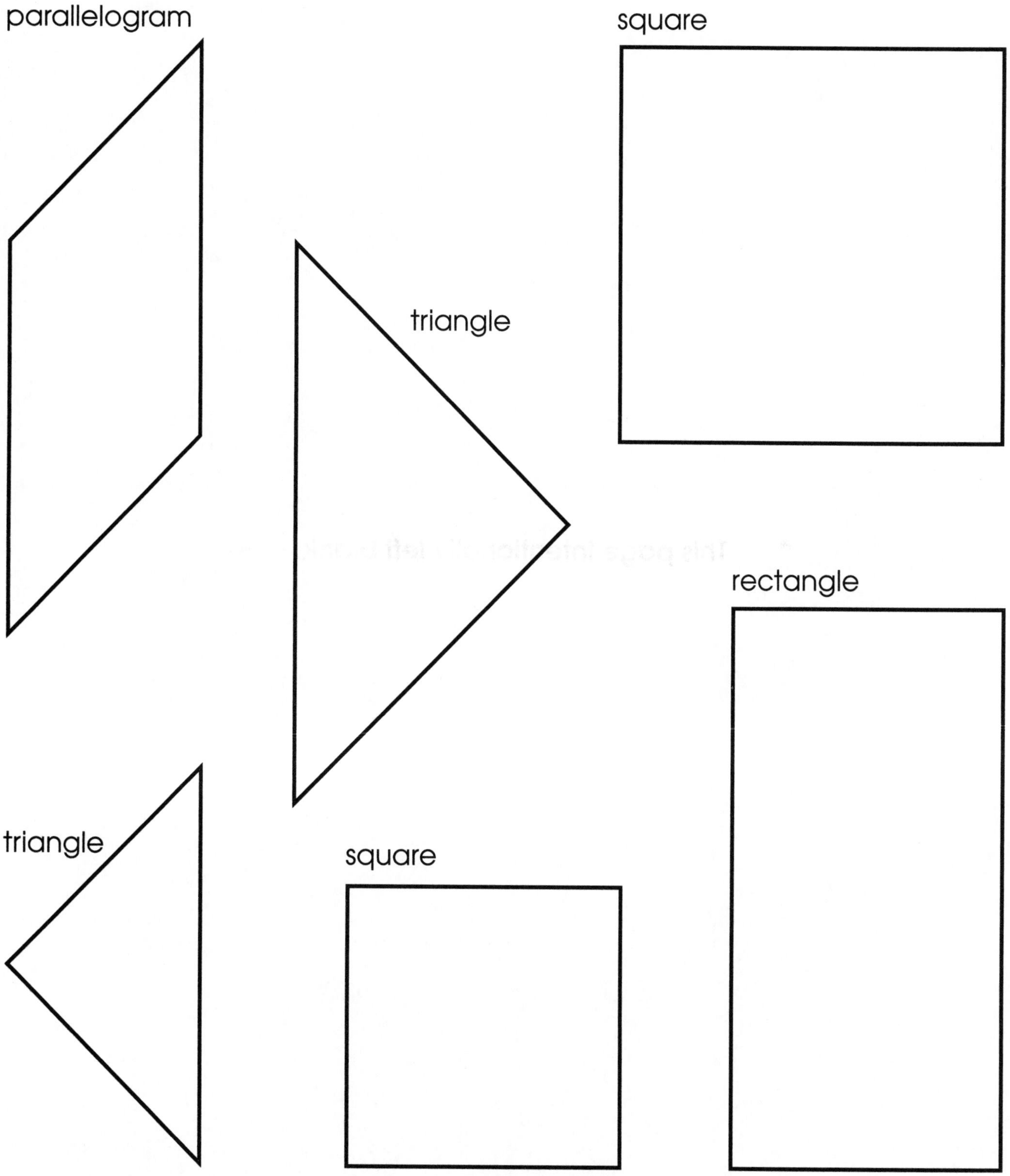

This page intentionally left blank.

Triangle Puzzle

square

trapezoid   parallelogram

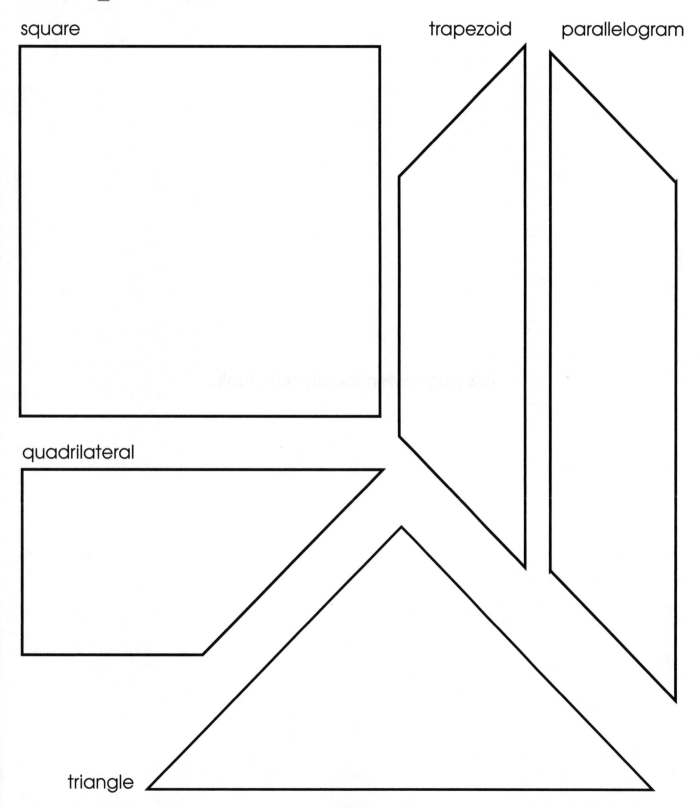

quadrilateral

triangle

This page intentionally left blank.

Name _____

A Native American Wall Hanging

Congruent figures have the same size and shape. They do not have to be the same color or in the same position.

Congruent figures

Not congruent figures

Directions: Draw two congruent figures to create a new shape. You can use triangles, squares, rectangles, pentagons, hexagons, octagons, semicircles, quarter-circles or trapezoids to make the shape. Use the new shape to create a wall hanging design. Connect the two congruent figures at one side. Color each part of the congruent pairs. Display your hanging on a wall of your house.

Who's New in the Zoo?

You are going to create a New Zoo by creating and naming all new animals. You may use the shapes from page 131 or use those as a pattern to make different-colored shapes.

Directions: Glue the shapes together to form the animals. Then, glue the animals onto a sheet of construction paper. Give your New Zoo Animal a name. Write the name on an index card along with a list of the shapes used to create the animal. The animal name should indicate some special feature, such as triangle toad, round-nosed runners, rectangle-tailed tootsie, etc. Try making the animals below.

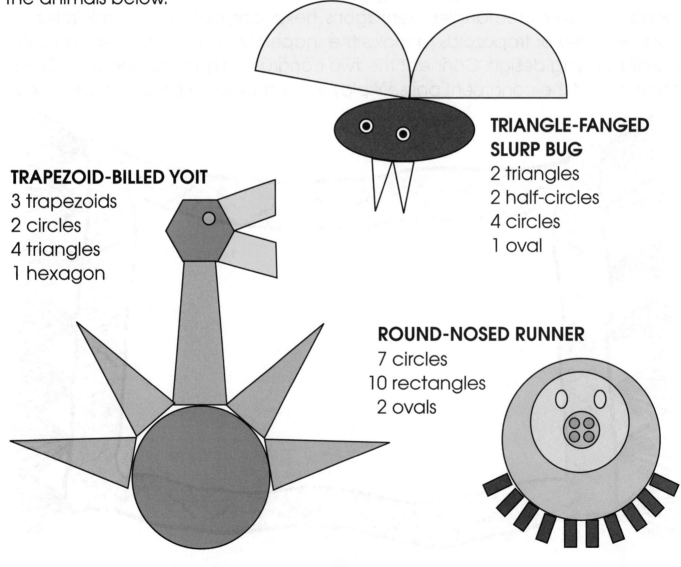

**TRIANGLE-FANGED
SLURP BUG**
2 triangles
2 half-circles
4 circles
1 oval

TRAPEZOID-BILLED YOIT
3 trapezoids
2 circles
4 triangles
1 hexagon

ROUND-NOSED RUNNER
7 circles
10 rectangles
2 ovals

Shape Up

Geometric Drop Art

You will need: a set of geometric shapes, an eraser, one sheet of 11" x 18" construction paper.

Directions: Hold one of the shapes above the paper and gently drop it on the paper. Trace the shape exactly where it lands. Repeat this process and erase the lines, if any, that the second shape covered on the first shape. For example, if the second shape, a rectangle, landed on the corner of a hexagon, then that hexagonal corner should be erased so that the rectangle actually appears to be "on top." (See illustration.) For a challenge, color the visible parts of each shape one color.

Shapely Stories

Directions: Make a geometric shape on white paper using a ruler and/or compass and cut it out. The shape should be nearly as large as the paper. Then, write a "shapely" story or poem by following around the inside perimeter of the shape. As the story continues, the center of the shape fills up. You can make an entire shape book by using additional pages and stapling them together.

Once upon a time, Sarah went to a toy store with her mom to buy a present for her brother Tom's birthday. She reached up to get a ball that she wanted to give him. Just as she got the ball to the cash register, it jumped out of her hand and . . .

Name _____

Perimeter Problems

The **perimeter** is the distance around the outside of a shape. **Find** the perimeters for the figures below by adding the lengths of all the sides.

Example:

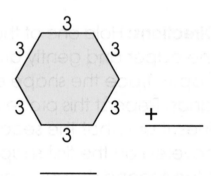

$$\begin{array}{r} 5 \\ 4 \\ 5 \\ + \ 4 \\ \hline 18 \end{array}$$

__18__

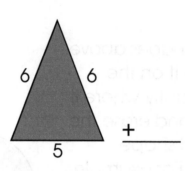

+ _____ _____

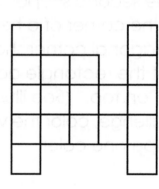

+ _____ _____

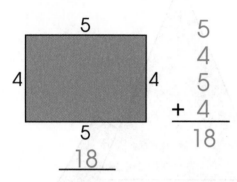

__20__

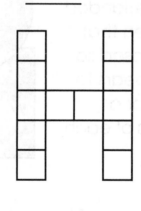

_____

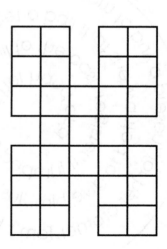

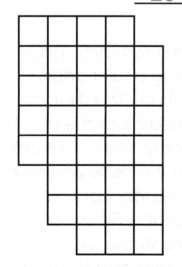

_____

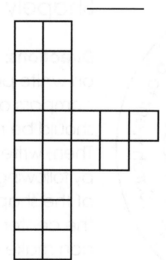

_____

_____

Figuring Distance

Find the perimeter of each figure.

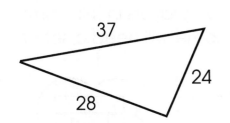

37
24
28

□
□
+ □
‾‾‾‾‾‾‾

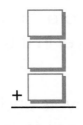

2   2
3
3
2

□
□
□
□
□
+ □
‾‾‾‾‾‾‾

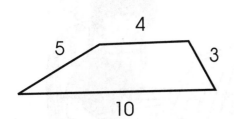

4
5
3
10

□
□
□
+ □
‾‾‾‾‾‾‾

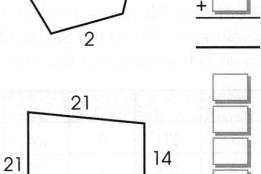

21
21
14
21

□
□
□
+ □
‾‾‾‾‾‾‾

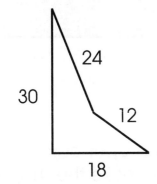

24
30
12
18

□
□
□
+ □
‾‾‾‾‾‾‾

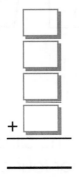

7
8
5
8

□
□
□
+ □
‾‾‾‾‾‾‾

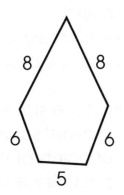

8   8
6   6
5

□
□
□
□
+ □
‾‾‾‾‾‾‾

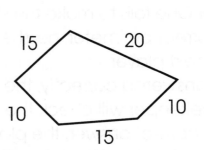

15   20
10   10
15

□
□
□
□
+ □
‾‾‾‾‾‾‾

Name _____

Four Shapes Make One Game

Preparation: Cut out all the game cards—the **Silhouette Shapes** on page 145 and **Four Shapes** cards on page 147. To make them last longer, glue them onto cardboard or index cards. If there will be more than two players in this game, make copies of the **Four Shapes**. Each player in the game will need a set of four **Four Shapes** cards.

Directions: This game involves 1 or more players and a timekeeper. Place the **Silhouette Shapes** cards face down in the center of the playing area.

Card #	Answer	Card #	Answer	Card #	Answer
1	20	6	24	11	28
2	22	7	22	12	22
3	26	8	26	13	22
4	28	9	24	14	28
5	22	10	22	15	24

RULES:

1. Each player takes four **Four Shapes** cards.
2. The first player is the one whose name is first alphabetically.
3. Player One draws a card from the top of the **Silhouette Shapes** card stack.
4. In 1 minute, Player One must use all his/her four cards to make the shape depicted on the card he/she drew.
5. The perimeter of the shape made should then be calculated.
6. If Player One fails to make the shape in 1 minute (timekeeper times), or gives an incorrect perimeter, he/she receives 0 points and the card is passed on to the next player.
7. When answered correctly, the card goes on the bottom of the stack.
8. The timekeeper will check the Answer Key and keep all players' scores.
9. For the correct answer, the player receives the number of points of the perimeter he/she calculated. The first player to reach 100 points is the winner.

Silhouette Shapes

1.	2.	3.
4.	5.	6.
7.	8.	9.
10.	11.	12.
13.	14.	15.

This page intentionally left blank.

Four Shapes Cards

This page intentionally left blank.

This page intentionally left blank.

Geometry

A Square Activity

The **area** is the number of square units covering a flat surface. **Find** the area by counting the square units.

Example: 2 squares x 5 squares = 10 squares

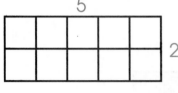

10

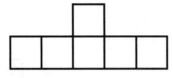

____

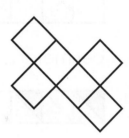

____

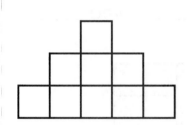

____

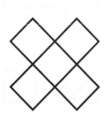

____

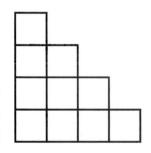

____

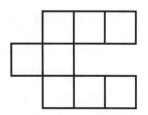

____

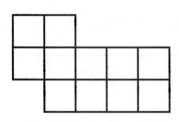

____

____

Name _____

Quilt Math

The area of a rectangle is calculated by multiplying the length of one side by the width of another side. **Find** the perimeter and area of each quilt.

1.
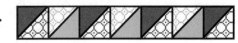

perimeter _____   area _____

2.
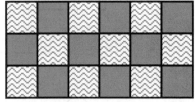

perimeter _____   area _____

3.
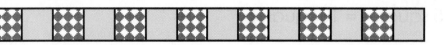

perimeter _____   area _____

4.

perimeter _____   area _____

5.
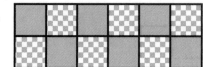

perimeter _____   area _____

6.
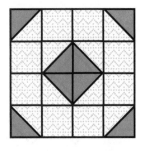

perimeter _____   area _____

7.
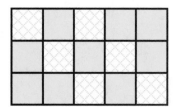

perimeter _____   area _____

8. What did you notice about the perimeter in problems 4, 5, 6 and 7?

_____

9. On another sheet of paper, lay out, then sketch a quilt that has 30 blocks in it.

10. On another sheet of paper, lay out, then sketch a quilt that has a perimeter of 14 units.

 Geometry

The Way Around Polygons

Use the cut-out shapes from pages 131–137. **Write** the name of each shape in the shape column. **Measure** the sides of each polygon and **record** its measurements. Then, **calculate** the perimeter of the polygon in the perimeter column. **Find** the area of every square and rectangle.

Shape	Each Side's Measurement	Perimeter side + side + side + side	Area 1 side x 1 side

Name _____

Suzy Spider, Interior Decorator

Suzy Spider is decorating her house. She is a very clever decorator, but she needs your help **calculating** the area and perimeter. **Draw** a picture to help.

1 Suzy is putting a silk fence around her garden. It is 12 inches long and 10 inches wide. What is the perimeter of the garden?

2 Suzy Spider wants to surround her house with a silk thread. Her house is 17 inches long and 12 inches wide. What is its perimeter?

3 Suzy wants to carpet her living room. It is 5 inches long and 4 inches wide. How much carpet should she buy for her living room?

4 Suzy wants to put wallpaper on a kitchen wall. The wall is 7 inches tall and 4 inches wide. What is its area?

5 Suzy has decided to hang a silk thread all the way around her porch. The porch is 4 inches long and 3 inches wide. How long should the thread be?

6 Suzy's bedroom is 6 inches long and 5 inches wide. How much carpet should she buy for it?

"State"istics

Choose ten states. Then, **research** their "lengths" and "heights" and **multiply** them to find their areas.

State Name	Approximate Miles E–W	Approximate Miles N–S	Area in Square Miles

Name _____

Turn Up the Volume

The **volume** is the measure of the inside of a shape. **Find** the volume of these shapes by counting the boxes. You might not be able to see all the boxes, but you can tell that they are there.

Example:

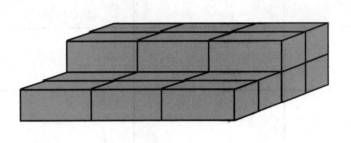

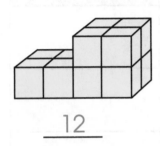

<u>12</u> _____ _____

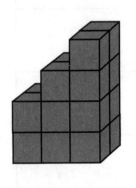

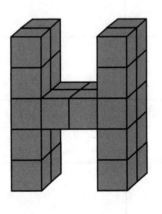

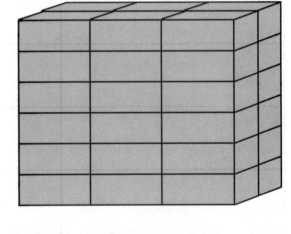

_____

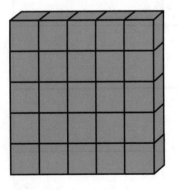

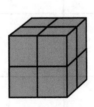

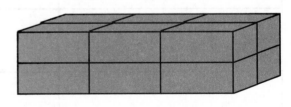

_____ _____ _____

How Much Can a Container Contain?

To find volume: Multiply length x width x height

1. Select four food boxes and draw and
   color one in each box below.
2. Measure the width, length and height
   (the sides) of each box and record
   it next to its picture.
3. Find the volume of each box and
   record it next to its picture.

H = _____
W = _____
L = _____

H

L   W

Name _____

Going in Circles

A **circle** is a round, closed figure. It is named by its center. A **radius** is a line segment from the center to any point on the circle.
A **diameter** is a line segment with both points on the circle. The diameter always passes through the center of the circle.

Name the radius, diameter and circle.

Example:

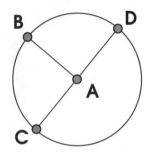

circle ___A___

radius _AB, AC, AD_

diameter _CD_

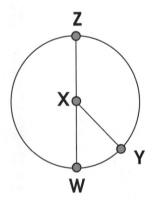

circle _____

radius _____

diameter _____

circle _____

radius _____

diameter _____

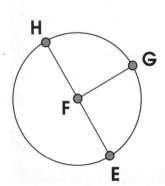

circle _____

radius _____

diameter _____

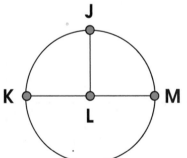

circle _____

radius _____

diameter _____

Perfect Symmetry

A figure that can be separated into two matching parts is **symmetric**. The **line of symmetry** is the line that divides the shape in half.

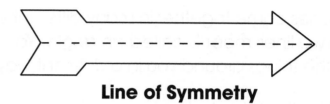

Line of Symmetry

Is the dotted line shown a line of symmetry?

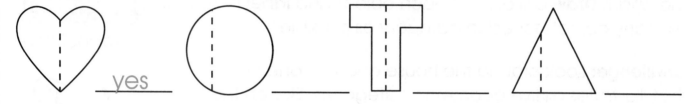

yes

Draw each matching part.

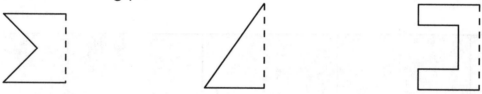

Complete the letters to make symmetric words.

Make two symmetric words of your own.

_ _ _ _ _ _ _ _ _ _ _ _ _ _ _

Look at the World From a Different Angle

Lines come together in many different ways. The point where two lines meet is called an **angle**. You may have to look at the things around you in a different way to find these angles.

Use the table below to **record** your observations from around the house. Look for objects that illustrate each **category** on the chart. **Draw** a sketch of each object and **label** it. **Find** as many objects for each category as possible.

perpendicular

Challenge: Look around the house and find one object that illustrates all five geometric categories. Sketch the object and label the various types of angles, lines or shapes that it has.

acute

 right	 acute	 obtuse	 straight	 perpendicular

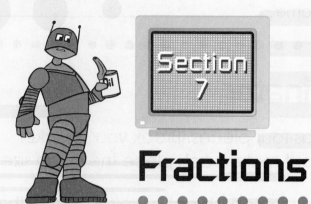

Fractions

RECIPES

INGREDIENTS

¹/₄ NUTS

¹/₄ MOTOROIL

¹/₄ BUTTONS

¹/₄ SCREWS

OIL

Graham Cracker Denominator

Find a cracker. If possible, use one that has four pieces. Break your cracker into as many or as few pieces as desired but make each piece the same size.

With fractions, the number of pieces into which an object is broken is how the bottom number, the **denominator**, obtains its numerical value. Remember that you started with one cracker that is in pieces now. **Write** the number of pieces as a denominator.

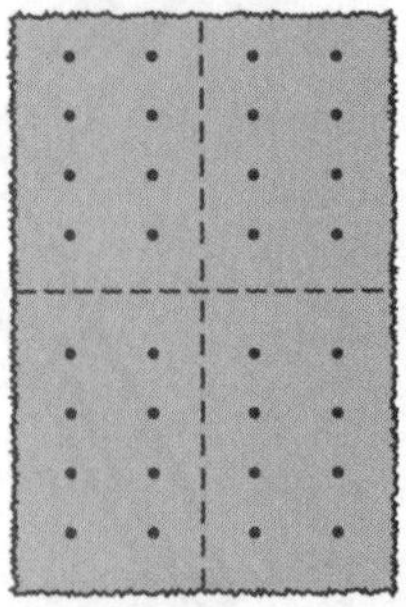

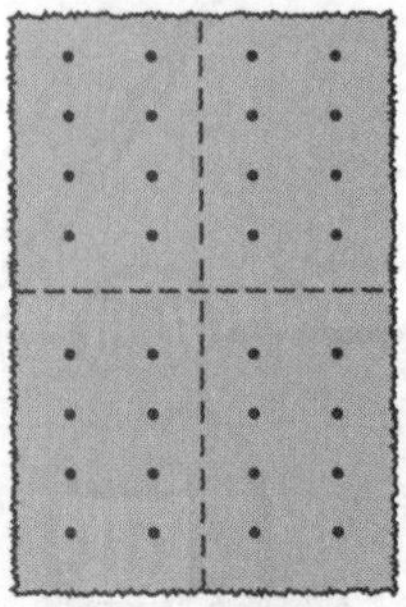

□ ← numerator

denominator → □

To determine the top number, the **numerator**, eat part of the cracker. In the diagram at the right, cross out the part you ate. This is the numerator.

Write two fractions—a fraction to show what is left and a fraction to show what was eaten.

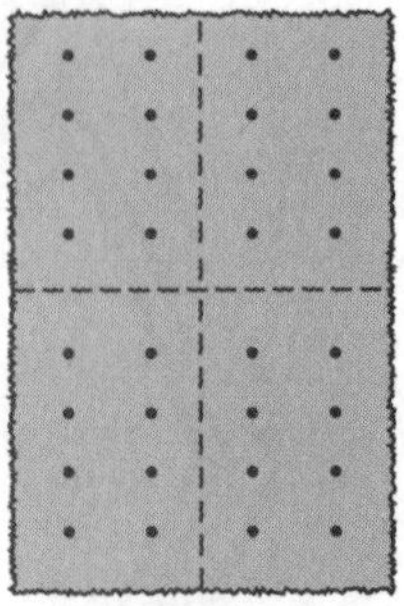

numerator □ of the cracker is left.
demoninator □

numerator □ of the cracker is gone.
denominator □

Eat another piece of the cracker. **Cross out** the part you ate in the diagram. Now, **write** how much is left.

numerator □ of the cracker is left.
denominator □

numerator □ of the cracker is gone.
denominator □

Eat another piece of the cracker. **Cross out** the part you ate in the diagram. Now, **write** how much is left.

numerator □ of the cracker is left.
denominator □

numerator □ of the cracker is gone.
denominator □

Which part changes, the numerator or the denominator?

SUPER!

Fantastic!

Awesome!

Excellent!

GREAT JOB!

Cool!

Wow!

TOTALLY!

IN9685617A

Fraction Fun

4 gloves are shaded. 9 gloves in all.

$\frac{4}{9}$ of the gloves are shaded.

What fraction of the balls is shaded? _____

cars? _____   trains? _____

dolls? _____   airplanes? _____

teddy bears? _____   rabbits? _____

hats? _____   boats? _____

Button Collection

Preparation: Use the boxes from **Equally Alike Boxes** on page 90 or collect sets of buttons. Count the number of buttons in each box or container. Create a response sheet like the one on the bottom of this page. You can choose how to group each of your objects. Those become the categories you write at the top of the response sheet.

Remember: A fraction has two numbers with a horizontal line drawn between them. The bottom number is called the **denominator**. The denominator tells how many equal parts or total pieces are in the whole. The top number is called the **numerator**. The numerator tells how many parts of the whole there are.

Example: $\dfrac{2}{5}$ the part of the total buttons with 2 holes

total number of buttons in the set

What is the fraction of buttons in this set with 2 holes?

		Fractions showing:					
Box #	# of buttons in box	Buttons with 2 holes	Buttons with 4 holes	White buttons	Gold buttons	Black buttons	Brown buttons

Response Sheet

The Mystery of the Missing Sweets

Some mysterious person is sneaking away with pieces of desserts from Sam Sillicook's Diner. Help him figure out how much is missing.

1 What fraction of Sam's Super Sweet Chocolate Cream Cake is missing?

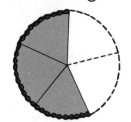

_____

4 What fraction of Sam's Heavenly Tasting Cherry Cream Tart is missing?

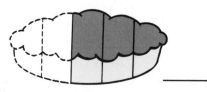

_____

2 What fraction of Sam's Tastee Toffee Coffee Cake is missing?

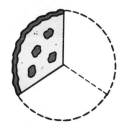

_____

5 Sam's Upside-Down Ice-Cream Cake is very famous. What fraction has vanished?

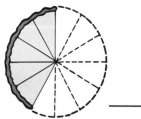

_____

3 What fraction of Sam's Tasty Tidbits of Chocolate Ice Cream is missing?

_____

6 What fraction of Sam's Luscious Licorice Candy Cake is missing?

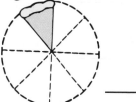

_____

Star Gazing

To find ½ of the stars, **divide** by 2.

Example:

$\dfrac{1}{2}$ of 10 = 5

$\dfrac{1}{2}$ of 6 = _____

$\dfrac{1}{2}$ of 8 = _____

$\dfrac{1}{3}$ of 9 = _____

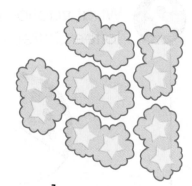

$\dfrac{1}{5}$ of 10 = _____

$\dfrac{1}{3}$ of 15 = _____

$\dfrac{1}{6}$ of 18 = _____

$\dfrac{1}{5}$ of 20 = _____

$\dfrac{1}{4}$ of 8 = _____

$\dfrac{1}{2}$ of 16 = _____

$\dfrac{1}{4}$ of 12 = _____

$\dfrac{1}{6}$ of 18 = _____

$\dfrac{1}{6}$ of 12 = _____

$\dfrac{1}{3}$ of 24 = _____

$\dfrac{1}{3}$ of 27 = _____

$\dfrac{1}{4}$ of 24 = _____

What Fraction Am I?

Identify the fraction for each shaded section.

Example: There are 5 sections on this figure.
2 sections are shaded. 2/5 of the sections
are shaded. 3 sections are not shaded.
3/5 of the sections are not shaded.

A. _____

B. _____

C. _____

D. _____

E. _____

F. _____

G. _____

H. _____

I. _____

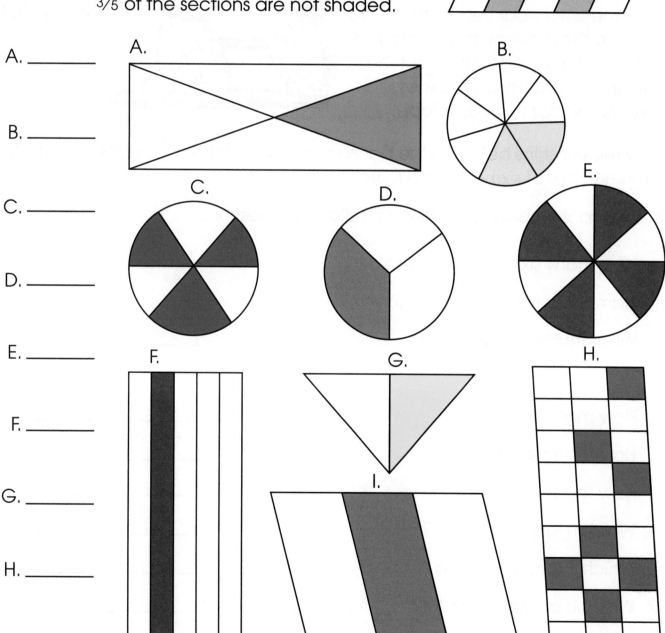

Fractions

Name _____

The Parts Equal the Whole

The one long **Fraction Bar** on page 167 is a whole. Each bar thereafter is broken up into equal parts.

Directions: Name what part of the whole each bar is. **Write** its fraction on it.

Color the whole bar yellow, the halves blue, the thirds green, the fourths red and the sixths orange. Then, **cut** the bars apart carefully on the lines. Store the pieces in an envelope.

Show relationships between the bar, such as the number of fourths in a whole or the number of sixths in a third, etc.

Use the fraction bars to **answer** the following questions:

1. How many sixths are in a whole? _____

2. Name four fractions that equal $1/2$. _____

3. What fractions equal $1/3$? _____

4. How many fourths are in $1/2$? _____

    How many sixths? _____

    How many eighths? _____

    How many tenths? _____

5. Which is larger, $3/4$ or $4/6$? _____

6. Which is larger, $1/3$ or $1/2$? _____

7. Which is smaller, $2/3$ or $4/4$? _____

8. Which is smaller, $1/2$ or $3/4$? _____

Fraction Bars

This page intentionally left blank.

The Whole Thing

Preparation: Cut 14 index cards in half. Write three copies of the following fractions on them (one per card): $-\dfrac{1}{3}$, $+\dfrac{1}{3}$, $-\dfrac{1}{6}$, $+\dfrac{1}{6}$, $-\dfrac{1}{2}$, $+\dfrac{1}{2}$, $-\dfrac{1}{4}$, $+\dfrac{1}{4}$.

On four more cards, write $+\dfrac{1}{3}$, $+\dfrac{1}{6}$, $+\dfrac{1}{2}$, $+\dfrac{1}{4}$.

Rules: This game involves 2–4 players. Put the stack of fraction cards upside down in the middle of the playing area. Use the **Fraction Bars** on page 167. Each player puts a whole bar in front of him/her and the fraction bars to the side. Fraction cards are always returned to the bottom of the stack after use.

The object of this game is to build a whole bar using a set of fractions. Players may build as many as four sets at a time.

Directions: Player One draws a fraction card. If a minus card is drawn and Player One has no bar, then Player One loses his/her turn. If an addition card is drawn, the fraction bar representing the fraction named on the card is placed on the whole bar. When a subtraction fraction card is drawn, the bar representing the fraction is taken away. If no fraction bar representing the fraction on the minus card is placed above the bar, the player simply loses his/her turn. The first player to build a whole bar is the winner.

Working With Fractions

Use the fraction bars to help you **find** the smallest fraction in each row.
Circle it.

1. $\dfrac{1}{2}$ $\dfrac{2}{3}$ $\dfrac{1}{6}$ $\dfrac{1}{3}$

2. $\dfrac{2}{3}$ $\dfrac{2}{6}$ $\dfrac{3}{3}$ $\dfrac{3}{6}$

3. $\dfrac{2}{2}$ $\dfrac{3}{6}$ $\dfrac{2}{3}$ $\dfrac{1}{3}$

4. $\dfrac{5}{6}$ $\dfrac{4}{6}$ $\dfrac{1}{2}$ $\dfrac{2}{3}$

5. $\dfrac{6}{6}$ $\dfrac{2}{3}$ $\dfrac{5}{6}$ $\dfrac{2}{2}$

1 Whole					
$\frac{1}{2}$			$\frac{2}{2}$		
$\frac{1}{3}$		$\frac{2}{3}$		$\frac{3}{3}$	
$\frac{1}{6}$	$\frac{2}{6}$	$\frac{3}{6}$	$\frac{4}{6}$	$\frac{5}{6}$	$\frac{6}{6}$

Use the fraction bars to help you **find** the greatest fraction in each row.
Circle it.

1 Whole							
$\frac{1}{2}$				$\frac{2}{2}$			
$\frac{1}{4}$		$\frac{2}{4}$		$\frac{3}{4}$		$\frac{4}{4}$	
$\frac{1}{8}$	$\frac{2}{8}$	$\frac{3}{8}$	$\frac{4}{8}$	$\frac{5}{8}$	$\frac{6}{8}$	$\frac{7}{8}$	$\frac{8}{8}$

1. $\dfrac{1}{2}$ $\dfrac{3}{4}$ $\dfrac{6}{8}$ $\dfrac{8}{8}$

2. $\dfrac{1}{4}$ $\dfrac{1}{8}$ $\dfrac{7}{8}$ $\dfrac{1}{2}$

3. $\dfrac{1}{8}$ $\dfrac{1}{2}$ $\dfrac{1}{4}$ $\dfrac{2}{8}$

4. $\dfrac{1}{4}$ $\dfrac{3}{8}$ $\dfrac{5}{8}$ $\dfrac{3}{4}$

5. $\dfrac{2}{8}$ $\dfrac{1}{8}$ $\dfrac{1}{4}$ $\dfrac{6}{8}$

Name _____

More Fractions

Compare the fractions below. **Write** < or > in each box.

Examples:

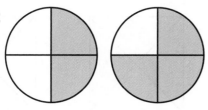

$\frac{2}{4}$ [<] $\frac{3}{4}$

less than

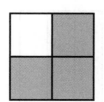

$\frac{3}{4}$ [>] $\frac{2}{4}$

greater than

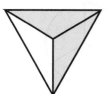 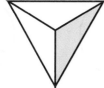  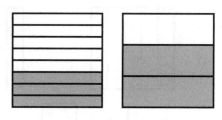

$\frac{2}{3}$ [ ] $\frac{1}{3}$ $\frac{1}{4}$ [ ] $\frac{5}{8}$ $\frac{3}{8}$ [ ] $\frac{2}{3}$

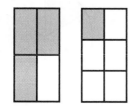 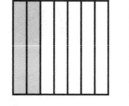 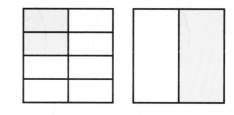

$\frac{3}{4}$ [ ] $\frac{1}{6}$ $\frac{2}{7}$ [ ] $\frac{4}{7}$ $\frac{2}{8}$ [ ] $\frac{1}{2}$

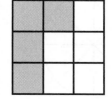 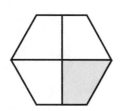 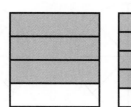

$\frac{4}{9}$ [ ] $\frac{2}{3}$ $\frac{1}{4}$ [ ] $\frac{3}{6}$ $\frac{3}{4}$ [ ] $\frac{4}{5}$

Dare to Compare

Compare the fractions below. **Write** =, < or > in each box.

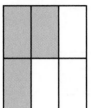 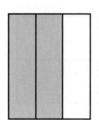

$\dfrac{3}{6}$ ☐ $\dfrac{2}{3}$

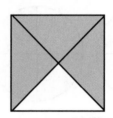 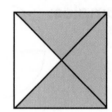

$\dfrac{3}{4}$ ☐ $\dfrac{3}{4}$

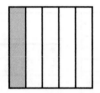

$\dfrac{1}{5}$ ☐ $\dfrac{3}{10}$

$\dfrac{1}{2}$ ☐ $\dfrac{1}{3}$

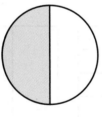 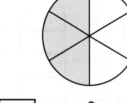

$\dfrac{1}{2}$ ☐ $\dfrac{3}{6}$

 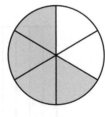

$\dfrac{4}{6}$ ☐ $\dfrac{4}{6}$

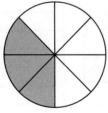

$\dfrac{3}{8}$ ☐ $\dfrac{6}{8}$

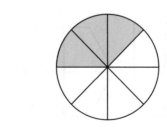 

$\dfrac{3}{8}$ ☐ $\dfrac{2}{8}$

Exploring Equivalent Fractions

Equivalent fractions are two different fractions which represent the same number. For example, on page 172, the picture shows that ½ and ⅜ are the same or equivalent fractions.

Complete these equivalent fractions. **Use** your fraction bars.

1. $\dfrac{1}{3} = \dfrac{}{6}$
2. $\dfrac{1}{2} = \dfrac{}{4}$
3. $\dfrac{3}{4} = \dfrac{}{8}$
4. $\dfrac{1}{3} = \dfrac{}{9}$

Circle the figure that shows a fraction equivalent to the first figure. **Write** the fractions for the shaded area under each figure.

5.
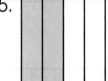   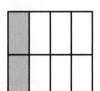

_____   _____   _____   _____

6.
        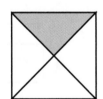   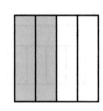

_____   _____   _____   _____

Write two equivalent fractions for each fraction.

7. $\dfrac{1}{4}$, __ , __
8. $\dfrac{1}{5}$, __ , __
9. $\dfrac{2}{3}$, __ , __
10. $\dfrac{3}{8}$, __ , __

To find an equivalent fraction, **multiply** both parts of the fraction by the same number.

Example: $\dfrac{2}{3} \times \dfrac{3}{3} = \dfrac{6}{9}$

11. $\dfrac{1}{4} = \dfrac{}{8}$
12. $\dfrac{3}{4} = \dfrac{}{8}$
13. $\dfrac{4}{5} = \dfrac{8}{}$
14. $\dfrac{3}{8} = \dfrac{}{24}$

Fractions

Match the Fractions

Above each bar, **write** a fraction for the shaded part. Then, **match** each fraction on the left with its equivalent fraction on the right.

1. _____

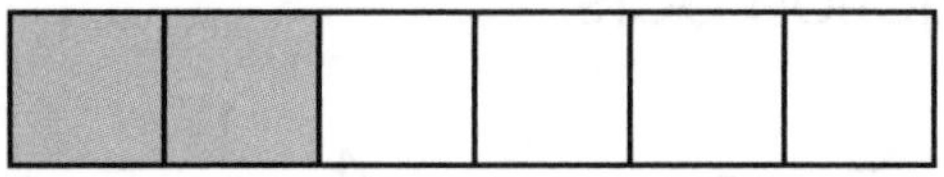

•   •

2. _____

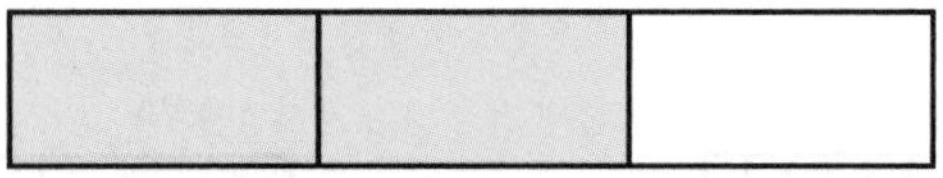

•   •

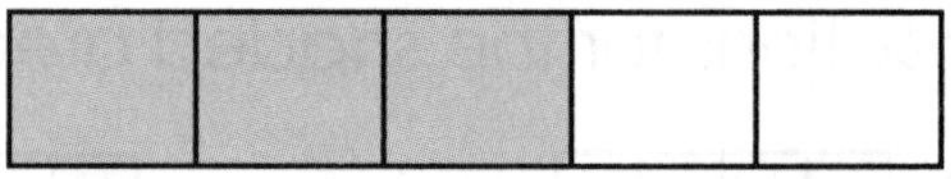

3. _____

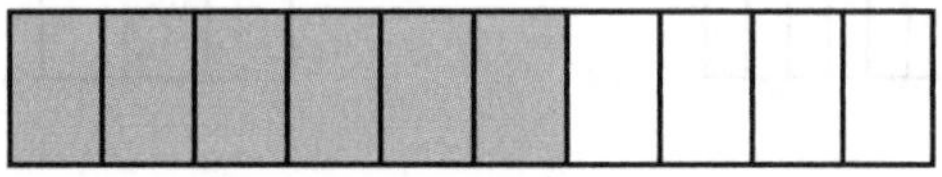

•   •

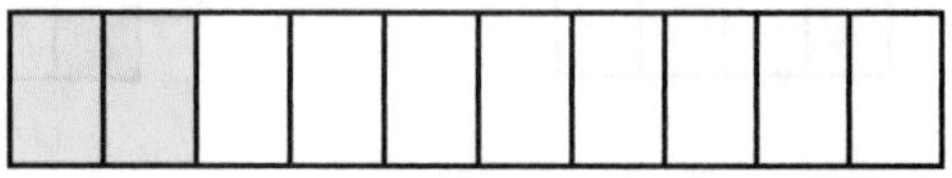

4. _____

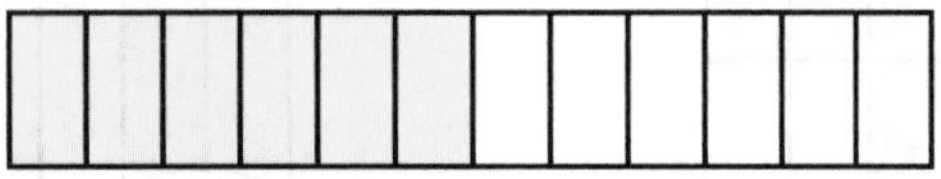

•   •

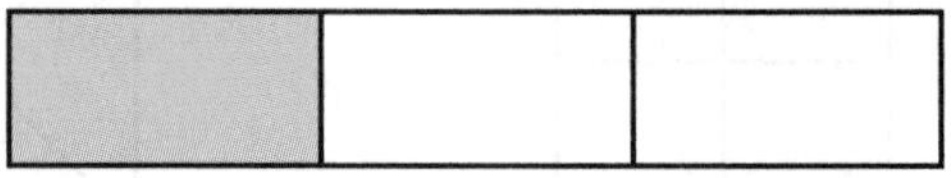

5. _____

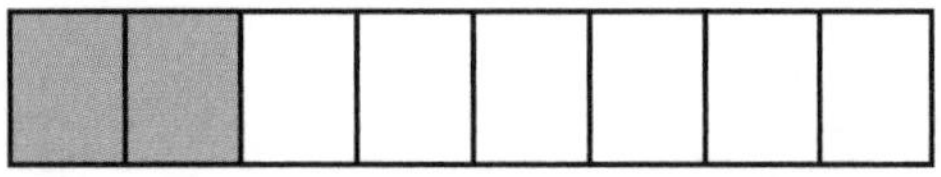

•   •

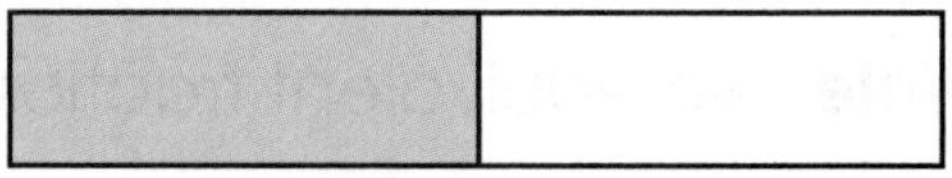

6. _____

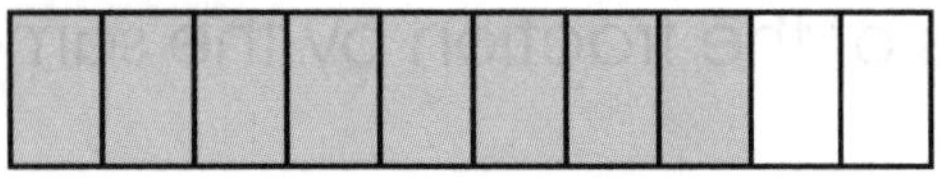

•   •

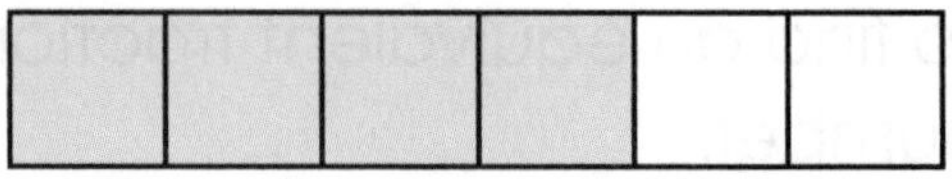

7. _____

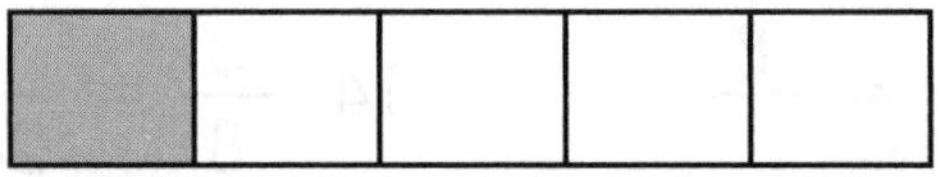

•   •

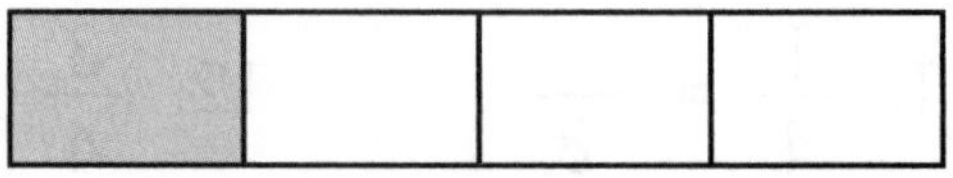

Name _____

Fraction Patterns

Each row contains equivalent fractions except for one. **Find** which three fractions are equivalent for each row.

Draw an **X** on the fraction that is not equivalent. On the line, **write** a fraction that could be in the set. If necessary, **draw** a picture to help.

Example:

| $\frac{1}{2}$ | $\frac{2}{4}$ | $\cancel{\frac{3}{5}}$ | $\frac{4}{8}$ |

$$\frac{\text{Numerator (N) x 2}}{\text{Denominator (D) x 2}}$$

New Fraction
$$\frac{8}{16}$$

New Fraction

1.

| $\frac{1}{8}$ | $\frac{2}{16}$ | $\frac{2}{24}$ | $\frac{4}{32}$ |

_____

2.

| $\frac{3}{4}$ | $\frac{6}{8}$ | $\frac{12}{16}$ | $\frac{20}{30}$ |

_____

3.

| $\frac{3}{10}$ | $\frac{9}{30}$ | $\frac{27}{90}$ | $\frac{36}{180}$ |

_____

4.

| $\frac{1}{5}$ | $\frac{3}{10}$ | $\frac{3}{15}$ | $\frac{4}{20}$ |

_____

5.

| $\frac{3}{7}$ | $\frac{6}{14}$ | $\frac{8}{21}$ | $\frac{12}{28}$ |

_____

6.

| $\frac{1}{2}$ | $\frac{4}{8}$ | $\frac{16}{32}$ | $\frac{62}{128}$ |

_____

7.

| $\frac{5}{8}$ | $\frac{9}{16}$ | $\frac{15}{24}$ | $\frac{20}{32}$ |

_____

Write a rule to find equivalent fractions.

_____

Alligator Problems

Complete each equivalent fraction below.

Example: $\dfrac{4 \times 3}{6 \times 3} = \dfrac{12}{18}$

$\dfrac{2}{3} = \dfrac{}{15}$ $\qquad$ $\dfrac{1}{6} = \dfrac{}{36}$ $\qquad$ $\dfrac{5}{7} = \dfrac{}{49}$ $\qquad$ $\dfrac{4}{5} = \dfrac{}{20}$

$\dfrac{1}{2} = \dfrac{6}{}$ $\qquad$ $\dfrac{1}{3} = \dfrac{}{12}$ $\qquad$ $\dfrac{4}{9} = \dfrac{}{27}$ $\qquad$ $\dfrac{7}{9} = \dfrac{14}{}$

$\dfrac{2}{3} = \dfrac{}{12}$ $\qquad$ $\dfrac{4}{9} = \dfrac{}{27}$ $\qquad$ $\dfrac{3}{8} = \dfrac{}{24}$ $\qquad$ $\dfrac{1}{6} = \dfrac{}{24}$

$\dfrac{1}{2} = \dfrac{4}{}$ $\qquad$ $\dfrac{1}{2} = \dfrac{}{16}$ $\qquad$ $\dfrac{1}{4} = \dfrac{4}{}$ $\qquad$ $\dfrac{4}{7} = \dfrac{}{28}$

$\dfrac{1}{8} = \dfrac{}{16}$ $\qquad$ $\dfrac{1}{3} = \dfrac{}{24}$ $\qquad$ $\dfrac{3}{6} = \dfrac{}{12}$ $\qquad$ $\dfrac{5}{10} = \dfrac{}{20}$

$\dfrac{2}{5} = \dfrac{4}{}$ $\qquad$ $\dfrac{2}{3} = \dfrac{4}{}$ $\qquad$ $\dfrac{3}{7} = \dfrac{}{21}$

$\dfrac{2}{3} = \dfrac{}{9}$

$\dfrac{2}{5} = \dfrac{}{25}$

$\dfrac{2}{7} = \dfrac{}{14}$

Name

More Than Peanuts

Write <, >, or = to compare the fractions below. **Draw** pictures or **write** equivalent fractions, if needed.

$\frac{3}{8}$ ☐ $\frac{2}{8}$ $\frac{2}{3}$ ☐ $\frac{3}{6}$ $\frac{3}{6}$ ☐ $\frac{1}{2}$

$\frac{4}{7}$ ☐ $\frac{4}{14}$ $\frac{1}{3}$ ☐ $\frac{6}{9}$ $\frac{7}{10}$ ☐ $\frac{2}{5}$

$\frac{8}{12}$ ☐ $\frac{3}{6}$ $\frac{7}{14}$ ☐ $\frac{1}{2}$ $\frac{4}{7}$ ☐ $\frac{3}{7}$ $\frac{4}{8}$ ☐ $\frac{8}{16}$

$\frac{1}{3}$ ☐ $\frac{2}{6}$ $\frac{2}{8}$ ☐ $\frac{1}{2}$ $\frac{1}{5}$ ☐ $\frac{3}{10}$ $\frac{6}{11}$ ☐ $\frac{5}{11}$

$\frac{6}{12}$ ☐ $\frac{1}{2}$ $\frac{2}{3}$ ☐ $\frac{2}{6}$ $\frac{7}{12}$ ☐ $\frac{2}{4}$ $\frac{5}{6}$ ☐ $\frac{1}{3}$

$\frac{7}{10}$ ☐ $\frac{3}{10}$ $\frac{1}{2}$ ☐ $\frac{8}{12}$ $\frac{1}{5}$ ☐ $\frac{8}{10}$ $\frac{7}{8}$ ☐ $\frac{2}{4}$

$\frac{3}{8}$ ☐ $\frac{1}{4}$ $\frac{2}{5}$ ☐ $\frac{5}{10}$

$\frac{5}{6}$ ☐ $\frac{2}{3}$ $\frac{6}{10}$ ☐ $\frac{2}{5}$

$\frac{6}{10}$ ☐ $\frac{3}{10}$ $\frac{3}{6}$ ☐ $\frac{6}{12}$

$\frac{1}{8}$ ☐ $\frac{1}{4}$ $\frac{1}{2}$ ☐ $\frac{1}{4}$

Name _____

Catch It If You Can

For each fraction below, determine if the fraction equals more or less than ½.
For each fraction, **cross out** the ball that does not describe the fraction.
Then, **fill in** the blanks with the letters left to solve the riddle at the bottom
of the page.

		Less than	More than
1.	$\frac{3}{8}$	Y	T
2.	$\frac{4}{5}$	H	O
3.	$\frac{1}{3}$	U	E
4.	$\frac{4}{6}$	S	R
5.	$\frac{1}{4}$	B	T

		Less than	More than
6.	$\frac{2}{3}$	L	R
7.	$\frac{5}{8}$	R	E
8.	$\frac{7}{8}$	O	A
9.	$\frac{1}{8}$	T	L
10.	$\frac{1}{6}$	H	P

What is harder to catch the faster you run?

___ ___ ___ ___ ___ ___   ___ ___ ___ ___ ___ ___

Reduce, Reduce

To reduce a fraction, **divide** each number in the fraction by a common factor. A fraction is reduced when the numerator and the denominator have only a common factor of 1. This is called a fraction's **lowest terms**.

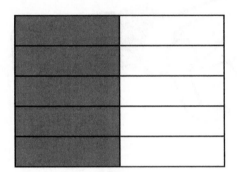 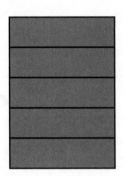 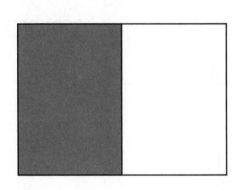

$$\frac{5}{10} \qquad \div \qquad \frac{5}{5} \qquad = \qquad \frac{1}{2}$$

5 is a common factor of 5 and 10. (It can be divided into groups of five.)
Is there another number these both can be divided by? (Only the number 1.)

Example: $\frac{16}{20} \div \frac{2}{2} = \frac{8}{10}$ **Ask:** Is this the lowest? Is there another number these both can be divided by? (Yes, 2.)

$\frac{8}{10} \div \frac{2}{2} = \frac{4}{5}$ Can this still divided by a common number? (No.)

Reduce these fractions.

$\frac{9}{12} =$ $\qquad$ $\frac{3}{15} =$ $\qquad$ $\frac{12}{16} =$ $\qquad$ $\frac{4}{5} =$ $\qquad$ $\frac{2}{8} =$

$\frac{1}{8} =$ $\qquad$ $\frac{4}{6} =$ $\qquad$ $\frac{3}{9} =$ $\qquad$ $\frac{7}{14} =$ $\qquad$ $\frac{18}{24} =$

Name _____

Reduce the Fat

Reduce each fraction to its lowest terms.

Example: $\dfrac{5}{25} \dfrac{\div 5}{\div 5} = \dfrac{1}{5}$

common factors

$\dfrac{8}{16} = \underline{\quad}$ $\qquad$ $\dfrac{12}{18} = \underline{\quad}$

$\dfrac{10}{25} = \underline{\quad}$ $\qquad$ $\dfrac{12}{30} = \underline{\quad}$ $\qquad$ $\dfrac{3}{30} = \underline{\quad}$ $\qquad$ $\dfrac{6}{30} = \underline{\quad}$

$\dfrac{12}{20} = \underline{\quad}$ $\qquad$ $\dfrac{3}{18} = \underline{\quad}$ $\qquad$ $\dfrac{3}{9} = \underline{\quad}$ $\qquad$ $\dfrac{4}{26} = \underline{\quad}$

$\dfrac{4}{28} = \underline{\quad}$ $\qquad$ $\dfrac{7}{21} = \underline{\quad}$ $\qquad$ $\dfrac{16}{20} = \underline{\quad}$ $\qquad$ $\dfrac{2}{10} = \underline{\quad}$

$\dfrac{3}{27} = \underline{\quad}$ $\qquad$ $\dfrac{5}{60} = \underline{\quad}$ $\qquad$ $\dfrac{21}{35} = \underline{\quad}$ $\qquad$ $\dfrac{3}{12} = \underline{\quad}$

$\dfrac{9}{36} = \underline{\quad}$ $\qquad$ $\dfrac{24}{40} = \underline{\quad}$ $\qquad$ $\dfrac{8}{24} = \underline{\quad}$

$\dfrac{16}{40} = \underline{\quad}$

Mix 'Em Up

A **mixed number** is a whole number with a fraction.

Example: $1\frac{2}{3}$

An **improper fraction** is a fraction representing a whole and a fraction. The numerator is larger than the denominator.

Example: $\frac{16}{3}$

To change a mixed number to an improper fraction, **multiply** the whole number by the denominator.

Example: $2\frac{3}{4}$ 2 x 4 = 8   (How many fourths?)

Add the numerator to that number. 8 + 3 = 11

Write the fraction with the resulting number as numerator over the original denominator. $\frac{11}{4}$

$1\frac{1}{3} =$ $3\frac{2}{5} =$ $4\frac{3}{4} =$ $2\frac{2}{7} =$

To change an improper fraction to a mixed number, **divide** the numerator by the denominator. $\frac{10}{3}$

(How many wholes can be made?) $3\overline{)10}$ $^{3\,R1}$

Write the quotient as the whole number and **write** any remainder as a fraction (with the denominator from the original problem).

$3\frac{1}{3} =$

$\frac{5}{2} =$ $\frac{7}{6} =$ $\frac{4}{3} =$ $\frac{10}{4} =$

Fractions

Name _____

Oh, My!

When the numerator is greater than the denominator (an improper fraction), write a mixed number or divide to write a whole number. A mixed number is made up of a whole number and a fraction. **Example:** $2\frac{1}{2}$

Draw the correct mouths on the animals by finding the whole or mixed number for each.

Example:

$$\frac{11}{2} =$$

$$\frac{20}{3}$$

$$\frac{21}{7}$$

$$\frac{24}{2}$$

$$11 \div 2 = 5\,R\,1 = 5\frac{1}{2}$$

$$\frac{16}{2}$$

$$\frac{49}{7}$$

$$\frac{16}{16}$$

$$\frac{16}{6}$$

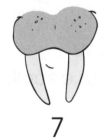

7

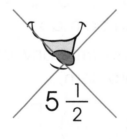

$$5\frac{1}{2}$$

$$2\frac{4}{6}$$

$$6\frac{2}{3}$$

3

8

1

12

Fractions

Figure It Out

Solve the problems. Then, **connect** the dots in the same order as the answers appear.

1. $3\frac{3}{4} = \frac{}{4}$ **2.** $\frac{30}{11} = 2\frac{}{11}$ **3.** $\frac{10}{6} = 1\frac{}{6}$ **4.** $4\frac{1}{5} = \frac{}{5}$

5. $\frac{13}{7} = 1\frac{}{7}$ **6.** $1\frac{5}{6} = \frac{}{6}$ **7.** $4\frac{1}{3} = \frac{}{3}$ **8.** $2\frac{2}{5} = \frac{}{5}$

9. $1\frac{1}{9} = \frac{}{9}$ **10.** $1\frac{2}{5} = \frac{}{5}$ **11.** $\frac{9}{2} = 4\frac{}{2}$ **12.** $8\frac{1}{2} = \frac{}{2}$

13. $4\frac{3}{8} = \frac{}{8}$ **14.** $\frac{11}{3} = 3\frac{}{3}$ **15.** $3\frac{5}{6} = \frac{}{6}$ **16.** $\frac{13}{5} = 2\frac{}{5}$

17. $\frac{12}{7} = 1\frac{}{7}$ **18.** $6\frac{2}{5} = \frac{}{5}$ **19.** $\frac{13}{8} = 1\frac{}{8}$ **20.** $1\frac{1}{8} = \frac{}{8}$

1

17

7

35

10

13   12

2

21

4

11

8

23

15   9   3

5   5

32

6

Name _____

The Ultimate Adding Machine

Find the sum for each problem. **Reduce** it to the lowest terms.

$\dfrac{7}{9} + \dfrac{1}{9} =$ 　　　　$\dfrac{4}{12} + \dfrac{3}{12} =$ 　　　　$\dfrac{3}{6} + \dfrac{2}{6} =$

$\dfrac{1}{9} + \dfrac{3}{9} =$ 　　　　$\dfrac{4}{10} + \dfrac{4}{10} =$ 　　　　$\dfrac{3}{6} + \dfrac{1}{6} =$

$\dfrac{5}{9} + \dfrac{3}{9} =$ 　　　　$\dfrac{2}{5} + \dfrac{1}{5} =$ 　　　　$\dfrac{5}{11} + \dfrac{5}{11} =$

$\dfrac{3}{7} + \dfrac{2}{7} =$ 　　　　$\dfrac{4}{8} + \dfrac{1}{8} =$ 　　　　$\dfrac{4}{12} + \dfrac{1}{12} =$

$\dfrac{5}{8} + \dfrac{2}{8} =$ 　　　　$\dfrac{6}{12} + \dfrac{4}{12} =$ 　　　　$\dfrac{4}{6} + \dfrac{1}{6} =$

$\dfrac{4}{11} + \dfrac{4}{11} =$ 　　　　$\dfrac{2}{5} + \dfrac{2}{5} =$

$\dfrac{5}{8} + \dfrac{5}{8} =$ 　　　　$\dfrac{1}{9} + \dfrac{2}{9} =$

$\dfrac{7}{10} + \dfrac{2}{10} =$ 　　**7 + 9 + 6 +**

Sea Math

Reduce each sum to a whole number or a mixed number in the lowest terms.

$$\frac{6}{9} + \frac{6}{9}$$  $$\frac{4}{5} + \frac{6}{5}$$ $$\frac{3}{4} + \frac{2}{4}$$ $$\frac{8}{11} + \frac{8}{11}$$ $$\frac{2}{5} + \frac{3}{5}$$

$$\frac{8}{9} + \frac{3}{9}$$ $$\frac{4}{8} + \frac{6}{8}$$ $$\frac{5}{4} + \frac{2}{4}$$ $$\frac{4}{3} + \frac{2}{3}$$ $$\frac{5}{7} + \frac{6}{7}$$

$$\frac{8}{11} + \frac{3}{11}$$ $$\frac{3}{12} + \frac{10}{12}$$ $$\frac{3}{6} + \frac{3}{6}$$ $$\frac{6}{12} + \frac{8}{12}$$ $$\frac{4}{8} + \frac{4}{8}$$ $$\frac{5}{12} + \frac{8}{12}$$

$$\frac{5}{12} + \frac{10}{12}$$  $$\frac{7}{13} + \frac{6}{13}$$ $$\frac{8}{15} + \frac{14}{15}$$ $$\frac{5}{7} + \frac{6}{7}$$

Fractions

Name _____

Soaring Subtraction

Solve each subtraction problem. **Reduce** each difference to the lowest terms.

$$\frac{7}{10} - \frac{3}{10}$$

$$\frac{14}{16} - \frac{7}{16}$$

$$\frac{7}{7} - \frac{3}{7}$$

$$\frac{6}{8} - \frac{2}{8}$$

$$\frac{9}{11} - \frac{7}{11}$$

$$\frac{16}{21} - \frac{9}{21}$$

$$\frac{9}{10} - \frac{6}{10}$$

$$\frac{17}{18} - \frac{6}{18}$$

$$\frac{9}{12} - \frac{7}{12}$$

$$\frac{15}{18} - \frac{7}{18}$$

$$\frac{11}{14} - \frac{8}{14}$$

$$\frac{17}{17} - \frac{8}{17}$$

$$\frac{14}{15} - \frac{8}{15}$$

$$\frac{11}{12} - \frac{2}{12}$$

$$\frac{9}{10} - \frac{5}{10}$$

$$\frac{8}{9} - \frac{7}{9}$$

$$\frac{4}{5} - \frac{3}{5}$$

$$\frac{8}{10} - \frac{5}{10}$$

$$\frac{2}{3} - \frac{1}{3}$$

$$\frac{4}{6} - \frac{3}{6}$$

$$\frac{8}{9} - \frac{5}{9}$$

Take a Closer Look

What is a stamp collector called?

To find out, **solve** the following subtraction problems and **reduce** to the lowest terms. Then, **write** the letter above its matching answer at the bottom of the page.

I. $\dfrac{10}{11} - \dfrac{9}{11} =$ H. $\dfrac{12}{12} - \dfrac{3}{12} =$ E. $\dfrac{13}{14} - \dfrac{8}{14} =$

A. $\dfrac{6}{8} - \dfrac{4}{8} =$ I. $\dfrac{6}{7} - \dfrac{5}{7} =$ P. $\dfrac{6}{6} - \dfrac{2}{6} =$

T. $\dfrac{13}{14} - \dfrac{6}{14} =$ L. $\dfrac{17}{20} - \dfrac{8}{20} =$

S. $\dfrac{10}{14} - \dfrac{6}{14} =$ T. $\dfrac{8}{10} - \dfrac{2}{10} =$

L. $\dfrac{14}{18} - \dfrac{8}{18} =$

$\dfrac{2}{3}$ $\dfrac{3}{4}$ $\dfrac{1}{7}$ $\dfrac{1}{3}$ $\dfrac{1}{4}$ $\dfrac{1}{2}$ $\dfrac{5}{14}$ $\dfrac{9}{20}$ $\dfrac{1}{11}$ $\dfrac{2}{7}$ $\dfrac{3}{5}$

Name _____

Finding a Common Denominator

When adding or subtracting fractions with different denominators, find a common denominator first. A **common denominator** is a common multiple of two or more denominators.

Cut a paper plate in half. **Cut** another paper plate into eighths. Use these models to help **solve** the following addition and subtraction problems.

$\frac{1}{2} + \frac{2}{8} =$ The common denominator is 8 because 2 x 4 = 8; 8 x 1 = 8.

$$\frac{1}{2} \times \frac{4}{4} = \frac{4}{8} \qquad\qquad \frac{4}{8} + \frac{2}{8} = \frac{6}{8}$$

$\frac{7}{8} - \frac{1}{2} =$ The common denominator is 8 because 1 x 4 = 8; 2 x 4 = 8.

$$\frac{7}{8} - \frac{4}{8} = \frac{3}{8}$$

To find a common denominator of two or more fractions, follow these steps:

1. Write equivalent fractions so that the fractions have the same denominator.
2. Write the fractions with the same denominator.

Example: Step 1   Step 2

$$\frac{1}{2} + \frac{2}{6} = \qquad\qquad \frac{1}{2} \times \frac{3}{3} = \frac{3}{6} \qquad\qquad \frac{3}{6} + \frac{2}{6} = \frac{5}{6}$$

Follow the steps above. Then, **add**. **Reduce** the answer to its lowest terms.

$$\frac{5}{9} + \frac{1}{3} = \qquad\qquad\qquad\qquad \frac{3}{8} - \frac{1}{4} =$$

$$\frac{1}{3} + \frac{5}{12} = \qquad\qquad\qquad\qquad \frac{5}{12} - \frac{1}{6} =$$

Name _____

 Fractions

Bug Me!

Solve the puzzle.

Down

1. $\frac{1}{15} + \frac{2}{5} = $ _____ fifteenths

4. $\frac{2}{12} + \frac{2}{6} = $ one _____

5. $\frac{3}{10} + \frac{7}{20} = $ thirteen _____

7. $\frac{1}{8} + \frac{1}{4} = $ three _____

8. $\frac{2}{6} + \frac{1}{12} = $ five _____

9. $\frac{3}{9} + \frac{1}{3} = $ two _____

11. $\frac{1}{8} + \frac{2}{16} = $ _____ fourth

Across

2. $\frac{1}{12} + \frac{1}{3} = $ five _____

3. $\frac{5}{10} + \frac{2}{5} = $ nine _____

5. $\frac{7}{15} + \frac{1}{5} = $ _____ thirds

6. $\frac{1}{2} + \frac{2}{6} = $ _____ sixths

8. $\frac{1}{6} + \frac{1}{2} = $ _____ thirds

9. $\frac{1}{5} + \frac{4}{10} = $ _____ fifths

10. $\frac{1}{3} + \frac{3}{6} = $ _____ sixths

12. $\frac{2}{7} + \frac{1}{14} = $ five _____

13. $\frac{8}{14} + \frac{2}{7} = $ _____ sevenths

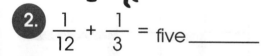

Name _____

Numeral Nibblers

Complete these equations. Use another sheet of paper to solve the problems, if needed.

$$\frac{15}{16} - \frac{1}{2} = \underline{\hphantom{00}}$$

$$-$$

$$\frac{3}{4} - \frac{10}{16} = \underline{\hphantom{00}}$$

$$= \qquad -$$

$$- \frac{1}{8} = \underline{\hphantom{00}}$$

$$- \qquad -$$

$$\frac{2}{3} - \frac{2}{12} = \underline{\hphantom{00}} \qquad \frac{1}{48}$$

$$- \qquad =$$

$$\frac{2}{9} \qquad \frac{21}{24} - \frac{5}{6} = \underline{\hphantom{00}}$$

$$= \qquad - \qquad -$$

$$\frac{3}{4} - \frac{7}{12} = \underline{\hphantom{00}}$$

$$= \qquad =$$

Make a Wish

Solve these problems.

Example: $\frac{2}{9}$ of 27 =   (27 ÷ 9) x 2 = 6

$\frac{7}{8}$ of 16 = $\frac{3}{7}$ of 49 = $\frac{4}{6}$ of 60 = $\frac{3}{6}$ of 54 =

$\frac{6}{8}$ of 24 = $\frac{9}{12}$ of 36 = $\frac{9}{12}$ of 24 = $\frac{2}{5}$ of 25 =

$\frac{3}{8}$ of 32 = $\frac{5}{7}$ of 42 = $\frac{3}{4}$ of 48 =

$\frac{3}{7}$ of 35 = $\frac{7}{9}$ of 36 =

$\frac{6}{8}$ of 64 = $\frac{8}{9}$ of 81 =

$\frac{3}{6}$ of 24 = $\frac{5}{6}$ of 30 =

$\frac{9}{10}$ of 40 = $\frac{6}{8}$ of 72 =

$\frac{9}{11}$ of 33 = $\frac{3}{8}$ of 48 =

Name _____

Make the Move

Complete the puzzle by writing the answers in words.

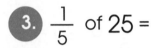

Down

Example: 1. $\dfrac{3}{4}$ of 12 =

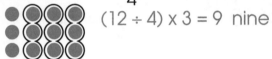

$(12 \div 4) \times 3 = 9$ nine

3. $\dfrac{1}{5}$ of 25 =

5. $\dfrac{8}{9}$ of 27 =

6. $\dfrac{3}{6}$ of 18 =

7. $\dfrac{3}{8}$ of 16 =

12. $\dfrac{2}{11}$ of 22 =

13. $\dfrac{3}{4}$ of 24 =

15. $\dfrac{1}{8}$ of 16 =

Across

2. $\dfrac{3}{10}$ of 20 =

4. $\dfrac{9}{10}$ of 20 =

8. $\dfrac{1}{3}$ of 15 =

9. $\dfrac{7}{9}$ of 9 =

10. $\dfrac{1}{3}$ of 12 =

11. $\dfrac{1}{8}$ of 16 =

12. $\dfrac{7}{8}$ of 16 =

14. $\dfrac{1}{5}$ of 15 =

15. $\dfrac{1}{6}$ of 18 =

16. $\dfrac{2}{5}$ of 10 =

Fractions

Animals Bit by Bit

Color each animal a different color. Be sure it's a color that doesn't cover the numbers. Then, **cut** the puzzle pieces apart and mix them up. Assemble the pieces by solving the problems.

Subtraction of Fractions

$= \frac{2}{5}$ $= 2\frac{1}{3}$ $= 1\frac{1}{2}$ $= \frac{1}{7}$ $= \frac{3}{4}$ $= 4$ $= 1\frac{1}{3}$ $= 2$

$-\frac{5}{10}$ $-\frac{1}{3}$ $-\frac{5}{6}$ $-\frac{6}{14}$ $-\frac{3}{12}$ $-\frac{2}{5}$ $-\frac{5}{9}$ $-\frac{0}{7}$

$\frac{9}{10}$ $\frac{8}{3}$ $\frac{14}{6}$ $\frac{8}{14}$ $\frac{12}{12}$ $\frac{22}{5}$ $\frac{17}{9}$ $\frac{14}{7}$

Addition of Fractions

$= 1\frac{1}{8}$ $= 1\frac{4}{7}$ $= 1$ $= 3$ $= 1\frac{7}{9}$ $= 1\frac{1}{3}$ $= 1\frac{4}{5}$ $= 3\frac{4}{5}$

$+\frac{5}{8}$ $+\frac{6}{7}$ $+\frac{8}{15}$ $+\frac{7}{4}$ $+\frac{14}{9}$ $+\frac{11}{6}$ $+\frac{13}{10}$ $+\frac{7}{5}$

$\frac{4}{8}$ $\frac{5}{7}$ $\frac{7}{15}$ $\frac{5}{4}$ $\frac{2}{9}$ $\frac{3}{6}$ $\frac{5}{10}$ $\frac{12}{5}$

Equivalent Fractions

$\frac{63}{126}$ 6 $\frac{6}{7}$ $\frac{105}{160}$ $\frac{16}{20}$ $\frac{152}{208}$ $\frac{126}{180}$ $\frac{35}{49}$ $\frac{6}{18}$

$\frac{25}{50}$ $\frac{24}{28}$ $\frac{21}{32}$ $\frac{32}{40}$ $\frac{19}{26}$ $\frac{14}{20}$ $\frac{40}{56}$ $\frac{18}{54}$

$\frac{40}{80}$ $\frac{72}{84}$ $\frac{63}{96}$ $\frac{88}{110}$ $\frac{38}{52}$ $\frac{56}{80}$ $\frac{15}{21}$ $\frac{24}{72}$

This page intentionally left blank.

Fractions

Name _____

Picture the Problem

Use the picture to **solve** each problem.

1. Andy had two ropes of the same length. He cut one rope into 2 equal parts and gave the 2 halves to Bill. The other rope he cut into fourths and gave 2 of the fourths to Sue. Circle who got the most rope.

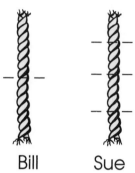

Bill　　　Sue

2. Mr. Johns built an office building with an aisle down the middle. He divided one side into 6 equal spaces. He divided the other side into 9 equal spaces. The Ace Company rented 5 of the ninths. The Best Company rented 4 of the sixths. Circle which company rented the larger space.

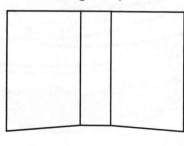

Best　　　Ace

3. Hannah cut an 8-foot log into 4 equal pieces and burned 2 of them in the fireplace. Joseph cut an 8-foot log into 8 equal pieces and put 3 of them in the fireplace. Circle who put the most wood in the fireplace.

Hannah　　　Joseph

4. The 4-H Club display area at the state fair was divided into 2 equal areas. One of these sections had 12 booths, the other had 9 booths. The flower display covered 2 of the ninths, and the melon display covered 4 of the twelfths. Circle which display had the most room.

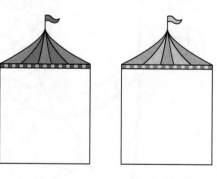

Flowers　　　Melons

Section 8

Decimals

Doing Decimals

Just as a fraction stands for part of a whole number, a decimal also shows part of a whole number. And with decimals, the number is always broken into ten or a power of ten (hundred, thousand, etc.) parts. These place values are named tenths, hundredths, thousandths, etc.

A **decimal point** is a dot placed between the ones place and the tenths place.

0.2 is read as "two tenths."   0.4 is four tenths

Write the answer as a decimal for the shaded parts.

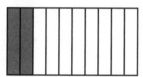   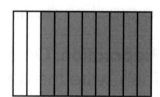

_____   _____   _____

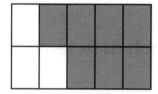   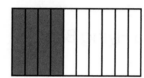   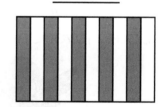

_____   _____   _____

Color the parts that match the decimal numbers.

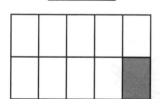   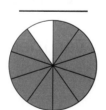   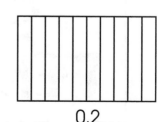

0.4   0.3   0.2

Decimal Fun

The **Hundredth Picture Grid** on page 94 is divided into one hundred parts.

Use colored pencils to **draw** a picture of a person, animal or object on the grid. Give it a title which includes how many hundredths are colored in the drawing.

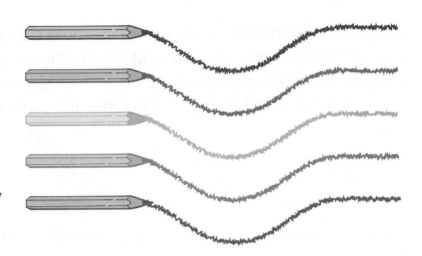

Example: "The 0.46 Flying Bird" or "A 0.82 Scuba Diver," etc.

To practice decimals, play this game with a friend.

Preparation: On index cards, write decimals in written form, such as six tenths. Then, write the decimal numbers on back.

Directions: Player One holds up either side of a card or says a decimal. Player Two writes the decimal or the words for the decimal on a sheet of paper. Player One checks his/her answer. Then, the players switch roles.

SIX TENTHS

0.6

Hundredth Picture Grid

Name _____

 Decimals

Decimal Divisions

Decimals are often used with whole numbers.

Examples: 2.8

3.5

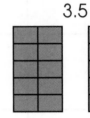 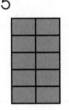 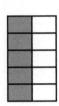

Write the decimal for each picture.

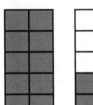 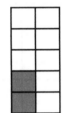    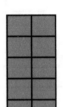 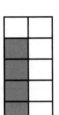 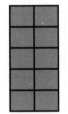

_____   _____   _____

Shade in the picture to show the decimal number.

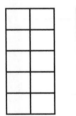 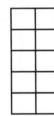   

1.9   3.5   0.4   4.1

When reading decimals with whole numbers, say "point" or "and" for the decimal point.

Write the word names for each decimal from above.

1.9 _____   0.4 _____

3.5 _____   4.1 _____

How Hot Are You?

Write the number for each word name. **Cross off** the number in the cloud. The number that is left is your body temperature. **Hint:** Remember to add a zero to hold any place value not given.

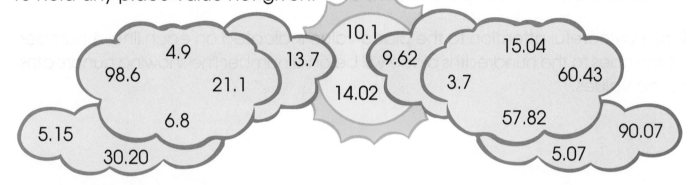

4.9
98.6
21.1
13.7
10.1
9.62
14.02
15.04
3.7
60.43
57.82
5.15
6.8
90.07
30.20
5.07

1. six and eight tenths _____

2. four and nine tenths _____

3. thirteen and seven tenths _____

4. twenty-one and one tenth _____

5. five and fifteen hundredths _____

6. nine and sixty-two hundredths _____

7. fifteen and four hundredths _____

8. fifty-seven and eighty-two hundredths _____

9. three and seven tenths _____

10. sixty and forty-three hundredths _____

11. ninety and seven hundredths _____

12. fourteen and two hundredths _____

13. five and seven hundredths _____

14. ten and one tenth _____

15. thirty and twenty hundredths _____

Your body temperature is: _____

 Decimals

Name _____

Order in the Line

Look at the number lines below. **Cut out** the decimal number squares on the next page. First, **find** the number line on which each number is located. **Glue** the decimals in their correct positions on the correct number line.

Hint: Pay careful attention to the place value indicated on each line. A number which goes to the hundredths place will be on a number line showing hundredths place values.

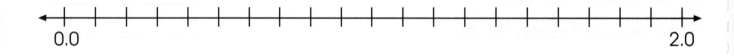

0.0   2.0

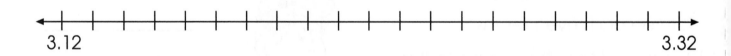

3.12   3.32

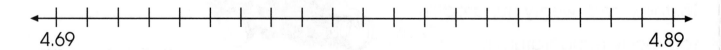

4.69   4.89

Decimals

Order in the Line

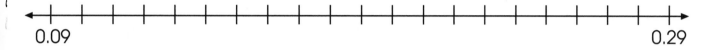

0.09   0.29

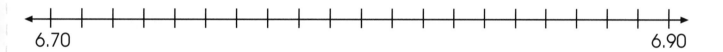

6.70   6.90

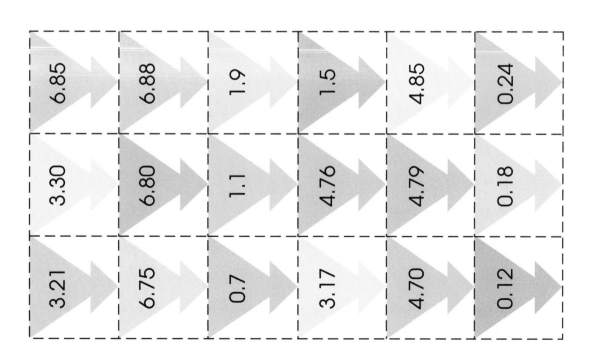

6.85	6.88	1.9	1.5	4.85	0.24
3.30	6.80	1.1	4.76	4.79	0.18
3.21	6.75	0.7	3.17	4.70	0.12

This page intentionally left blank.

Get the Point

When you add or subtract decimals, remember to include the decimal point.

Add.
$$
\begin{array}{r}
3.6 \\
+3.3 \\
\hline
6.9
\end{array}
$$

Subtract.
$$
\begin{array}{r}
6.8 \\
-2.6 \\
\hline
4.2
\end{array}
$$

Solve these problems.

4.2 +5.2	6.4 +1.4	3.1 +7.8	4.7 +3.2	4.9 +2.0	4.2 7 +5.5 2
5.9 −3.2	6.7 −5.6	7.8 −2.5	5.8 −3.3	3.9 −1.5	4.8 6 −1.7 6
0.2 3 +0.2 5	0.4 3 +0.1 6	0.2 6 +0.4 2	0.6 4 +0.1 5	0.6 8 +0.3 1	6.7 3 +1.1 5
0.8 7 −0.4 2	0.9 8 −0.3 5	0.7 9 −0.1 5	0.8 7 −0.6 7	0.8 3 −0.1 2	5.8 6 −3.8 3
3.1 3 +2.2 6	4.7 2 +1.1 5	6.8 7 +2.1 1	4.9 8 −2.3 2	5.9 7 −2.5 4	6.9 8 −1.4 5

Name _____

Animal Trivia

1 An earthworm is 14.9 cm long. A grasshopper is 8.7 cm long. What is the difference?

2 A pocket gopher has a hind foot 3.5 cm long. A ground squirrel's hind foot is 6.4 cm long. How much longer is the ground squirrel's hind foot?

3 A porcupine has a tail 30.0 cm long. An opossum has a tail 53.5 cm long. How much longer is the opossum's tail?

4 A wood rat has a tail which is 23.6 cm long. A deer mouse has a tail 12.2 cm long. What is the difference between the two?

5 A cottontail rabbit has ears which are 6.8 cm long. A jackrabbit has ears 12.9 cm long. How much shorter is the cottontail's ear?

6 The hind foot of a river otter is 14.6 cm long. The hind foot of a hog-nosed skunk is 9.0 cm long. What is the difference?

7 A rock mouse is 26.1 cm long. His tail adds another 14.4 cm. What is his total length from his nose to the tip of his tail?

Dueling Decimals

Preparation: To play "Dueling Decimals," you need 2 players. Each player needs a spinner and a place value card (see the example shown).

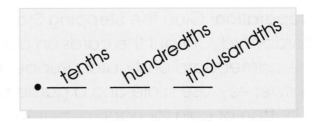

Directions: Player One should spin the spinner. The number that comes up should be recorded under the thousandths place column on the player's place value card. Player Two repeats the process. Player One then spins again, this time placing the number under the hundredths place column on his/her place value card.

Repeat until both players have a complete decimal number. Players should then compare the two numbers. The player with the larger number earns a point. Players have now completed the first round and should continue for four more rounds. The player with the most points after the fifth round wins "Dueling Decimals"!

Extension: Add your five decimal numbers. Compare the sums. Is the winner of the game also the player with a higher sum? _____

Why? _____

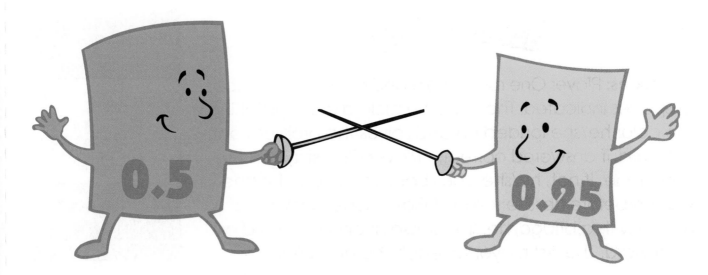

Decimals

Name _____

Stepping Stones

Preparation: Glue the **Stepping Stones** gameboard on page 209 onto cardboard. Cut out the cards on pages 211–220. You may choose to laminate the gameboard and cards. Rubber band the cards together and make an answer key. Use a die and a game piece for each player. (You may also use a button or coin for each player to mark his/her place.)

Rules: This game involves 2–4 players. The player who rolls the lowest number is first. Play goes counterclockwise. Separate the stack of cards. Place them in five piles upside down by the board. Cards should always be returned to the bottom of the stack.

Each group of cards is different.

The pink set gives a game obstacle.

The gray set gives an addition problem with decimals.

The blue set gives a subtraction problem with decimals.

The yellow set gives two decimals to compare.

The purple set gives a decimal number to round.

Directions: Player One rolls the die and moves the number of spaces indicated. Then, he/she picks a card matching the color he/she landed on and solves the problem on the card. If answered correctly, Player One stays on the new stone. If not, he/she goes back to the one he/she was on before he/she rolled. If Player One lands on a space with a bridge, he/she crosses it either forward or backward. The first player to reach the end wins.

Oops! Lost your balance. Move back 1 stone.

$$0.307$$
$$+0.900$$

$$1.040$$
$$-0.216$$

7.2 ◯ 7.5

< or >

3.5<u>3</u>5

Round to the underlined number.

 Decimals

Stepping Stones Gameboard

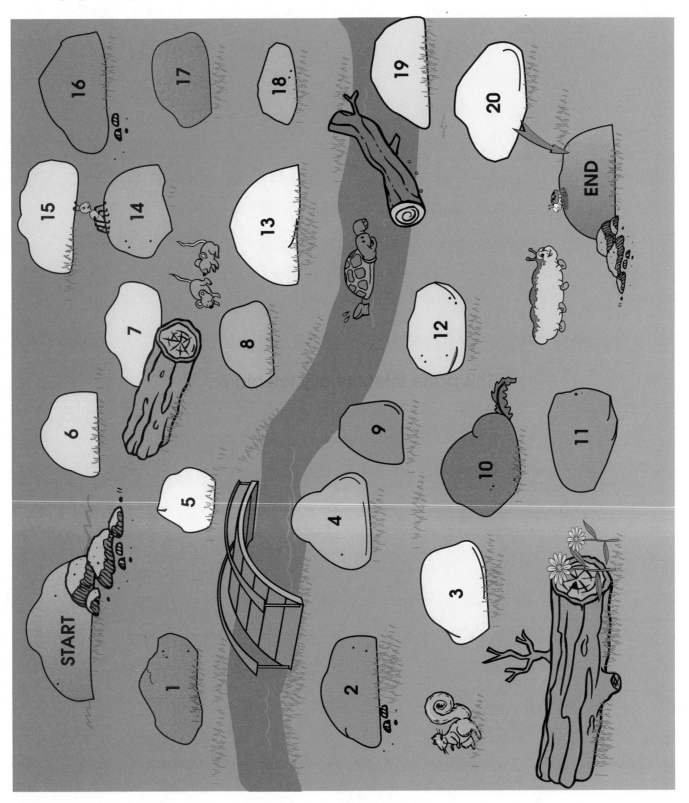

This page intentionally left blank.

Subtraction Cards

1.0 4 0 − 0.2 1 6	5.5 − 3.2
0.3 5 0 − 0.1 2 8	8.6 − 4.8
0.6 0 9 − 0.3 1 7	1.3 0 − 0.1 7
0.8 7 − 0.4 9	0.9 4 − 0.5 3
0.7 0 4 − 0.3 2 6	2.3 − 1.4

Name _____

Rounding Cards

3.5<u>3</u>5 Round to the underlined number.	<u>9</u>.7 Round to the underlined number.
0.<u>3</u>34 Round to the underlined number.	<u>2</u>.09 Round to the underlined number.
<u>5</u>.48 Round to the underlined number.	6.<u>8</u>3 Round to the underlined number.
0.6<u>1</u>2 Round to the underlined number.	0.<u>0</u>51 Round to the underlined number.
7.7<u>1</u>7 Round to the underlined number.	<u>1</u>.842 Round to the underlined number.

Comparison Cards

7.2 ◯ 7.5
< or >

0.3 ◯ 3.0
< or >

4.9 ◯ 4.8
< or >

1.5 ◯ 1.7
< or >

3.23 ◯ 3.32
< or >

6.19 ◯ 6.2
< or >

2.08 ◯ 2.40
< or >

0.86 ◯ 0.88
< or >

5.61 ◯ 5.62
< or >

8.3 ◯ 8.06
< or >

Decimals

Name _____

Addition Cards

```
  0.3 0 7
+ 0.9 0 0
_____
```

```
  0.6 4
+ 0.3 3
_____
```

```
  0.7 8
+ 0.2 1
_____
```

```
  0.6 5
+ 0.6 5
_____
```

```
  1.2 9
+ 4.5 0
_____
```

```
  0.4 4 2
+ 0.7 8 4
_____
```

```
  0.7 0 4
+ 0.1 2 7
_____
```

```
  0.9 4 6
+ 0.0 3 5
_____
```

```
  4.7 6
+ 2.2 5
_____
```

```
  2.1 2
+ 3.7 9
_____
```

Game Obstacle Cards

Cross the closest bridge.

Cross the closest bridge.

There's a butterfly on the next rock.
Step back one stone.

Step ahead to the next blue stone.
If there isn't one, go to 14.

Oops! Lost your balance.
Move back 1 stone.

You're a great leaper—
jump ahead 1 stone.

No need to rest—
take another turn.

Stop to tie your shoe.
Lose a turn.

Rest for a minute—
lose your turn.

Catch up with the sunbeam—
take another turn.

Name _____

Decimal Riddles

Read the clues to **write** the numbers.

1. Numbers: 4, 8, 2, 2
   Clues:
   - The numbers in the tens place and the tenths place are the same.
   - The greatest number is in the hundredths place.

2. Numbers: 1, 2, 3, 8
   Clues:
   - The number in the tens place is 5 less than the number in the hundredths place.
   - The number in the tenths place is twice the number in the ones place.

3. Numbers: 3, 5, 8, 9
   Clues:
   - The greatest number is in the hundredths place.
   - The number in the tenths place is 2 less than the number in the tens place.

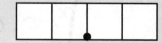

4. Numbers: 2, 3, 4, 6
   Clues:
   - The 3 is in the tenths place.
   - The number in the hundreds place is half the number in the tens place.
   - The number in the ones place is the sum of the numbers in the hundreds place and the tens place.

5. Numbers: 0, 5, 6, 7, 8
   Clues:
   - The number in the hundredths place is 8 more than the number in the tenths place.
   - The 6 is in the tens place.
   - The number in the hundreds place is greater than the number in the ones place.

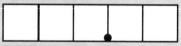

6. Numbers: 2, 4, 6, 7, 8
   Clues:
   - The number in the hundredths place is twice the number in the tenths place.
   - The 7 is in the ones place.
   - The number in the hundreds place is three times the number in the tens place.

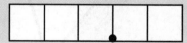

Section 9

Graphs, Tables and Diagrams

Flower Graph

A **pictograph** is a graph using pictures to give information.
Cut out the flowers and **glue** them onto the pictograph.

Daisies					
Sunflowers					
Tulips					
Roses					

How many tulips? _____

       sunflowers? _____

       roses? _____

       daisies? _____

How many more tulips than roses? _____

How many more daisies than sunflowers? _____

How many sunflowers and tulips? _____

How many roses and daisies? _____

Each picture stands for 2 flowers.

This page intentionally left blank.

Frog Bubbles

Complete the line graph to show how many bubbles each frog blew.

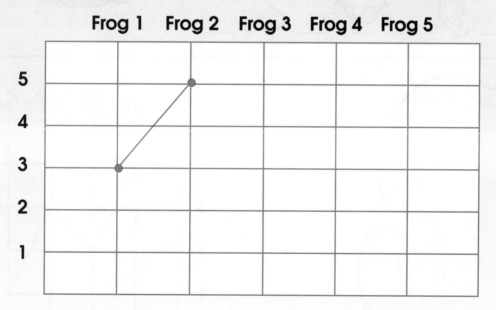

How many bubbles? Frog 1:_____   2:_____   3:_____   4:_____   5:_____

Which frog blew the most bubbles?_____

Which frog blew the fewest?_____

Potato Face

Read the line graphs to **draw** the potato faces.

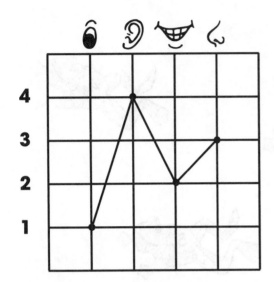

How many?

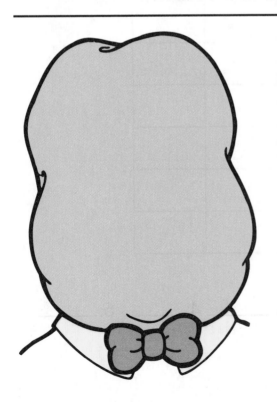

How many?

Name _____

Vote for Me!

Middletown school had an election to choose the new members of the Student Council. Grace, Bernie, Laurie, Sherry and Sam all ran for the office of president. On the chart below are the five students' names with the number of the votes each received.

Grace	21	36	39
Bernie	47	32	26
Laurie	25	44	38
Sherry	34	37	40
Sam	48	33	29

Use the information and the clues below to see who became president and how many votes he or she received.

- The winning number of votes was an even number.

- The winning number of votes was between 30 and 40.

- The two digits added together are greater than 10.

_____ became the president
of the Student Council with
_____ votes.

Who would have become president if
the winning number was **odd** and the
other clues remained the same?

_____

Name _____

School Statistics

Read each graph and follow the directions.

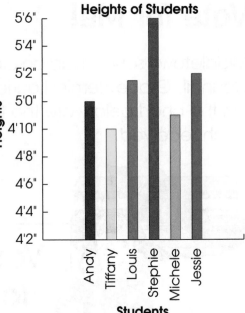

Heights of Students

List the names of the students from the shortest to the tallest.

1. _____   4. _____

2. _____   5. _____

3. _____   6. _____

Lunches Bought

List how many lunches the students bought each day, from the day the most were bought to the least.

1. _____   4. _____

2. _____   5. _____

3. _____

List the months in the order of the most number of outside recesses to the least number.

1. _____   6. _____

2. _____   7. _____

3. _____   8. _____

4. _____   9. _____

5. _____   10. _____

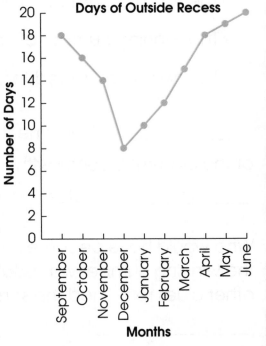

Days of Outside Recess

Candy Sales

Every year the students at Lincoln Elementary sell candy as a fund-raising project. These are the results of the sales for this year.

Grade Level	Number of Sales
Kindergarten	40
First	70
Second	50
Third	80
Fourth	85
Fifth	75

Color the bar graph to show the number of sales made at each grade level.

Number of Sales

90
85
80
75
70
65
60
55
50
45
40
35
30
25
20
15
10
5

K   1   2   3   4   5

Grade Level

Write the grade levels in order starting with the one that sold the most.

1. _____
2. _____
3. _____
4. _____
5. _____
6. _____

Name _____

Hot Lunch Favorites

The cooks in the cafeteria asked each third- and fourth-grade class to rate the hot lunches. They wanted to know which food the children liked the best.

The table shows how the students rated the lunches.

Key: Each 👤 equals 2 students.

Food	Number of students who liked it best
hamburgers	👤 👤 👤 👤 👤 👤
hot dogs	👤 👤 👤 👤 👤 👤 👤
tacos	👤 👤 👤 👤 👤
chili	
soup and sandwiches	👤
spaghetti	👤 👤
fried chicken	👤 👤 👤 👤
fish sticks	👤 👤 👤

Color the bar graph to show the information on the table. Remember that each 👤 equals 2 people. The first one is done for you.

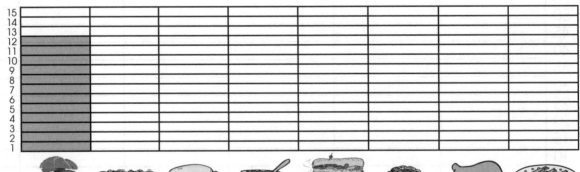

Number of Students

15 14 13 12 11 10 9 8 7 6 5 4 3 2 1

Write the food in order starting with the one that students liked most.

1. _____   5. _____

2. _____   6. _____

3. _____   7. _____

4. _____   8. _____

Gliding Graphics

Draw the lines as directed from point to point for each graph.

Draw a line from:

- F,7 to D,1
- D,1 to I,6
- I,6 to N,8
- N,8 to M,3
- M,3 to F,1
- F,1 to G,4
- G,4 to E,4
- E,4 to B,1

- B,1 to A,8
- A,8 to D,11
- D,11 to F,9
- F,9 to F,7
- F,7 to I,9
- I,9 to I,6
- I,6 to F,7

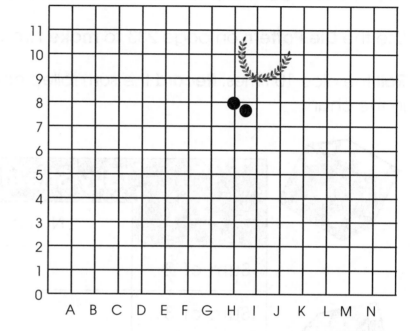

Draw a line from:

J, 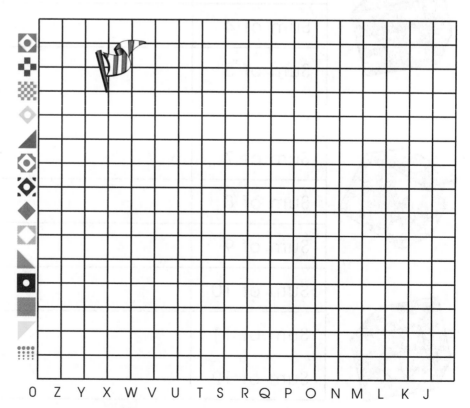 to N,
N, to U,
U, to Z,
Z, to X,
X, to U,
U, to S,
S, to N,
N, to N,
N, to J,
J, to L,
L, to Y,
Y, to Z,
Z, to L,
L, to J,

Name _____

Tally Ho!

A **tally mark** is a line to represent one. The fifth tally mark is written diagonally over the first four marks for easy reading of the results. (**Example:** ⲎⲎⳠ = 5.)

Use the **Die Pattern** on page 233 to **make** two dice.

Roll the dice 10 times. **Record** the sum rolled each time by making a tally mark in the chart.

Tally Sheet	
	Number of rolls
Sum of 2	
Sum of 3	
Sum of 4	
Sum of 5	
Sum of 6	
Sum of 7	
Sum of 8	
Sum of 9	
Sum of 10	
Sum of 11	
Sum of 12	

Die Pattern

You will need: tape, glue, construction paper, two copies of this pattern

Directions: Glue the patterns to construction paper and cut them out. Fold on the dotted lines so that all the edges meet to form a cube. Glue the tabs in place and tape the edges of the cube together carefully.

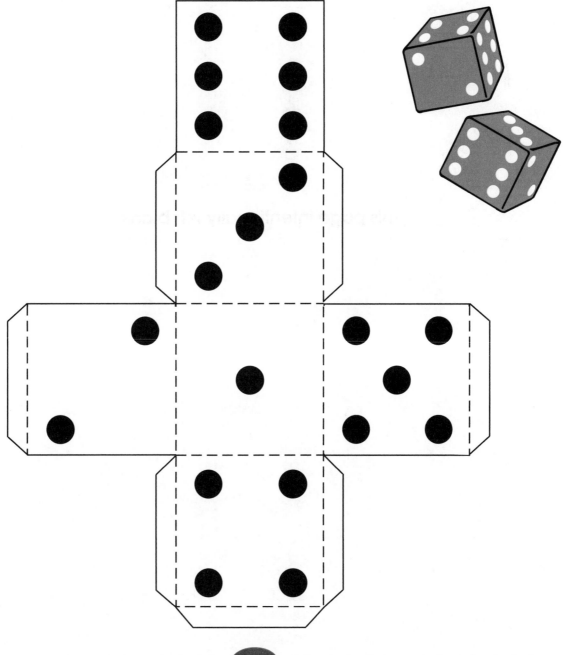

This page intentionally left blank.

Roll 'Em!

Roll the die 20 times in a row. **Use** the following tally sheet to keep track of the number you roll each time.

Tally Sheet

Number rolled	Number of rolls
Number 1 ⚀	
Number 2 ⚁	
Number 3 ⚂	
Number 4 ⚃	
Number 5 ⚄	
Number 6 ⚅	

Answer the following questions about the tally sheet.

1. Which number was rolled most frequently? _____

2. Which number was rolled least frequently? _____

3. Were any numbers rolled the same number of times?_____

    Which ones? _____

    Why do you think this happened?_____

Extension:

Do this exercise again and compare the first results with the second results.

Why did the results turn out the way they did?_____

Was there anything that could have been done to change the results?

_____

Predict what would happen if the die were rolled 40 times?_____

_____

Pie Graph Survey

Step 1: Conducting a Survey

A **survey** is a mini-interview of many people to find out what they like or do not like. Possible topics might be a favorite television show, a food or a career choice. Choose a survey topic to create the survey table.

Directions: Create a title for the survey. Write it across the top of the chart below. Next, provide several choices for the survey. For example, if the title of the survey is "Favorite Subject," you would choose some popular subjects and write them vertically along the left margin of the chart. Next, you will survey sixteen people.

You may want to discuss the sample population and perhaps set limits. Will you survey a group of people that are all the same? Will you survey only friends your age? The first sixteen people you see on the street? Relatives?

Favorite Desserts	
Ice cream	III
Pecan pie	I
Apple pie	II
Chocolate cake	III
Candy bar	II
Milkshake	ℍℍ

Title:

Pie Graph Survey

Step 2: Creating Fractions
Directions: Convert the results of your survey into fractions. The denominator will be 16, because that is the number of people who make up the whole survey. Determine the numerator by counting the number of people who chose an item. (For example, if four people chose math as their favorite subject, the fraction would be 4/16.) When all tallied results have been converted into fractions, you are ready to create the pie graph.

Chocolate cake = 3/16 means three children out of sixteen picked the cake as their favorite dessert.

Step 3: Creating the Pie Graph
Directions: Shade in the number of sections that each numerator indicates, using a different color for each numerator, or choice from the survey. Write the choice, fraction and the color in the key. Now, copy your pie graph and key, cut them out, mount them and share them with the people you surveyed.

Key:
Pecan pie 1/16
Apple pie 2/16
Chocolate cake 3/16
Candy bar 2/16
Milkshake 5/16
Ice cream 3/16

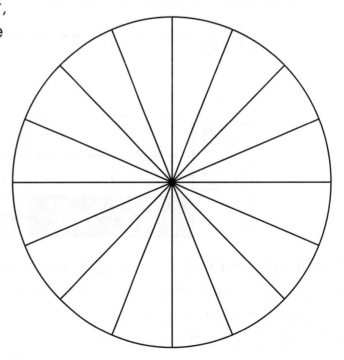

Key:

Name _____

Guess the Color

Probability shows the chance that a given event will happen. To show probability, write a fraction. The number of different possibilities is the denominator. The number of times the event could happen is the numerator. (Remember to reduce fractions to the lowest terms.)

Look at the spinner. What is the probability that the arrow will land on . . .

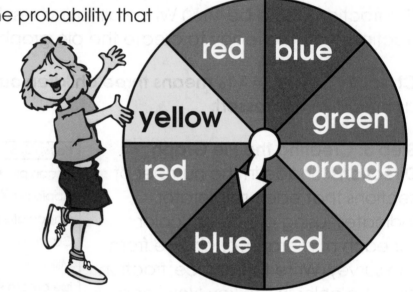

1. red? $\frac{3}{8}$

2. blue?   _____

3. yellow?   _____

4. green?   _____

5. orange?   _____

Complete the bar graph showing your answers (the data) from above.

Number of Probability					
8					
6					
4					
2					
	red	blue	yellow	orange	green

Circle the best title for the above bar graph.
a. Probability of Arrow Landing on a Color
b. Eight Turns of the Spinner
c. Which Color Is the Winner?

Spinner Fun

You will need: 2 brass fasteners, a piece of cardboard

Directions: Glue the patterns below to a piece of cardboard and cut them out. Pierce a hole in the arrows and in the center of each spinner. Using the brass fasteners, connect an arrow to each spinner.

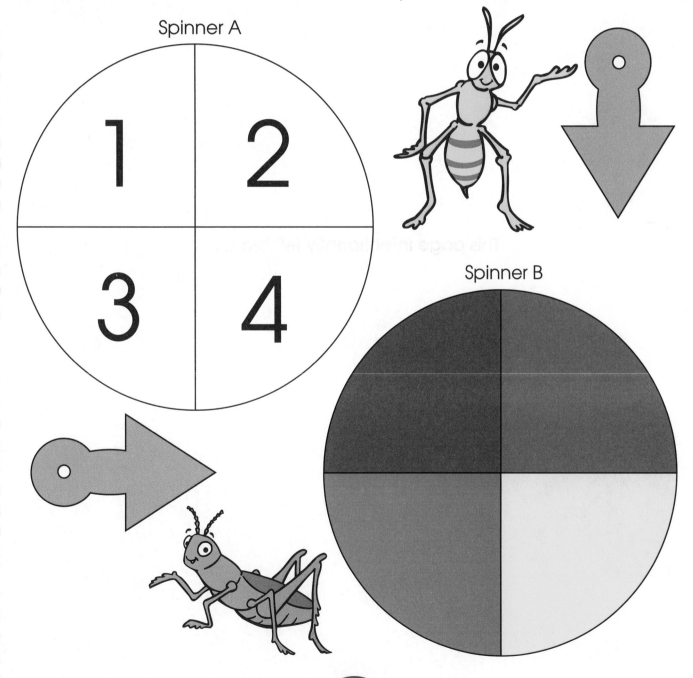

Spinner A

Spinner B

This page intentionally left blank.

Trees

Possible combinations of two events can be organized on trees. **Use** the spinners from page 239.

Part A: Complete the tree diagram by doing the following: Assume that you first spin Spinner A. Write the possibilities on the diagram. Then, spin Spinner B. Write the possibilities on the diagram. On the right, write the probability for each combination if you spun both spinners 16 times. Then, below the tree diagram, list all the possible combinations of the two spinners.

Probability

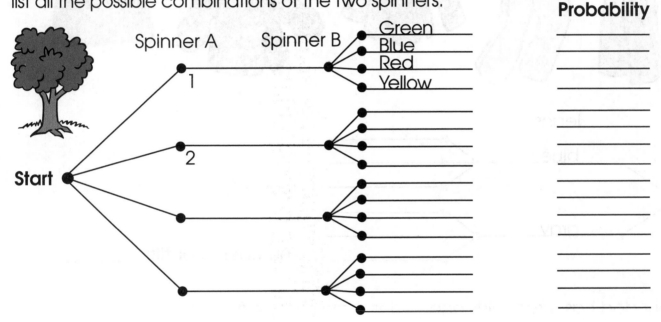

Spinner A   Spinner B
Green
Blue
Red
Yellow

1

2

Start

Part B: Spin Spinner A, then spin Spinner B. Do this 16 times. Record the outcomes below and compare them with the probabilities and possible combinations you listed above.

1. _____   5. _____   9. _____   13. _____
2. _____   6. _____   10. _____   14. _____
3. _____   7. _____   11. _____   15. _____
4. _____   8. _____   12. _____   16. _____

What do you notice? Why do you think that is? _____

_____

Name _____

How Many Outfits?

Suppose you had two pairs of jeans (one blue and the other gray) and three shirts (orange, red and green). How many different outfits could you wear? **Use** a tree to help you with the answer.

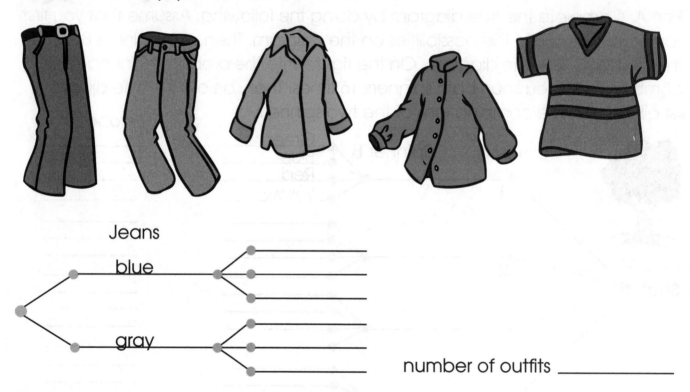

Jeans

blue

gray

number of outfits _____

Your dad has three shirts and six ties. How many different ways can he wear his shirts and ties? **Draw** a tree to help you figure out the answer.

number of outfits _____

Keep Your Heads Up!

Collect 21 pennies. **Predict** the numbers of heads and tails that will turn up before you toss the pennies. Then, **toss** the coins ten times.

Does anything change about your predictions the more you guess?

_____

Toss	Guess Heads	Tails	Actual Heads	Tails
1				
2				
3				
4				
5				
6				
7				
8				
9				
10				

Measurement

Make a Tape Measure

Directions:

1. Cut out the rectangle pattern below on the solid lines.
2. Cut the rectangle into six strips by cutting on the dotted lines.
3. Put a little glue on the shaded end of one strip and glue it to the end of another strip. Press the strips together. Repeat this step until all the strips are joined to make one long strip.
4. Cut off the one leftover shaded end. You now have a tape measure.

5. Lay your tape measure out flat. Starting from the left side, mark off inches, 1/2 inches and 1/4 inches. Number the inches.
6. Reinforce your tape measure by putting clear tape on the back of it.

This page intentionally left blank.

Name _____

How Does Your Home Measure Up?

Directions: Take a "measuring journey" through your house. To begin, brainstorm a list of various destinations around your house. Then, **list** five objects found in each room and **write** them on the left-hand side of a sheet of paper.

Example:

Kitchen	**Bathroom**	**Bedroom**
stove	toothbrush	books
teaspoon	hairbrush	desk/table
cookbook	soap	pillow
can opener	mirror	clock
box of cereal	bandage	hanger

Read through the objects on the list and **write** estimations of their measurements. Decide on a unit of measurement to use and whether to measure length, width or both. Then, **measure** the objects. (A tape measure or string may be used to measure the size or circumference of any oddly shaped objects.) Finally, compare your estimations with the actual measurements.

Object	Estimate	Actual

Name _____

Growing String Beans

All plants with green leaves make food from the sun. They take water and nutrients from the soil, but they make their food from light.

You will measure in inches how fast a string bean plant grows. Record this information on the **Growing String Beans Bar Graph** on page 249.

You will need:
string bean seeds
potting soil
16 oz. plastic cup
12-inch ruler

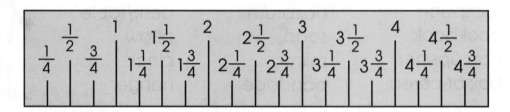

Directions:
1. Fill the cup 3/4 full with potting soil.
2. Use a pencil to make a hole 1-inch deep and drop in a bean seed. Gently cover the seed and lightly water it.
3. Water the plant regularly so that the soil does not become dried out.
4. Wait for the new plant to germinate and peek out of the soil.
5. Measure and record the plant's growth using the ruler. Record it on the bar graph at each specified interval.
6. When it has grown, enjoy the delicious string beans as a treat!

How To Measure: Place the ruler next to the plant, resting it on the soil. Measure from the top of the plant down to the soil.

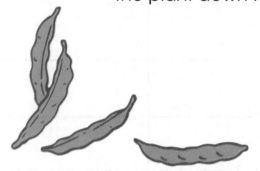

Name _____

Growing String Beans
Bar Graph

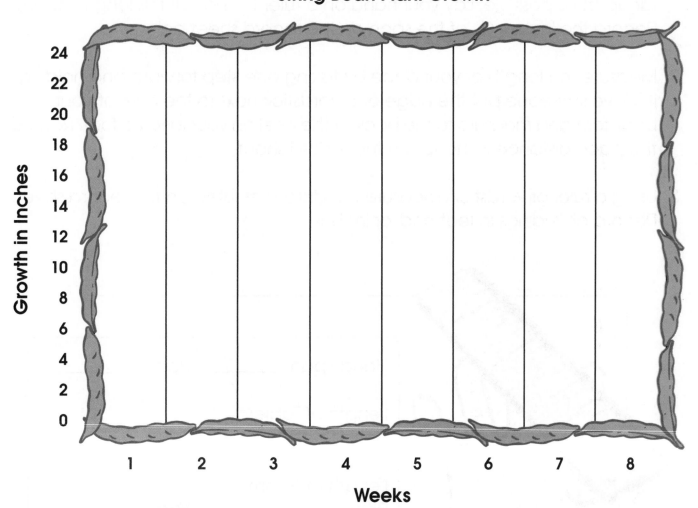

String Bean Plant Growth

Growth in Inches

24
22
20
18
16
14
12
10
8
6
4
2
0

1   2   3   4   5   6   7   8

Weeks

Other Ideas:

Try growing a few other interesting plants like:
1. Carrot tops cut off and placed in a pie tin filled with water.
2. Plain popcorn seeds from the store (no oiled or treated). Plant them in the ground.
3. Go to your local plant nursery or hardware store and look at the selection of plant seeds available.
4. Plant a young tree in your yard and measure its growth each year.

Name _____

Hand—Foot—Ruler

Directions:

1. Measure the span of your hand by stretching your thumb and little finger as far apart as possible. Lay your hand on a ruler to find out this length (span). Record the inches (") of the span on the record sheet below.

2. Measure the length of your pace by taking one step forward and holding it. Have someone put the edge of a yardstick next to the heel of your back foot and measure to the back of the heel on your forward foot. Record the pace distance in inches on the record sheet.

3. Using a ruler or yardstick, measure the distances listed on the record sheet. Record all findings in feet and/or inches.

Hand Span _____"   Pace _____"

Length of Table:
Hand Span _____   Ruler _____"

Length of Room:
Pace _____   Yardstick _____"

Height of Bookcase:
Hand Span _____   Ruler _____"

Width of Kitchen:
Pace _____   Yardstick _____"

A Measurement of Our Own

Create your own new system of measurement. Brainstorm ideas on what and how you should base the new unit. For example, you may use the length of your finger, the length of a juice box, the length of your backpack, etc. as a base.

Next, **create** a ruler using your new unit of measurement. A foot is made of inches and a meter is made of centimeters. Break your standard unit into smaller units and **add** these to the ruler. When the ruler is complete, fill out the form below.

Answer the questions below.

1. What is the name of your unit of measurement? _____

2. What would your unit of measurement be best suited for measuring—long

   distances or microscopic organisms? _____

   Why? _____

3. Would you rather use your new unit of measurement versus the standard

   unit? _____ Why or why not? _____

4. Measure an object using your new ruler. What did it measure? _____
   If you were to tell someone that the object you measured was that long, do

   you think that person would be able to picture its length? _____

   Why or why not? _____

5. Why do you think everyone in the entire country uses the exact same unit

   of measurement? _____

Name _____

Krab E. Krabby

Krab E. Krabby carries a yardstick with him everywhere he goes and he measures everything he can.

Key:
12 inches = 1 foot
36 inches = 3 feet = 1 yard

1 Krab E. Krabby wanted to measure the length of a grasshopper. Would he use a ruler or a yardstick?

2 Krab E. measured a garter snake that was 44 inches long. How many yards and inches is this?

_____ yard _____ inches

3 Krab E. measured a monarch butterfly that was 4 inches wide. How many inches less than a foot is the butterfly?

4 Krab E. Krabby scolded Rollo Rattlesnake because Rollo wouldn't straighten out and cooperate. Should Krab E. use a ruler or a yardstick to measure Rollo?

5 Krab E. measured a tomato hornworm that was 5 inches long. How many inches less than a foot is this?

6 Krab E. measured a lazy tuna that was 1 foot 11 inches long. How many total inches is the tuna?

Calculating Lengths

Use your yardstick to **calculate** and **write** the following lengths. Remember to write feet or yards. Some lengths may not be exactly in feet or yards, so be sure to write the inches too. Have a friend or parent help you **measure** these lengths.

1. How long is the biggest step you can take? _____

2. How far can a paper airplane fly? _____

3. From start to finish, how much distance do you cover when you do a

   somersault? _____

4. How far can you throw a feather? _____

5. How wide is your driveway? _____

6. How far can you walk balancing a book on your head? _____

7. How high can you stack wooden blocks before they fall? _____

8. How high can you jump? (Measure from where your finger touches to the

   floor.) _____

9. How far can you jump? (Begin with your feet together.) _____

10. How much distance is covered if you skip 10 times? _____

11. What is the distance you can hit a softball with your bat before it hits the

    ground? _____

12. What is the distance you can throw a baseball? _____

13. How far away were you when you caught your friend's throw? _____

14. How far can you spit a seed? _____

15. How much distance do you cover when you sprint for 3 seconds? _____

    _____

Animal Math

The chart below lists some of the body statistics of 15 endangered animals.
Use these measurements to **solve** the problems below the chart.

Animal	Height	Weight	Length
Mountain gorilla	6 feet	450 pounds	
Black rhinoceros	5.5 feet	4,000 pounds	12 feet
Cheetah	2.5 feet	100 pounds	5 feet
Leopard	2 feet	150 pounds	4.5 feet
Spectacled bear	2.5 feet	300 pounds	5 feet
Giant armadillo		100 pounds	4 feet
Vicuna	2.5 feet	100 pounds	
Siberian tiger	38 inches	600 pounds	6 feet
Orangutan	4.5 feet	200 pounds	
Giant panda		300 pounds	6 feet
Polar bear		1,600 pounds	8 feet
Yak	5.5 feet	1,200 pounds	

1. What is the total height of a mountain gorilla, a vicuna and a yak? _____

2. What is the total weight of a leopard, a cheetah and a polar bear? _____

3. What is the total weight of a giant panda and a giant armadillo? _____

4. Add the lengths of a black rhinoceros, a spectacled bear and a Siberian
   tiger. _____

5. Add the heights of two leopards, three yaks and four orangutans. _____

6. Subtract the height of a vicuna from the height of a cheetah. _____

7. Add the weights of all the animals. _____

8. Write the lengths of the animals from longest to shortest.

   _____

   _____

   _____

Finding Weight Equivalents

In the United States, we use a standard weight system that includes ounces (oz.), pounds (lb.) and tons (tn.). Develop your own standard weight system below.

You will need: marbles, paper clips, ice-cream sticks, crayons, pencils, spoons, etc. (anything that has weight and can be counted), a scale or balance

Directions: Your standard weight is _____.

Now, use your scale to find out how much different objects weigh.

1. Place the object to be weighed on one side of the scale.
2. Find out, for example, how many of your standard weight it takes to equal the object being weighed.
3. When the scale is level, you have found your equivalent weight.
4. Weigh different objects and record the results below.

Example: bottle of glue   weight: 16 crayons

object: _____   weight: _____

object: _____   weight: _____

object: _____   weight: _____

object: _____   weight: _____

object: _____   weight: _____

object: _____   weight: _____

object: _____   weight: _____

object: _____   weight: _____

object: _____   weight: _____

object: _____   weight: _____

object: _____   weight: _____

Discovering Capacity

Capacity measures how much can fit inside an object.

You will need:

    measuring cup (2 cup capacity) tablespoon
    pie tin   cake pan
    1 cup of salt   1 cup of ice
    bathroom sink   baking pan
    1 gallon plastic jug   1 gallon freezer bag
    2 liter plastic jug

Complete the tasks below to discover the capacity of objects around your house.

1. How many cups of water are there in a 1-gallon plastic jug? _____

2. How many tablespoons of salt does it take to fill up 1 cup? _____

    How many tablespoons of water does it take to fill up ½ cup? _____

3. Plug your bathroom sink. How many cups of water will it hold? _____

    How many gallons is that? _____

5. How many cups of water does it take to fill a pie tin? _____

6. Does a gallon-size plastic freezer bag really hold a gallon of something?

    _____ Count how many cups of water you can fit inside one. _____

    _____ Is that a gallon?

7. Fill a cake pan with water. Count how many cups it takes. _____

    If 2 cups = 1 pint, how many pints does it hold? _____

    If 2 pints = 1 quart, what is the quart capacity of your cake pan? _____

Discovering Capacity Equivalents

Gallons, quarts, cups and pints are used for measuring capacity in the U.S.A. You use them every day, but you probably don't measure them every time. When you pour milk on your cereal in the morning, you are estimating how much milk you need to cover your breakfast. We are always making estimates.

You will need:

1 cup capacity measuring cup, pint, quart and half gallon containers, two 1-gallon capacity plastic jugs, water

Directions:

Set the two 1-gallon jugs beside each other. Fill one with water. Then, fill the measuring cups with water from the jug to determine the number of cups, pints, quarts and gallons of water it will take to fill the other jug.

> **1 cup** — How many cups do you think it will take to fill
>
> 1 gallon? _____
>
> The actual amount _____

> **1 pint (2 cups)** — How many pints do you think it will take to fill
>
> 1 gallon? _____
>
> The actual amount _____

> **1 quart (2 pints)** — How many quarts do you think it will take to fill
>
> 1 gallon? _____
>
> The actual amount _____

> **1 half gallon (2 quarts)** — How many half gallons do you think it will take to fill
>
> 1 gallon? _____
>
> The actual amount _____

Name _____

Comparing Temperatures

Temperatures tell how warm or cold something is.
You will need: Fahrenheit thermometer
measuring cup (1 or 2 cup capacity)

Measure and **record** the temperatures of:

_____ 1. Water from the tap

_____ 2. The dairy section at the grocery store (Call or visit store to ask.)

_____ 3. A pet's body temperature (Call or visit veterinarian.)

_____ 4. Your freezer (Have your parents help you.)

_____ 5. Bathtub water (Fill a cup from the bathtub and place the
thermometer in it.)

_____ 6. A cup of water outside in the sun

- Place a cup of water in a safe place with the thermometer
resting inside.
- Let it set until the temperature stops rising.
- Record the temperature.

Is it the same as the temperature outside? _____

_____ 7. A cup of ice water

_____ 8. Your body temperature

Now, **compare**.

1. How many degrees warmer is the bathtub water than the tap water?

_____

2. How many degrees difference is a pet's body temperature than yours?
_____ Who is warmer?_____

3. What is the difference between your freezer's temperature and the
temperature in the dairy section of your grocery store?_____

4. What is the difference in temperature between a cup of water that has
set out in the sun and a cup of ice water?_____

Weather Page

Examine the weather page from the newspaper for two or more consecutive days (preferably the two days prior to this activity).

Look for the following information:
    time of sunrise and sunset for each day,
    low temperature for each day,
    high temperature for each day,
    high and low tides (if applicable.)

How accurate was the forecast for:
    time of sunrise and sunset for each day?
    low temperature for each day?
    high temperature for each day?
    high and low tides?

time of sunrise	
time of sunset	
low temperature	
high temperature	
times of high tides	
times of low tides	

Today's Temperature

Record the indoor and outdoor temperatures in degrees Celsius and Fahrenheit. Post the daily temperature on poster paper on your refrigerator. If desired, use an almanac or newspaper to share record high and low temperatures for each day.

Indoor temperature
(8 A.M. and 3 P.M.)

Outdoor temperature
(8 A.M. and 3 P.M.)

Extension: Create ongoing line graphs to show temperature differences. Each day, plot the temperatures. Display them near the daily temperature recordings.

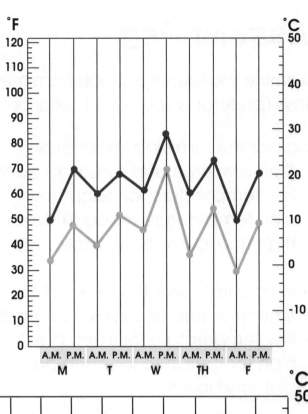

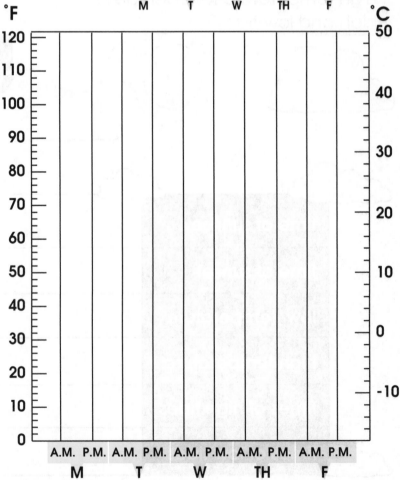

Name _____

Super Shadows

Go outside to **measure** your shadow every hour on a sunny day. Have someone help you by **drawing** around your shadow with colored chalk. **Record** the time and length on your chart. Stand in the same place each time. Predict what will be different.

Were your predictions accurate? _____

8 A.M. Shadows

Everyone's shadow is taller than really,
The shadows of giants are taller than trees.
The shadows of children are big as their parents,
And shadows of trotting dogs bend at the knees.
Everyone's shadow is taller than really,
Everyone's shadow is thinner than thin,
8 A.M. shadows are long at the dawning,
Pulling the night away,
Coaxing the light to say:
"Welcome, all shadows,
Day, please begin!"

Patricia Hubbel

Time	Length of shadow

Section 11

Time

Name _____

My Schedule

Keep track of what you do all day for a week on several copies of this page. **Write** the day and date at the start of the day. Then, **write** what you do and the time you do it. Each time you change activities, you should **write** a new time entry. At the end of the day, **add** how much time was spent in each type of activity. Some activities can be grouped together (i.e., breakfast, lunch, dinner = eating; social studies, language, math = school subjects; etc.). Tally up your activities on Friday.

Extension: Use the information collected to plot a pie graph, bar graph, line graph or pictograph.

Day and date

Time	Activity

Totals

Name _____

Timely Fun

Predict how many times you can do each activity in 1 minute. Then, **time** yourself and see how accurate your predictions were.

Say the alphabet.

Estimate: _____   Actual: _____

Clap your hands.

Estimate: _____   Actual: _____

Do 20 jumping jacks.

Estimate: _____   Actual: _____

Count to 20.

Estimate: _____   Actual: _____

Hop on one foot.

Estimate: _____   Actual: _____

Count backward from 20 to 1.

Estimate: _____   Actual: _____

Name _____

Time on My Hands

Draw the hour and minute hands to show each time below.

Example:

3:35

10:05

4:55

8:10

12:50

9:20

7:25

1:15

11:45

3:30

6:40

12:55

2:00

5:35

3:15

10:50

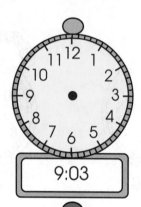

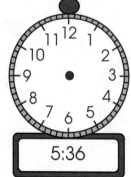

Time

Minute Men

Draw the hour and minute hands on these clocks.

Example:

| 4:42 | 9:03 | 6:51 |

| 1:24 | 7:33 | 10:11 |

| 3:58 | 12:01 | 2:49 |

| 4:17 | 5:36 | 8:23 |

Name _____

Take Time for These

Write the time shown on these clocks.

Example:

_6:47_ _____ _____ _____

_____ _____ _____ _____

_____ _____ _____ _____

Name ____________________

Father Time Teasers

Write the times below.

Example:

25 minutes ago

5:35

10 minutes later

40 minutes ago

35 minutes ago

50 minutes later

15 minutes ago

20 minutes later

45 minutes ago

5 minutes ago

30 minutes later

55 minutes later

25 minutes ago

Name _____

Time "Tables"

Draw the hands on these clocks.

10 minutes before
12:17

36 minutes after
8:19

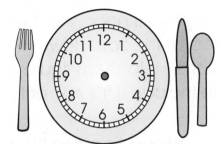

8 minutes before
1:05

21 minutes after
8:40

16 minutes before
4:30

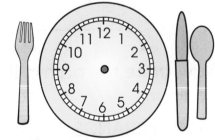

46 minutes after
10:11

32 minutes before
5:25

11 minutes after
3:16

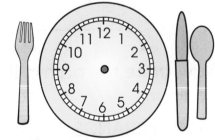

24 minutes before
12:30

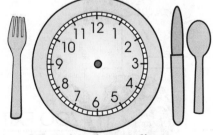

17 minutes after
1:31

43 minutes before
2:01

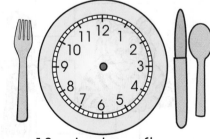

18 minutes after
6:45

Feeding Time

The abbreviations **A.M.** and **P.M.** help tell the time of day. At midnight, A.M. begins. At noon, P.M. begins. Ken and Angie enjoy watching the animals being fed at the zoo. However, when they arrived, they were a little confused by the signs. Help them figure out the feeding time for each kind of animal. Be sure to include if it's A.M. or P.M.

Zebras: Feeding time is 2 hours after the monkeys.

_____

Tigers: Feeding time is 2 hours after 9:00 A.M.

_____

Elephants: Feeding time is 1:00 P.M.

Giraffes: Feeding time is 1 hour before the lions.

_____

Monkeys: Feeding time is 3 hours before the giraffes.

_____

Lions: Feeding time is 3 hours after the elephants.

_____

Now, **trace** the path in the zoo that Ken and Angie would take so that they could see all the animals being fed.

ZOO ENTRANCE

ZOO EXIT

Monkeying Around

Nat can't tell time. He needs your help to **solve** these problems.

1. Nat is supposed to be at school in 10 minutes. What time should he get there?

_____

2. Nat started breakfast at 7:10 A.M. It took him 15 minutes to eat. Mark the time he finished.

3. Nat will leave school in 5 minutes. What time will it be then?

_____

4. Nat's family will eat dinner in 15 minutes. When will that be?

_____

5. It is now 6:45 P.M. Nat must start his homework in 5 minutes. Mark the starting time on the clock.

6. Nat will go to the park in 15 minutes. It is now 1:25 P.M. Mark the time he will go to the park.

Name _____

Minutes Make Up the Hours

Preparation: Cut out the game cards on pages 273 and 275. There are 12 pairs of cards. One card of each pair has minutes written on it. The other card has hours and minutes written on it (see the examples shown). M is on the back of the Minute cards. HM is on the back of the Hour/Minute cards. Put a rubber band around the Minute cards and one around the Hour/Minute cards. Make an answer key telling which Hour/Minute card matches each Minute card.

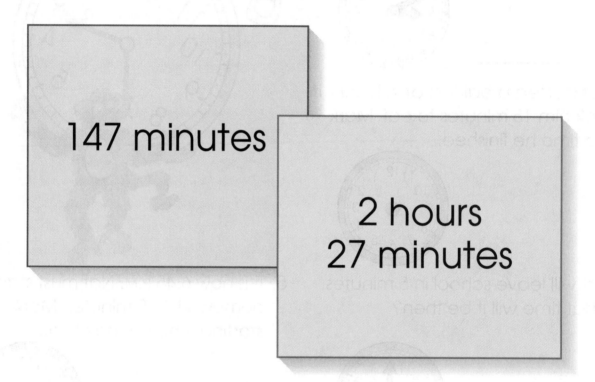

Rules: This game involves 2–4 players. The youngest player goes first and play goes clockwise. Lay the Minute cards facedown on one side of the playing area. Lay the Hour/Minute cards facedown on the other side. For another challenge, mix them together and lay them all in rows.

Directions: The game is played like "Memory." Player One turns a card up from each set of cards. If the cards are a pair, the player may take them. Otherwise, the cards should be put back facedown. Play continues until all pairs are matched. The player with the most pairs is the winner and goes first if playing another game. Use the key only if the players do not agree on a match.

Minute Cards

233 minutes	200 minutes	120 minutes
65 minutes	280 minutes	147 minutes
74 minutes	35 minutes	360 minutes
122 minutes	97 minutes	109 minutes

Minute Cards

M	M	M
M	M	M
M	M	M
M	M	M

Hour/Minute Cards

3 hours 53 minutes	3 hours 20 minutes	2 hours
1 hour 5 minutes	4 hours 40 minutes	2 hours 27 minutes
1 hour 14 minutes	(0 hours) 35 minutes	6 hours (0 minutes)
2 hours 2 minutes	1 hour 37 minutes	1 hour 49 minutes

Time

Name _____

Hour/Minute Cards

HM	HM	HM
HM	HM	HM
HM	HM	HM
HM	HM	HM

Name _____

How Far Is It?

Drawing pictures can be a good problem-solving strategy. **Draw** pictures to help you **solve** the problems below. Each problem requires three answers.

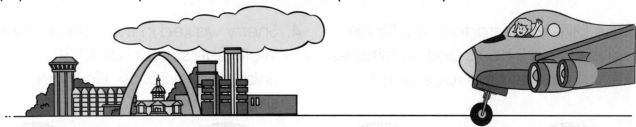

1. Jimmy has to walk 12 blocks to get to the park where he likes to play ball. It takes him 3 minutes to walk one block. How many minutes will it take him to walk to the park?

   Distance _____   Speed _____   Time _____

2. An airplane leaves the airport at 9:00 A.M. It flies at 200 miles per hour. When it lands at 11:00 A.M., how far will it have gone?

   Distance _____   Speed _____   Time _____

3. It is 50 miles between Dakota City and Blue Falls. It takes Mr. Oliver 1 hour to make the drive. How fast does he drive?

   Distance _____   Speed _____   Time _____

4. Tad rides his bike to his grandmother's house. It takes him 45 minutes to ride there. She lives 5 miles from his house. How many minutes does it take him to ride 1 mile?

   Distance _____   Speed _____   Time _____

5. Rachel loves to visit her grandparents who live 150 miles from her house. When they make the trip, her dad drives. He averages 50 miles an hour. How many hours will the trip take?

   Distance _____   Speed _____   Time _____

Time

Name _____

Time Problems

Draw the hands on the clocks to show the starting time and the ending time. Then, **write** the answer to the question.

1. The bike race started at 2:55 P.M. and lasted 2 hours and 10 minutes. What time did the race end?

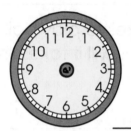 _____

4. Sherry walked in the 12-mile Hunger Walk. She started at 12:30 P.M. and finished at 4:50 P.M. How long did she walk?

 _____

2. The 500-mile auto race started at 11:00 A.M. and lasted 2 hours and 25 minutes. What time did the race end?

 _____

5. The chili cook-off started at 10:00 A.M., and all the chili was cooked by 4:30 P.M. How long did it take to cook the chili?

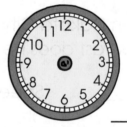 _____

3. The train left Indianapolis at 7:25 A.M. and arrived in Chicago at 10:50 A.M. How long did the trip take?

 _____

6. The chili judging began at 4:30 P.M. After 3 hours and 45 minutes the chili had all been eaten. At what time was the chili judging finished?

 _____

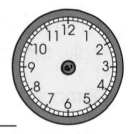

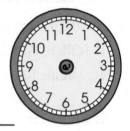

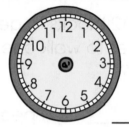

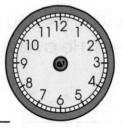

Time Zones

Clocks in various parts of the world do not show the same time. Suppose they did show the same time—3 P.M., for example. At that time, people in some countries would see the sun rise and people in other lands would see it high in the sky. In other countries, the sun could not be seen because 3 P.M. would occur at night. Instead, clocks in all locations show 12 o'clock at midday.

Alaska Time	Pacific Time	Mountain Time	Central Time	Eastern Time	Atlantic Time
3 A.M.	4 A.M.	5 A.M.	6 A.M.	7 A.M.	8 A.M.

The United States and Canada each have six standard time zones. Each zone uses a time 1 hour different from its neighboring zones. The hours are earlier to the west of each zone and later to the east. The Newfoundland Time Zone is not a true standard time zone because it differs from its neighboring zones by only a half hour. The boundaries between the zones are irregular so that neighboring communities can have the same time.

3:00 A.M.

St. Louis, MO

Directions:
Color each time zone a different color on **Map of North America** on page 280. Cut out **Hour Cards** from page 281 and **City Cards** from page 283.

Lay the **City Cards** facedown in a stack and spread out the **Hour Cards** faceup. Select one **Hour Card** and one **City Card**. This **City Card** will be referred to as the original city. Take another **City Card** from the stack. Find the **Hour Card** that tells what the time would be in this city. Do this several times, choosing other **City Cards** before changing the original city and time.

Map of North America

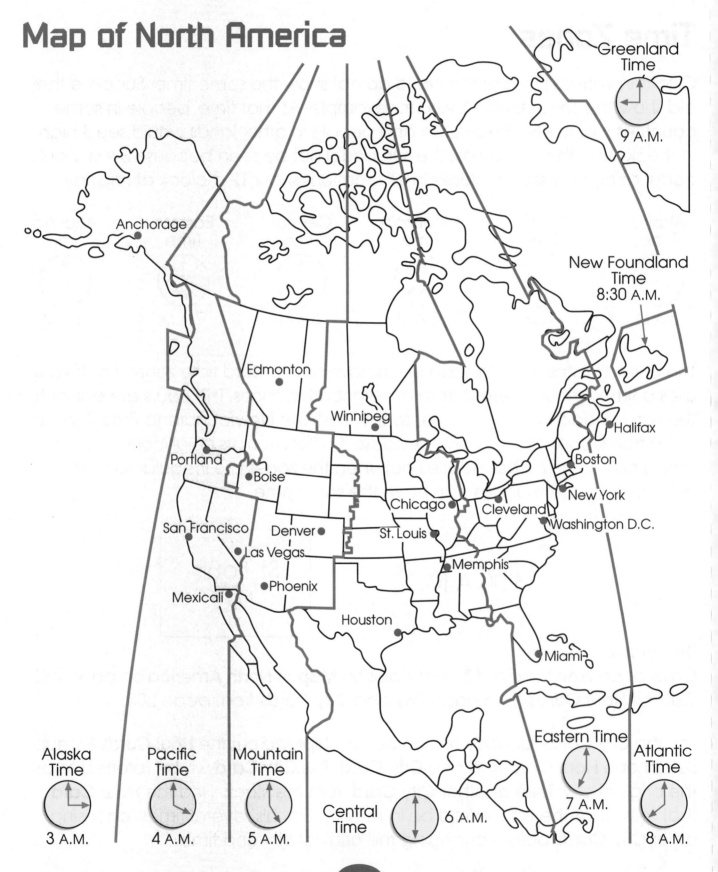

Greenland Time
9 A.M.

New Foundland Time
8:30 A.M.

Anchorage

Edmonton

Winnipeg

Halifax

Portland

Boise

Boston

New York

Chicago

Cleveland

Washington D.C.

San Francisco

Denver

St. Louis

Las Vegas

Memphis

Phoenix

Mexicali

Houston

Miami

Alaska Time
3 A.M.

Pacific Time
4 A.M.

Mountain Time
5 A.M.

Central Time
6 A.M.

Eastern Time
7 A.M.

Atlantic Time
8 A.M.

Hour Cards

12:00 A.M.	1:00 A.M.	2:00 A.M.	3:00 A.M.
4:00 A.M.	5:00 A.M.	6:00 A.M.	7:00 A.M.
8:00 A.M.	9:00 A.M.	10:00 A.M.	11:00 A.M.
12:00 P.M.	1:00 P.M.	2:00 P.M.	3:00 P.M.
4:00 P.M.	5:00 P.M.	6:00 P.M.	7:00 P.M.
8:00 P.M.	9:00 P.M.	10:00 P.M.	11:00 P.M.

City Cards

Halifax, N.S.	Boston, MA	New York, NY	Miami, FL
Washington, D.C.	St. Louis, MO	Chicago, IL	Cleveland, OH
Winnipeg, MB	Houston, TX	Memphis, TN	Edmonton, AB
Denver, CO	Phoenix, AZ	Boise, ID	Las Vegas, NV
Portland, OR	Anchorage, AK	San Francisco, CA	Mexicali, Mexico

Name _____

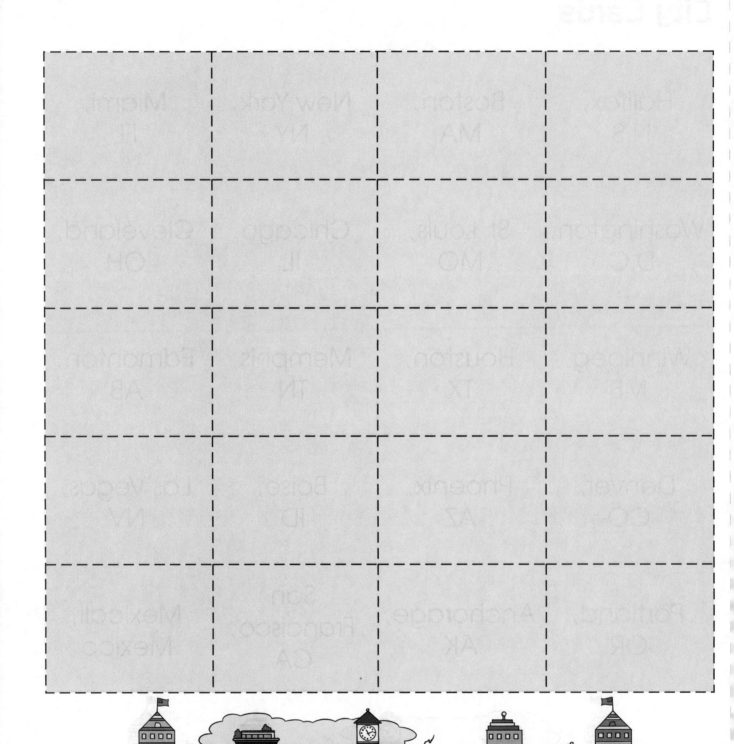

Racing Chimps 🍌

One chimpanzee in the forest always likes to brag that it can get more fruit than any other animal in the forest. So an older and wiser chimpanzee decided to challenge him to a race.

"Let us see who can bring back more bananas in 1 hour," said the older chimp. The race began.

Quickly, the younger chimp picked a bunch of five bananas and carried it back. He continued doing this every 5 minutes.

The older chimp was not quite as fast. Every 10 minutes he carried back eight bananas.

After 45 minutes, the young chimp decided to stop and eat one of his bananas before continuing. By the time he finished, the hour was over and the older chimp called out, "The race is over. Whose pile of bananas is bigger?"

Using the information above, figure out how many bananas were in each pile and which chimp won the race.

The younger chimp had _____ bananas in his pile.

The older chimp had _____ bananas in his pile.

The winner was the _____ chimp!

Section 12

Money

Garage Sale

Use the fewest number of coins possible to equal the amount shown in each box. **Write** or **draw** the coins you would use in each box.

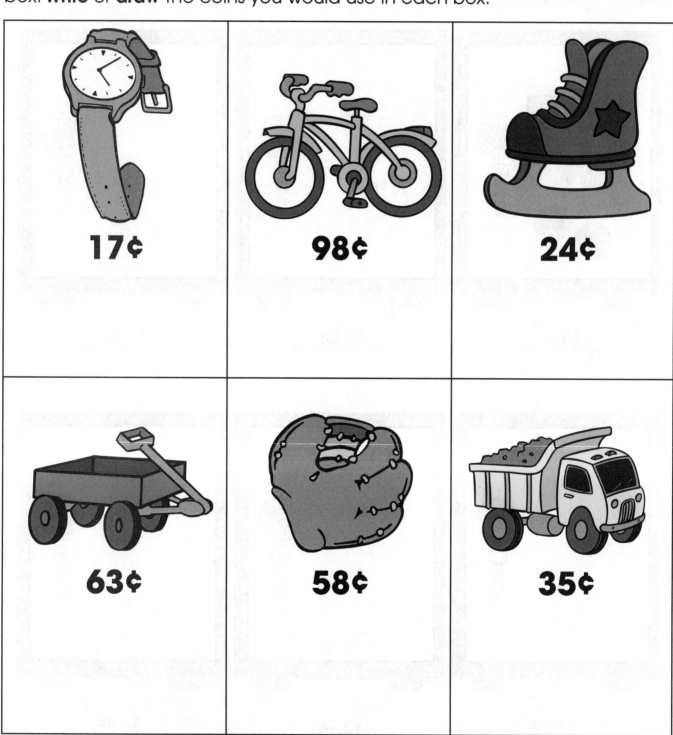

17¢

98¢

24¢

63¢

58¢

35¢

Name _____

Your Answer's Safe With Me

Find the right "combination" to open each safe. **Draw** the bills and coins needed to make each amount.

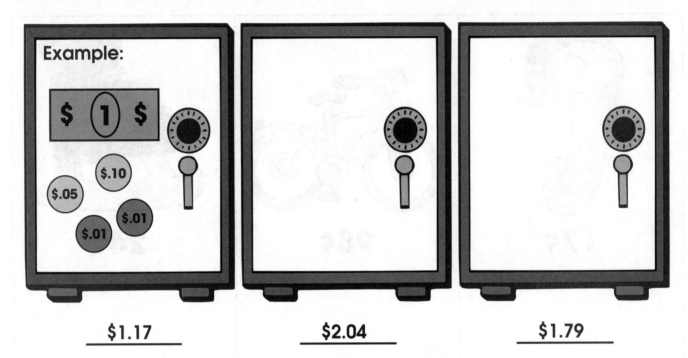

Example:

$ (1) $

$.10

$.05

$.01

$.01

_____$1.17_____   _____$2.04_____   _____$1.79_____

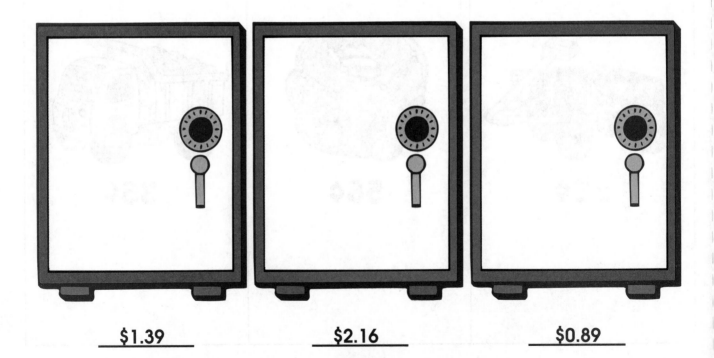

_____$1.39_____   _____$2.16_____   _____$0.89_____

Name _____

Easy Street

What is each house worth? **Count** the money in each house on Easy Street.
Write the amount on the line below it.

Example:

$2.40

_____   _____   _____   _____   _____

Name _____

A Collection of Coins

Write the number of coins needed to make the amount shown.

Money	Quarters	Dimes	Nickels	Pennies
76¢				
45¢				
98¢				
40¢				
84¢				
62¢				
31¢				
$1.42				
$1.98				

Monetary Message

What's the smartest thing to do with your money? To find out, **solve** the following problems and **write** the matching letter above the answer.

$\overline{}$ $\overline{}$ $\overline{}$ $\overline{}$ $\qquad$ $\overline{}$ $\overline{}$,
$42.71 $33.94 $50.42 $100.73 $45.70 $2.39

$\overline{}$ $\overline{}$ $\overline{}$ $\quad$ $\overline{}$ $\overline{}$ $\quad$ $\overline{}$ $\overline{}$ $\overline{}$ $\overline{}$
$33.94 $26.13 $88.02 $45.70 $2.39 $51.12 $45.70 $11.01 $11.01

$\overline{}$ $\overline{}$ $\overline{}$ $\quad$ $\overline{}$ $\overline{}$!
$33.94 $88.02 $88.02 $55.76 $42.79

$$V = \begin{array}{r} \$42.13 \\ +\ \ 8.29 \end{array} \qquad A = \begin{array}{r} \$\ 4.56 \\ +\ 29.38 \end{array} \qquad N = \begin{array}{r} \$\ 4.65 \\ +\ 21.48 \end{array} \qquad S = \begin{array}{r} \$23.46 \\ +\ 19.25 \end{array}$$

$$P = \begin{array}{r} \$\ 9.31 \\ +\ 33.48 \end{array} \qquad L = \begin{array}{r} \$\ 6.73 \\ +\ \ 4.28 \end{array} \qquad E = \begin{array}{r} \$81.49 \\ +\ 19.24 \end{array} \qquad T = \begin{array}{r} \$\ \ .42 \\ 1.94 \\ +\ \ \ .03 \end{array}$$

$$U = \begin{array}{r} \$50.84 \\ +\ \ 4.92 \end{array} \qquad I = \begin{array}{r} \$\ 7.49 \\ +\ 38.21 \end{array}$$

$$D = \begin{array}{r} \$\ 3.04 \\ +\ 84.98 \end{array} \qquad W = \begin{array}{r} \$\ 1.89 \\ +\ 49.23 \end{array}$$

Name _____

Add 'Em Up!

Write the prices, then **add. Regroup**, when needed.

1.   skateboard
   + _____ hat

2.   dictionary
   + _____ radio

3.   wallet
   + _____ goldfish

4.   hot dog
   + _____ watch

5.   dictionary
   + _____ kite

6.   in-line skates
   + _____ trumpet

7.   hot dog
   + _____ rocket

8.   skateboard
   + _____ goldfish

9.   hat
   + _____ kite

10.   radio
    + _____ trumpet

11.   rocket
    + _____ goldfish

12.   skateboard
    + _____ in-line skates

Name _____

Making Change

When you do not have the exact change to buy something at a store, the clerk must give you change. The first amount of money is what you give the clerk. The second amount is what the item costs. In the box, **list** the fewest number of coins and bills you will receive in change.

	Amount I Have	Cost of Item	Change
1	$3.75	$3.54	
2	$10.00	$5.63	
3	$7.00	$6.05	
4	$7.25	$6.50	
5	$7.50	$6.13	
6	$0.75	$0.37	
7	$7.00	$6.99	
8	$15.00	$12.75	

Name _____

The Money Shuffle

Cut out the game board on pages 295 and 297 and laminate it, if possible. To play the game, you will need two players. Place the gameboard on the floor or table top.

Player One takes his/her turn by placing a penny at the bottom of the paper and flicking it with his/her thumb and forefinger. The penny should land on a coin. (If it does not, Player One counts it as zero. Or, if desired, the player may "shoot" again.)

Player One must then remember that coin value while Player Two takes his/her turn and repeats the process. (If the players are still learning coin values, they may use paper and pencil.) Player One then receives a second turn. This time, however, Player One must add the new coin value to the coin value from his/her first turn. This procedure is repeated until one player makes a mental addition error and is "caught" by another player. His/her score returns to zero and the player must start all over. Players may use a calculator to help check the other players' sums.

Name _____

The Money Shuffle Gameboard

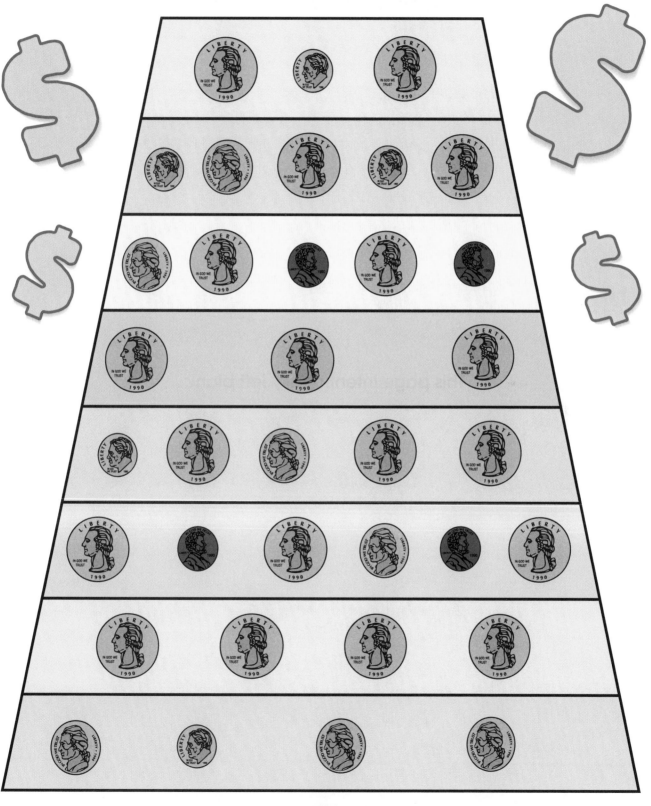

This page intentionally left blank.

The Money Shuffle Gameboard

This page intentionally left blank.

Super Savers!

Add to find the amounts of money each person saved.

Sam's
Account

$8.03
0.84
+ 5.47
_____

Debbie's
Account

$45.32
2.41
+ 34.28
_____

Sarah's
Account

$85.42
12.58
+ 2.21
_____

Roberto's
Account

$41.46
+ 8.89
_____

Alex's
Account

$ 4.06
81.23
+ 2.84
_____

Eva's
Account

$89.42
3.06
+ 0.94
_____

Bill's
Account

$62.41
3.84
+ 64.21
_____

Monica's
Account

$20.04
3.42
+ 25.81
_____

Tom's
Account

$ 8.05
21.21
+ 0.98
_____

Andy's
Account

$ 0.47
31.24
+ 2.38
_____

Earl's
Account

$50.42
3.84
+ 0.98
_____

Mark's
Account

$21.46
20.00
+ 5.58
_____

Katelyn's
Account

$ 0.42
0.59
+ 3.42
_____

Kimberly's
Account

$ 5.42
40.64
+ 3.89
_____

Whose account
is the largest? _____

Whose is
the smallest? _____

Whose is closest
to $50? _____

Fast Food

Mealwormy is the latest restaurant of that famous fast food creator, Buggs I. Lyke. His Mealwormy Burger costs $1.69. An order of Roasted Roaches cost $0.59 for the regular size and $0.79 for the larger size. A Cricket Cola is $0.89.

1 You buy a Mealwormy Burger and a regular order of Roasted Roaches. What is the total?

4 Your best friend orders a Mealwormy Burger, a large order of Roasted Roaches and Cricket Cola. How much will it cost?

2 Your teacher buys a Cricket Cola and a regular order of Roasted Roaches. What does it cost her?

5 The principal is very hungry, so his bill comes to $14.37. How much change will he get from $20.00?

3 Your mom goes to Mealwormy to buy your dinner. She spends $3.37. How much change does she get from a $5.00 bill?

6 You have $1.17 in your bank. How much more do you need to pay for a Mealwormy Burger?

Spending Spree

Use the clues to figure out what each person bought. Then, **subtract** to find out how much change each had left.

$12.49

Clue:

1. David began with: $40.25   He loves to see things zoom into the sky!
   − _____

$9.31

2. Mark started with: $50.37   He likes to travel places with his hands free and a breeze in his face!
   − _____

$21.52

3. Eva started with: $14.84   She loves to practice her jumping and exercise at the same time!
   − _____

$13.45

$15.29

4. Bill brought: $61.49   He wants to see the heavens for himself!
   − _____

$2.43

5. Michelle brought: $40.29   Fuzzy companions make such great friends!
   − _____

$3.95

$52.28

6. Cheryl started with: $16.80   She loves to hear music that is soft and beautiful!
   − _____

$32.51

7. Heather arrived with: $20.48   She loves to put it down on paper for everyone to see!
   − _____

$47.29

Name _____

One-Stop Shopping

Stash McCash is shopping. **Add** to find the total cost of the items. Then, **subtract** to find how much change Stash should receive.

$3.99 $2.68 $3.36 $0.27 $0.77 $3.15

$3.61 $1.54 $1.27 $2.55 $2.49

$1.49 $0.88 $4.25 $1.94

Example:

Stash has $5.00. He buys:	Stash has $8.50. He buys:	Stash has $7.04. He buys:	Stash has $9.00. He buys:

$ 0.88
     0.77
 + 1.54
    $ 3.19
 	
  $ 5.00
  − 3.19
  $ 1.81 Change
	
	Change
		
		Change
			
			Change

Stash has $10.95. He buys:	Stash has $10.00. He buys:	Stash has $9.24. He buys:	Stash has $8.09. He buys:
  Change	 Change	 Change	 Change

Match the Sale

Which item did each child purchase? **Calculate** the amount. **Write** each purchase price below.

Jessica:

$17.43

−_____

$9.14

Tammy:

$43.21

−_____

$34.86

Heather:

$10.06

−_____

$1.64

Mark:

$52.46

−_____

$14.17

Eva:

$65.04

−_____

$36.94

Monica:

$6.99

−_____

$3.56

Katelyn:

$9.06

−_____

$5.24

David:

$15.25

−_____

$6.82

Curt:

$63.45

−_____

$46.16

Michele:

$32.45

−_____

$13.50

Gwen:

$19.24

−_____

$6.38

Thomas:

$9.43

−_____

$5.59

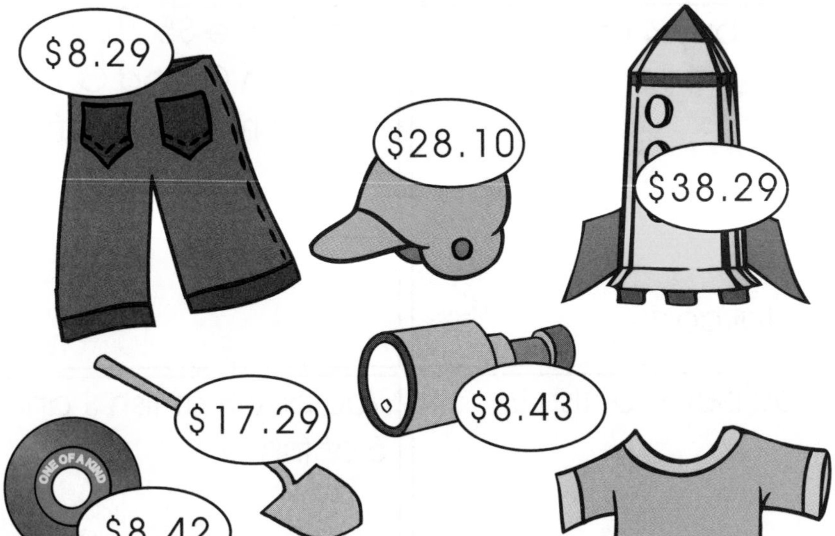

$8.29

$28.10

$38.29

$17.29

$8.43

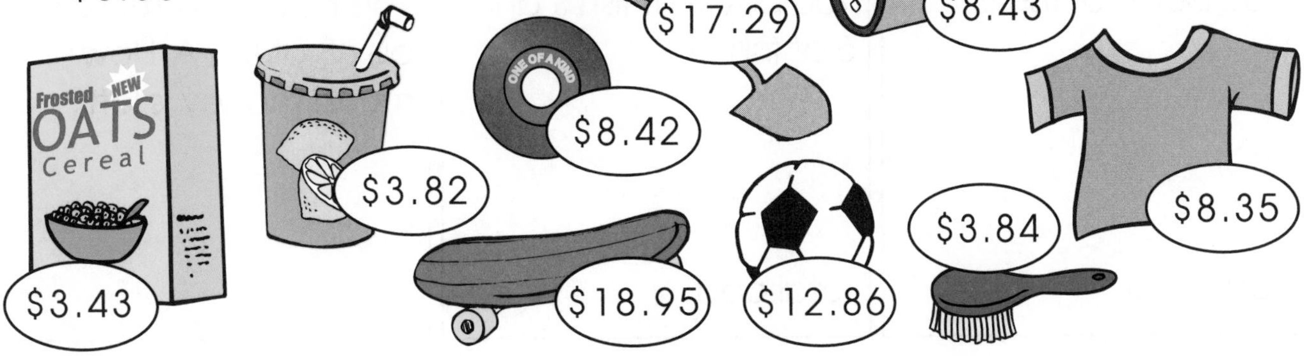

$8.42

$3.82

$3.43

$18.95

$12.86

$3.84

$8.35

Name _____

What a Great Catch!

Solve these problems.

A $2.47
B $1.69
C $2.18
G $1.77
D $2.36
E $3.29
I $4.39
F $3.62
H $2.54
J $3.76

You buy fish A, C and H. Total cost: $2.47 2.18 + 2.54 $7.19	You have $4.00. You buy fish D. How much money is left?	You have $10.00. You buy fish E and J. How much money is left?
You buy 4 of fish I. Total cost:	You have $5.75. You buy fish G and C. How much money is left?	You buy fish D, F, J and B. Total cost:
You buy 6 of fish E. Total cost:	You buy 3 of fish J and 6 of fish D. Total cost:	You have $10.76. You buy 3 of fish A. How much money is left?

Name _____

Dessert Included

Brenda and Doug really like chocolate—chocolate-covered raisins, chocolate candy, chocolate cake and hot chocolate! Most of all, they love chocolate sundaes with chocolate chip ice cream. When they find out that the Eats and Sweets Restaurant is offering a free chocolate dessert with any meal costing exactly $5.00, they decide to go there for dinner.

Menu

Meat
Chicken $1.95
Roast Beef $3.05
Shrimp $3.50
Roast Pork $2.75

Potatoes/Vegetables
Mashed Potatoes $1.00
French Fries $0.85
Sweet Corn $0.65
Green Beans $0.50

Salad
Cole Slaw $0.60
Potato Salad $0.95
Dinner Salad $0.75
Macaroni Salad $1.10

Drinks
Milk $0.40
Chocolate Milk $0.45
Orange Juice $0.95
Soda Pop $0.55

Choosing one item from each of the four categories, **list** four different meals Brenda and Doug could eat for exactly $5.00.

Meal # 1 _____ , _____ , _____ , _____

Meal # 2 _____ , _____ , _____ , _____

Meal # 3 _____ , _____ , _____ , _____

Meal # 4 _____ , _____ , _____ , _____

What's for Lunch?

Solve these problems.

Lunch Menu

Salad $2.25	**Beverages**	
Hot Dog $1.10	Milk $0.50	
Grilled cheese .. $1.00	Orange Juice $0.60	
Pizza $0.90	Soda $0.75	

Dessert
Pudding $0.90
Ice Cream $0.85

1. Craig, Thomas and Laura stopped for lunch on their long trip. Craig had a late breakfast and only wanted some milk to drink. Thomas was feeling a little carsick, so he simply wanted a soda. Laura was very hungry. They spent a total of $4.25. What could Laura have had for lunch?

   _____

2. Beth and Michelle stopped for lunch during their busy day of shopping. They had worked up quite an appetite after all their bargain hunting! Beth exclaimed, "I'll buy you lunch today, Michelle. After all, you've helped me carry these packages all day!" "Thank you," Michelle replied. Beth reached into her pocket to be sure of the amount of money she had left. "Oh, no!" Beth cried, "I must have lost some money! I only have $3.50 left!" What could they have eaten for lunch?

   _____

3. Diane spent $1.60 on lunch. She was too full to get dessert. What could she have had for lunch?

   _____

4. The twins had too much pizza for dinner last night and certainly did not want it today. They each had the same meal, including pudding for dessert. They spent $5.50. What could they have eaten for lunch?

   _____

5. Sue is a vegetarian and she's allergic to milk. Bob ate two slices of pizza and a soda. Together, their lunch cost them $5.40. What did Sue have for lunch?

   _____

Multiplying Money

Money is multiplied in the same way other numbers are. The only difference is a dollar sign and a decimal point are added to the final product.

Steps:

Multiply.

1. Multiply by ones.
1. 4 x 8 = 32 (Carry the 3.)
2. 4 x 2 = 8 + 3 = 11 (Carry the 1.)
3. 4 x 4 = 16 + 1 = 17

```
    1 3
  $4.2 8
x    3 4
  1 7 1 2
```

```
  $3.4 2
x    2 5
_____
```

```
  $5.4 2
x    6 1
_____
```

2.
1. Cross out the carried digits.
2. Add the zero.

```
   ✗✗
  $4.2 8
x    3 4
_____
  1 7 1 2
        0
```

3. Multiply by tens.
1. 3 x 8 = 24 (Carry the 2.)
2. 3 x 2 = 6 + 2 = 8
3. 3 x 4 = 12

```
        2
  $4.2 8
x    3 4
_____
  1 7 1 2
1 2 8 4 0
```

```
  $3.8 1
x    4 6
_____
```

```
  $8.2 0
x    5 5
_____
```

4. Add.
1,712 + 12,840 = 14,552

```
  $4.2 8
x    3 4
_____
  1 7 1 2
+1 2 8 4 0
_____
  14,5 5 2
```

5. Add the dollar sign and the decimal point.

```
  $4.2 8
x    3 4
_____
  1 7 1 2
+1 2 8 4 0
_____
$1 4 5.5 2
```

```
  $9.4 2
x    3 1
_____
```

```
  $4.2 3
x    9 6
_____
```

Name _____

Foxy Felix's Shop

Solve these problems.

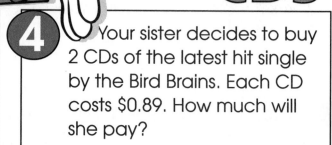

SALE 10% off 50% off on all CDs

1 Mighty Man comics cost $0.13 at Foxy Felix's. You buy 4 of these comics. How much should you pay?

2 Your best friend bought 9 marbles at Foxy Felix's. Each marble cost $0.19. How much money did he spend?

3 Baseball cards are $0.11 each at Foxy Felix's. How much will it cost you for 8 cards?

4 Your sister decides to buy 2 CDs of the latest hit single by the Bird Brains. Each CD costs $0.89. How much will she pay?

5 Crazy stickers cost $0.21 each at Foxy Felix's. You buy 7 of them. How much should you pay?

6 Stinky Stickers have a skunk odor. Your best friend bought 7 Stinky Stickers which cost $0.18 each. How much did he spend?

Money Math

Solve these problems. Remember the decimal point and dollar sign in your answers.

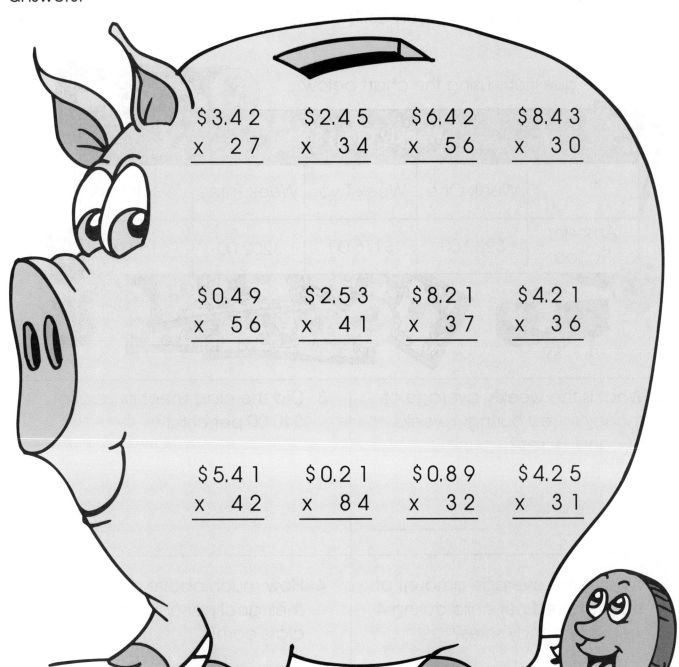

$3.42
x   27

$2.45
x   34

$6.42
x   56

$8.43
x   30

$0.49
x   56

$2.53
x   41

$8.21
x   37

$4.21
x   36

$5.41
x   42

$0.21
x   84

$0.89
x   32

$4.25
x   31

Name _____

Science Trip

The science class is planning a field trip to Chicago to visit the Museum of Science and Industry. There are 18 students in the class and each student needs $40.00 to cover the expenses. The class decided to sell candy to raise money.

Answer the questions using the chart below.

Weekly Class Sales				
	Week One	Week Two	Week Three	Week Four
Amount Raised	$282.00	$176.00	$202.00	$150.00

1. What is the weekly average of money raised during 4 weeks of candy sales?

    _____

2. What is the average amount of dollars raised per child during 4 weeks of candy sales?

    _____

3. Did the class meet its goal of $40.00 per child?

    _____

4. How much above or beneath their goal per child did the class earn?

    _____

Too Much Information

Cross out the information not needed and **solve** the problems.

1 All 20 of the students from Sandy's class went to the movies. Tickets cost $3.50 each. Drinks cost $0.95 each. How much altogether did the students spend on tickets?

2 Five students had ice cream, 12 others had candy. Ice cream cost $0.75 per cup. How much did the students spend on ice cream?

3 Seven of the 20 students did not like the movie. Three of the 20 students had seen the movie before. How many students had not seen the movie before?

4 Six of the students spent a total of $16.50 for refreshments and $21.00 for their tickets. How much did each spend for refreshments?

5 Of the students, 11 were girls and 9 were boys. At $1.50 per ticket, how much did the boys' tickets cost altogether?

6 Mary paid $0.95 for an orange drink and $0.65 for a candy bar. Sarah paid $2.50 for popcorn. How much did Mary's refreshments cost her?

7 Ten of the students went back to see the movie again the next day. Each student paid $3.50 for a ticket, $2.50 for popcorn and $0.95 for a soft drink. How much did each student pay?

Name _____

Sam Sillicook's Donut Shop

Solve these problems.

1 Your mom bought 32 Jam-filled Cream Puffs. They cost $0.89 each. How much did your mom spend?

2 Harry D. Hulk bought 14 Banana Cream Donuts for his breakfast at $0.65 each. How much did they cost Harry?

3 Your best friend bought 12 Cinnamon Twists at $0.29 each. How much did he spend?

4 You love Jam-filled Cream Puffs. Your mother buys 17 for your birthday party at $0.89 each. How much do they cost?

5 Your dad decided to take the whole family out. He bought 24 Super Duper Jelly Donuts at $0.49 each. What was the total cost?

6 You took 40 Banana Cream Donuts to school. They cost $0.65 each. What was the total?

Perplexing Problems

Solve these problems.

Mark, David, Curt and Jordan rented a motorized skateboard for 1 hour. What was the cost for each of them—split equally 4 ways?	Five students pitched in to buy Mr. Foley a birthday gift. How much did each of them contribute?
Total: $17.36 $ _____	**Total:** $9.60 $ _____

Mary, Cheryl and Betty went to the skating rink. What was their individual cost?	Carol, Katelyn and Kimberly bought lunch at their favorite salad shop. What did each of them pay for lunch?	Debbie, Sarah, Michele and Kelly earned $6.56 altogether collecting cans. How much did each of them earn individually?
Total: $7.44 $ _____	**Total:** $12.63 $ _____	**Total:** $6.56 $ _____
Five friends went to the Hot Spot Café for lunch. They all ordered the special. What did it cost?	Lee and Ricardo purchased an awesome model rocket together. What was the cost for each of them?	The total fee for Erik, Bill and Steve to enter the science museum was $8.76. What amount did each of them pay?
Total: $27.45 $ _____	**Total:** $9.52 $ _____	**Total:** $8.76 $ _____

Name _____

Let's Take a Trip!

You will plan a car trip to calculate approximately how much the trip will cost. You will calculate distances between locations and the amount of gasoline needed based upon miles per gallon of the car. Then, you will estimate the cost of the gasoline, hotel, food and entertainment.

Directions: Using graph paper, plot out your trip starting and ending at "point A." The trip should have five points of travel, including point A. Each square on the graph paper represents 10 miles. Calculate the mileage between points.

Use a copy of the **Expense Chart** on page 143 to keep track of your calculations. Use newspapers, travel brochures and menus to help you estimate the cost of food, gas, hotels, entertainment, etc. You will also want to use a calculator. When you have completed the **Expense Chart**, answer the questions below.

1. If two people go on this trip, how will the cost change? _____
2. If a family of four goes on the trip, how will the cost change? _____
3. Would the cost of gas change? _____
   Why or why not? _____
4. What else could change the cost of the trip? _____
5. Why is this just an estimate? _____
   _____

Expense Chart

Distance to travel

Miles from Point A to Point B: _____

Miles from Point B to Point C: _____

Miles from Point C to Point D: _____

Miles from Point D to Point E: _____

Miles from Point E to Point A: _____

Total miles to travel: _____

Your car gets 22 miles per gallon of gas.

Total gas needed: _____

Gas costs $1.19 per gallon.

Total amount needed for gas: _____

You will stay at a hotel/motel for four nights at $79.00 per night.

Total cost for four nights: _____

Estimated food cost per day (5 days)

breakfast—$2.50

lunch—$4.75

dinner—$9.25

Total per day: _____

Total for 5 days: _____

Estimated entertainment expenses

Admission to movies: _____

Admission to museums: _____

Admission to theme parks: _____

Admission to sports events: _____

Add all the entries to get a total estimate for the cost of the trip.

Total estimated cost of the trip: _____

Mind-Bogglers

Solve these problems. Then, explain your strategies.

1. Marta receives an allowance of $2.25 a week. This week, her mom pays her in nickels, dimes and quarters. She received more dimes than quarters.

   What coins did her mom use to pay her? _____

   Strategy I used: _____

2. Mr. Whitman takes his family on a trip to the amusement park. He brings $75 with him to buy the entrance tickets, food and souvenirs for the family. The tickets to get into the amusement park are $12.75 for adults and $8.45 for children. How much money will Mr. Whitman have for food and souvenirs after he buys entrance tickets for himself, Mrs. Whitman and their two children?

   Amount of money? _____

   Strategy I used: _____

3. There are four children who worked at the car wash. Kelly worked 4 hours. Jack worked for 3 hours. Matt and Tammy worked for 2 hours. They made $110.

   How much of that did Kelly earn? _____

   Jack? _____   Matt and Tammy? _____

   Strategy I used: _____

4. Mrs. Downs gives her three children a weekly allowance. She pays them in dollar bills. Lauren is the first to get paid. She receives half the number of dollar bills her mom has. Don gets his allowance second. He receives half of the remaining dollar bills plus one. Mrs. Downs now has $2 left, which is Edith's allowance. How much allowance do Lauren and Don receive?

   Lauren _____   Don _____

   Strategy I used: _____

Glossary

Acute angle: Any angle that is less than a right angle or 90°.

Angle: The part of a shape where two lines come together.

Area: The number of square units needed to cover a flat surface.

Average: A number that tells about how something is normally. Find an average by adding all the numbers together and dividing by the number of addends.

Capacity: The measure of how much can fit inside an object.

Circle: A round, closed figure.

Common denominator: One number that is a common multiple of two or more denominators.

Congruent figures: Figures that have the same shape and size.

Decimal: A dot placed between the ones place and the tenths place in a number.

Denominator: The bottom number of a fraction that numbers the total amount of equal pieces.

Diameter: A line segment with both points on the circle, which always passes through the center of the circles.

Difference: The answer in a subtraction problem.

Dividend: The number to be divided in a division problem.

Divisor: The number to divide by in a division problem.

Equivalent fractions: Two different fractions that represent the same number.

Factors: The two numbers multiplied together in a multiplication problem.

Fraction: One or more equal parts of a whole or part of a group.

Improper fractions: A fraction representing a whole and a fraction. The numerator is larger than the denominator.

Like Fractions: Fractions with the same denominator.

Mixed number: A number made up of a whole number and a fraction.

Multiplication: A quick way to add.

Numerator: The top number of a fraction that numbers the parts.

Obtuse angle: Any angle that is more than a right angle or 90°.

Ordered pair: A set of numbers used to find a point on a grid.

Perimeter: The distance around the outside of a shape.

Pictograph: A graph using pictures to give information.

Place value: The value of a numeral determined by its place in a number.

Polygon: A closed shape with straight sides.

Probability: The chance that a given event will happen.

Product: The answer in a multiplication problem.

Quotient: The answer in a division problem.

Radius: A line segment from the center of a circle to any point on the circle.

Regrouping: Borrowing or carrying numbers between places.

Remainder: The amount left over after dividing a number.

Right angle: Any angle that measures 90°. It forms a square corner.

Rounding: Changing an exact amount to an estimate of the number.

Sum: The answer in an addition problem.

Survey: A mini-interview of many people to find out what they like or do not like.

Symmetry: A figure with two parts that match exactly.

Tally mark: A line to represent one. The fifth tally of any grouping is written diagonally over the first four marks. **Example:** 卌

Temperature: The measure of how warm or cold something is.

Unlike fractions: Fractions with different denominators.

Volume: The measure of the inside of a shape.

Answer Key

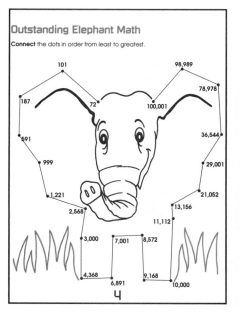

Outstanding Elephant Math

Connect the dots in order from least to greatest.

101
98,989
187
72
100,001
78,978
591
36,544
999
29,001
1,221
21,052
2,568
13,156
11,112
3,000 7,001 8,572
4,368 6,891 9,168 10,000

4

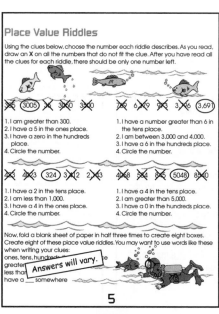

Place Value Riddles

Using the clues below, choose the number each riddle describes. As you read, draw an **X** on all the numbers that do not fit the clue. After you have read all the clues for each riddle, there should be only one number left.

~~355~~ (3005) ~~3050~~ ~~3500~~   ~~369~~ ~~6319~~ ~~639~~ ~~3169~~ (3,691)

1. I am greater than 300.
2. I have a 5 in the ones place.
3. I have a zero in the hundreds place.
4. Circle the number.

1. I have a number greater than 6 in the tens place.
2. I am between 3,000 and 4,000.
3. I have a 6 in the hundreds place.
4. Circle the number.

~~243~~ ~~4023~~ (324) ~~3412~~ ~~2443~~   ~~4068~~ ~~584~~ ~~845~~ (5048) ~~8540~~

1. I have a 2 in the tens place.
2. I am less than 1,000.
3. I have a 4 in the ones place.
4. Circle the number.

1. I have a 4 in the tens place.
2. I am greater than 5,000.
3. I have a 0 in the hundreds place.
4. Circle the number.

Now, fold a blank sheet of paper in half three times to create eight boxes. Create eight of these place value riddles. You may want to use words like these when writing your clues:
ones, tens, hundreds
greater
less than
have a ___ somewhere

Answers will vary.

5

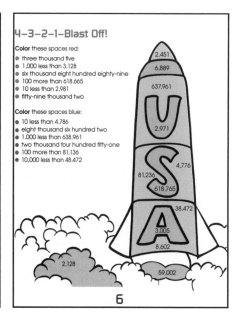

4-3-2-1-Blast Off!

Color these spaces red:
- three thousand five
- 1,000 less than 3,128
- six thousand eight hundred eighty-nine
- 100 more than 618,665
- 10 less than 2,981
- fifty-nine thousand two

Color these spaces blue:
- 10 less than 4,786
- eight thousand six hundred two
- 1,000 less than 638,961
- two thousand four hundred fifty-one
- 100 more than 81,136
- 10,000 less than 48,472

2,451
6,889
637,961
U S A
2,971
4,776
81,236
618,765
38,472
3,005
8,602
2,128
59,002

6

Place Value Puzzles

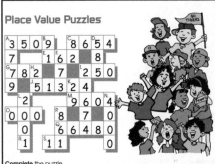

A3	5	0	9		C8	6	D5	4
7			E1	F6	2		8	
G7	H8	2		7		I2	5	0
9	J5	1	3	2	4			
L2					M9	6	N0	4
O0	0	0		P8			0	
0			Q6	6	4	8	0	
R1		S1	1				0	

Complete the puzzle.

ACROSS
- A. 3 thousand 5 hundred 9
- C. 100 less than 8,754
- E. one hundred sixty-two
- G. seven hundred eighty-two
- I. 100, 150, 200, ___
- J. 1, 2, 3, 4, 5 mixed up
- L. two
- M. 100 less than 9,704
- O. three zeros
- P. eight
- Q. 10,000 more than 56,480
- R. one
- S. 1 ten, 1 one

DOWN
- A. 10 more than 3,769
- B. ninety-one
- C. 28 backwards
- D. 5 hundreds, 8 tens, 5 ones
- F. 100 less than 773
- H. 5, 10, 15, 20, ___
- I. ten less than 24,684
- K. 2 tens, 9 ones
- L. two thousand one
- N. 1000, 2000, 3000, ___
- P. eight hundreds, 6 tens, 1 one

7

Write That Number

Write the numeral form for each number.

Example: three hundred forty-two = 342

1. six hundred fifty thousand, two hundred twenty-five **650,225**

2. nine hundred ninety-nine thousand, nine hundred ninety-nine **999,999**

3. one hundred six thousand, four hundred thirty-seven **106,437**

4. three hundred fifty-six thousand, two hundred two **356,202**

5. Write the number that is two more than 356,909. **356,911**

6. Write the number that is five less than 448,394. **448,389**

7. Write the number that is ten more than 285,634. **285,644**

8. Write the number that is ten less than 395,025. **395,015**

Write the following numbers in word form.

9. 3,208 **three thousand, two hundred eight**

10. 13,656 **thirteen thousand, six hundred fifty-six**

8

Place Value

1, 2 3 4 , 5 6 7

millions / hundred thousands / ten thousands / thousands / hundreds / tens / ones

Write each numeral in its correct place.

1. The number 8,672,019 has:
- **2** thousands
- **8** millions
- **0** hundreds
- **1** ten
- **9** ones
- **6** hundred thousands
- **7** ten thousands

2. What number has:
- 6 ones
- 7 hundreds
- 5 hundred thousands
- 3 millions
- 4 ten thousands
- 9 tens
- 8 thousands

The number is **3,548,796**.

3. The number 6,792,510 has:
- **9** ten thousands
- **0** ones
- **7** hundred thousands
- **6** millions
- **2** thousands
- **5** hundreds
- **1** ten

4. What number has:
- 5 millions
- 1 hundred
- 0 hundred thousands
- 3 tens
- 8 ten thousands
- 6 thousands
- 4 ones

The number is **5,086,134**.

9

Big Numbers Game

Preparation: Cut out the spinners, number cards and gameboard pattern on the next page. Glue the spinners and gameboard onto cardboard and let them dry. Cut them out. Attach a large paper clip or safety pin to the spinner base with a brad or paper fastener. The paper clip (or safety pin) should spin freely.

Give each player one set of ten cards. Also, each player will need a marker and a copy of the gameboard.

Rules: This game involves 2–6 players. The first player is the one who has the most letters in his/her last name. Play goes in a clockwise direction.

Directions: Player One spins the place value spinner first. Then, he/she spins the numerical spinner. Player One then puts the number marker on the place indicated by the spinner. (For example, if Player One spins hundreds on the place value spinner and 8 on the numerical spinner, he/she should put an 8 number marker in the hundreds place on the gameboard.) If the number shown on either spinner is already filled on the board, Player One loses his/her turn. The first player who fills all the spaces on his/her board and is able to read the number aloud is the winner.

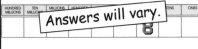

HUNDRED MILLIONS	TEN MILLIONS	MILLIONS			TENS	ONES

Answers will vary.

10

Estimate by Rounding Numbers

Estimate by rounding numbers to different place values. Use these rules.

Example: Round 283 to the nearest hundred.

- Find the digit in the place to be rounded. 283
- Now, look at the digit to its right. 283
- If the digit to the right is less than 5, the digit being rounded remains the same.
- If the digit to the right is 5 or more, the digit being rounded is increased by 1. 283 Rounds to 300
- Digits to the right of the place to be rounded become 0's. Digits to the left remain the same.

Examples: Round 4,385 . . .

to the nearest thousand	to the nearest hundred	to the nearest ten
4,385	4,385	4,385
3 is less than 5.	8 is more than 5.	5 = 5.
The 4 stays the same.	The 3 is rounded up to 4.	The 8 is rounded up to 9.
4,000	4,400	4,390

Complete the table.

NUMBERS TO BE ROUNDED	ROUND TO THE NEAREST THOUSAND	NEAREST HUNDRED	NEAREST TEN
2,725	3,000	2,700	2,730
10,942	11,000	10,900	10,940
6,816	7,000	6,800	6,820
2,309	2,000	2,300	2,310
7,237	7,000	7,200	7,240
959	1,000	1,000	960

13

Round, Round, Round You Go

Round each number to the nearest ten.

| 45 | **50** | 72 | **70** | 61 | **60** | 255 | **260** |
| 27 | **30** | 184 | **180** | 43 | **40** | 97 | **100** |

Round each number to the nearest hundred.

| 562 | **600** | 1,246 | **1,200** | 761 | **800** | 4,593 | **4,600** |
| 347 | **300** | 859 | **900** | 238 | **200** | 76 | **100** |

Round each number to the nearest thousand.

| 6,543 | **7,000** | 83,246 | **83,000** | 3,741 | **4,000** | 66,357 | **66,000** |
| 7,219 | **7,000** | 9,814 | **10,000** | 2,166 | **2,000** | 8,344 | **8,000** |

Round each number to the nearest ten thousand.

| 32,467 | **30,000** | 871,362 | **870,000** | 334,212 | **330,000** |
| 57,891 | **60,000** | 45,621 | **50,000** | 79,356 | **80,000** |

Round each number to the nearest hundred thousand.

| 116,349 | **100,000** | 946,477 | **900,000** | 732,166 | **700,000** |
| 762,887 | **800,000** | 365,851 | **400,000** | 225,631 | **200,000** |

Round each number to the nearest million.

2,765,437	**3,000,000**	7,762,997	**8,000,000**
1,469,876	**1,000,000**	5,564,783	**6,000,000**
14,537,123	**15,000,000**	4,117,655	**4,000,000**

14

The First State

What state is known as the first state? Follow the directions below to find out.

1. If 31,842 rounded to the nearest thousand is 31,000, put an **A** above number 2.
2. If 62 rounded to the nearest ten is 60, put an **E** above number 2 .
3. If 4,234 rounded to the nearest hundred is 4,200, put an **R** above number 7.
4. If 677 rounded to the nearest hundred is 600, put an **L** above number 3.
5. If 344 rounded to the nearest ten is 350, put an **E** above number 5.
6. If 5,599 rounded to the nearest thousand is 6,000, put an **A** above number 4.
7. If 1,549 rounded to the nearest hundred is 1,500, put an **A** above number 6.
8. If 885 rounded to the nearest hundred is 800, put a **W** above number 2.
9. If 521 rounded to the nearest ten is 520, put an **E** above number 8.
10. If 74 rounded to the nearest ten is 80, put an **R** above number 6.
11. If 3,291 rounded to the nearest thousand is 3,000, put an **L** above number 3.
12. If 248 rounded to the nearest hundred is 300, put an **R** above number 4.
13. If 615 rounded to the nearest ten is 620, put a **D** above number 1.
14. If 188 rounded to the nearest ten is 200, put a **W** above number 1.
15. If 6,817 rounded to the nearest thousand is 7,000, put a **W** above number 5.

Peach Blossom State Flower

Blue Hen Chicken State Bird

Fort Christina—site of the first state's first permanent settlement. Built by the Swedes and Finns.

D **E** **L** **A** **W** **A** **R** **E**
1   2   3   4   5   6   7   8

15

Dial-A-Word

Use the phone pad to calculate the "value" of the words.

Example: PHONE = 74663
PHONE = 7 + 4 + 6 + 6 + 3 = 26

(your name) =	Answers will vary	= ____
CALCULATOR =	2+2+5+2+8+5+2+8+6+7	= 47
DICTIONARY =	3+4+2+8+4+6+6+2+7+9	= 51
PET TRICKS =	7+3+8+8+7+4+2+5+7	= 51
BASEBALL GAME =	2+2+7+3+2+2+5+5+4+2+6+3	= 43
COMPUTERS =	2+6+6+7+8+8+3+7+7	= 54
TENNIS SHOES =	8+3+6+6+4+7+7+4+6+3+7	= 61
ADDITION =	2+3+3+4+8+4+6+6	= 36
MENTAL MATH =	6+3+6+8+2+5+6+2+8+4	= 50

17

Using Number Concepts 2 7 5 4 8

Cut out the set of cards on the next page. Use them to form number sentences that answer the questions below.

Sample answers below.

1. Use only two cards to list all the ways you can make the sum of 10.
There are 11 different combinations.

| 6 + 4 = 10 | 3 + 7 = 10 | 4 + 6 = 10 | 7 + 3 = 10 |

2. Use only two cards to list all the ways you can make the sum of 13.
14 combinations

| 8 + 5 = 13 | 10 + 3 = 13 |

3. Use only two cards to list all the ways you can make the sum of 16.
17 combinations

4. Use only two cards to list all the ways you can make the sum of 12.
13 combinations

5. Use only two cards to list all the ways you can make the sum of 15.
16 combinations

6. Use only two cards to list all the ways you can make the sum of 17.
18 combinations

7. How did you know you found all the ways?
Answers will vary.

Extension: Repeat this exercise using three cards to make each sum.

18

Mushrooming Addition

Follow the arrows to **add**.

Example: 52 + 28 = 80
28 + 91 = 119
119 + 80 = ?

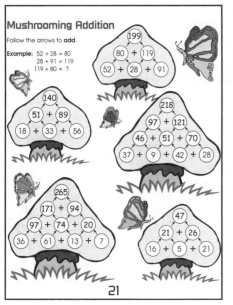

199
80 + 119
52 + 28 + 91

140
51 + 89
18 + 33 + 56

218
97 + 121
46 + 51 + 70
37 + 9 + 42 + 28

265
171 + 94
97 + 74 + 20
36 + 61 + 13 + 7

47
21 + 26
16 + 5 + 21

21

Fishy Addition

Add the ones.	Regroup, if needed.	Add the tens.
47 +18 82	47 +18 5	47 +18 65

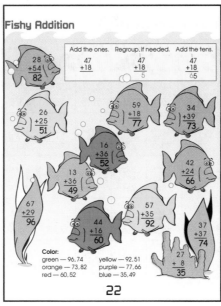

28 +54 = 82
26 +25 = 51
59 +18 = 77
34 +39 = 73
16 +36 = 52
13 +36 = 49
42 +24 = 66
67 +29 = 96
57 +35 = 92
44 +16 = 60
37 +37 = 74
27 + 8 = 35

Color:
green — 96, 74   yellow — 92, 51
orange — 73, 82   purple — 77, 66
red — 60, 52   blue — 35, 49

22

Make the Windows Shine!

Add.

476 +319 795	248 +629 877	327 +544 871
572 +318 890	815 +177 992	527 +144 671
429 +343 772	462 +319 781	462 +529 991	648 +238 886
756 +127 883	563 +208 771	646 +248 894	924 + 66 990
628 +259 887	526 +347 873	927 + 46 973	765 +218 983

23

Addition Ace

Add. Color the ribbon according to the code below.

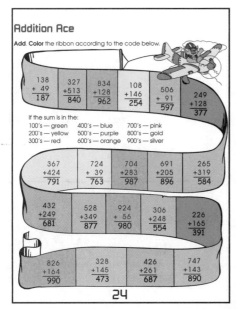

| 138
+ 49
187 | 327
+513
840 | 834
+128
962 | 108
+146
254 | 506
+ 91
597 | 249
+128
377 |

If the sum is in the:
100's — green   400's — blue   700's — pink
200's — yellow   500's — purple   800's — gold
300's — red   600's — orange   900's — silver

367 +424 791	724 + 39 763	704 +283 987	691 +205 896	265 +319 584
432 +249 681	528 +349 877	924 + 56 980	306 +248 554	226 +165 391
826 +164 990	328 +145 473	426 +261 687	747 +143 890

24

Space Shuttle Addition

Add the ones.	Regroup.	Add the tens and regroup.	Add the hundreds.
362 +439	362 +439	362 +439 01	362 +439 801

Add.

371 +439 810	629 +184 813	146 +587 733	264 +483 747	438 +290 728
347 +328 675	362 +459 821	528 +391 919	382 +249 631	327 +649 976
283 +346 629	409 +292 701		465 +193 658	566 +283 849
			283 +519 802	423 +392 815
			625 +246 871	498 +123 621

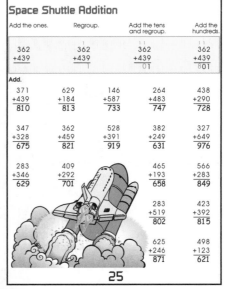

25

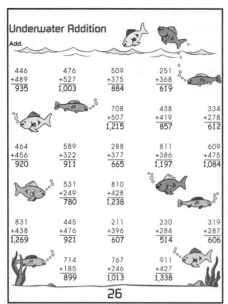

Underwater Addition

Add.

446 +489 935	476 +527 1,003	509 +375 884	251 +368 619
	708 +507 1,215	438 +419 857	334 +278 612
464 +456 920	589 +322 911	288 +377 665	811 +386 1,197	609 +475 1,084
531 +249 780	810 +428 1,238		
831 +438 1,269	445 +476 921	211 +396 607	230 +284 514	319 +287 606
714 +185 899	767 +246 1,013	911 +427 1,338	

26

Let's Climb to the Top!

Add.

328 +449 777	246 +492 738	462 +781 1,243	621 +489 1,110	429 +636 1,065
	409 +736 1,145	921 + 87 1,008	562 +614 1,176	824 +597 1,421
	982 +220 1,202	207 +913 1,120		826 + 95 921
	547 +782 1,329	284 +493 777		506 +214 720
200 +489 689	684 +519 1,203	425 +594 1,019	536 +184 720	623 +192 815

27

Picnic Problems

Help the ant find a path to the picnic. **Solve** the problems. **Shade** the box if an answer has a 9 in it.

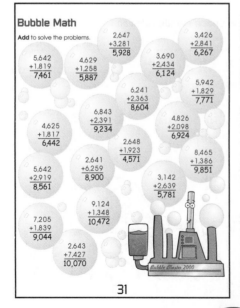

836 + 90 926	536 +248 784	952 + 8 960	362 + 47 409	486 +293 779	368 +529 897
789 526 +214 1,529	2,846 +6,478 9,324	932 +365 1,297	374 +299 673	835 +552 1,387	956 874 + 65 1,895
4,768 +2,894 7,662	38 456 +3,894 4,388	4,507 +2,743 7,250	404 +289 693	1,843 +6,752 8,595	4,367 +3,574 7,941
639 + 77 716	587 342 +679 1,608	5,379 1,865 +2,348 9,592	450 +145 595	594 +278 872	459 +367 826
29 875 +2,341 3,245	387 29 +5,614 6,030	462 379 +248 1,089			

28

Grand Prix Addition

Solve each problem. Beginning at 7,000, run through this racetrack to find the path the race car took. When you reach 7,023, you're ready to exit and gas up for the next race.

3,536 +3,482 7,018	1,792 +5,225 7,017	3,838 +3,178 7,016	3,767 +3,248 7,015	1,874 +5,140 7,014	4,809 +2,204 7,013
3,561 +3,458 7,019	4,162 +2,858 7,020	3,771 +4,213 7,984	4,123 +2,887 7,010	5,879 +1,132 7,011	1,725 +5,287 7,012
3,544 +3,478 7,022	1,273 +5,748 7,021	2,435 +5,214 7,649	4,853 +2,156 7,009	3,589 +3,419 7,008	5,218 +1,789 7,007
5,997 +1,026 7,023	5,289 +1,713 7,002	3,698 +3,305 7,003	4,756 +2,248 7,004	4,248 +2,757 7,005	4,658 +2,348 7,006
4,853 +2,147 7,000	2,216 +4,785 7,001	1,157 +6,412 7,569	3,720 +3,698 7,418	3,612 +3,552 7,164	1,687 +5,662 7,349

29

Gearing Up

Add the ones. Regroup.	Add the tens. Regroup.	Add the hundreds. Regroup.	Add the thousands. Regroup.
7,465 +4,978 3	7,465 +4,978 43	7,465 +4,978 443	7,465 +4,978 12,443

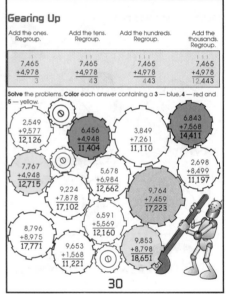

Solve the problems. **Color** each answer containing a 3 — blue, 4 — red and 5 — yellow.

2,549
+9,577
12,126

6,456
+4,948
11,404

3,849
+7,261
11,110

6,843
+7,568
14,411

7,767
+4,948
12,715

5,678
+6,984
12,662

9,764
+7,459
17,223

2,698
+8,499
11,197

9,224
+7,878
17,102

6,591
+5,569
12,160

8,796
+8,975
17,771

9,653
+1,568
11,221

9,853
+8,798
18,651

30

Bubble Math

Add to solve the problems.

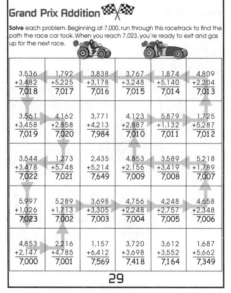

2,647
+3,281
5,928

3,426
+2,841
6,267

5,642
+1,819
7,461

4,629
+1,258
5,887

3,690
+2,434
6,124

6,241
+2,363
8,604

5,942
+1,829
7,771

6,843
+2,391
9,234

4,826
+2,098
6,924

4,625
+1,817
6,442

2,648
+1,923
4,571

8,465
+1,386
9,851

5,642
+2,919
8,561

2,641
+6,259
8,900

3,142
+2,639
5,781

9,124
+1,348
10,472

7,205
+1,839
9,044

2,643
+7,427
10,070

31

Cotton Pickin' Math

Solve the problems.

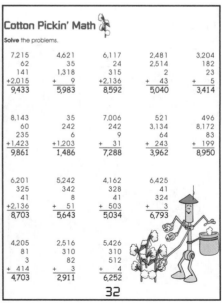

7,215 62 141 +2,015 9,433	4,621 35 1,318 + 9 5,983	6,117 24 315 +2,136 8,592	2,481 2,514 2 + 43 5,040	3,204 182 23 + 5 3,414
8,143 60 235 +1,423 9,861	35 242 6 +1,203 1,486	7,006 242 9 + 31 7,288	521 3,134 64 + 243 3,962	496 8,172 83 + 199 8,950
6,201 325 41 +2,136 8,703	5,242 342 8 + 51 5,643	4,162 328 41 + 503 5,034	6,425 41 324 + 3 6,793	
4,205 81 3 + 414 4,703	2,516 310 82 + 3 2,911	5,426 310 512 + 4 6,252		

32

Palindrome Sums

A **number palindrome** is similar to a word palindrome in that it reads the same backward or forward.

Examples:
75,457
1,689,861

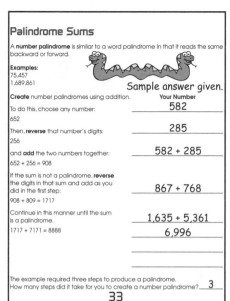

Sample answer given.

Create number palindromes using addition.

To do this, choose any number:
652

Then, **reverse** that number's digits:
256

and **add** the two numbers together:
652 + 256 = 908

If the sum is not a palindrome, **reverse** the digits in that sum and add as you did in the first step:
908 + 809 = 1717

Continue in this manner until the sum is a palindrome.
1717 + 7171 = 8888

Your Number
582

285

582 + 285

867 + 768

1,635 + 5,361

6,996

The example required three steps to produce a palindrome.
How many steps did it take for you to create a number palindrome? 3

33

Mountaintop Getaway

Solve the problems. **Find** a path to the cabin by shading in all answers that have a 3 in them.

98 −52 46	46 −12 34	68 −17 51
79 −53 26	65 −23 42	63 −31 32	86 −32 54
59 −45 14	75 −64 11	67 −24 43	87 −54 33	55 −43 12
87 −65 22	44 −32 12	57 −24 33	88 −25 63	75 −61 14	48 −26 22
69 −25 44	95 −24 71	48 −13 35	58 −16 42	35 −13 22	39 −17 22

SECRET PATHS

35

Stay on Track

Add or **subtract**. **Write** each answer in the puzzle.

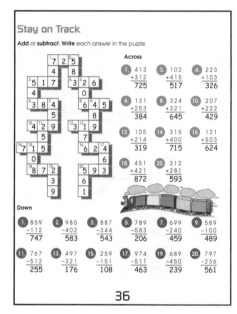

Across

1. 413 +312 725
3. 102 +415 517
4. 223 +103 326
6. 131 +253 384
8. 324 +321 645
10. 207 +222 429
12. 105 +214 319
14. 315 +400 715
16. 121 +503 624
18. 451 +421 872
20. 312 +281 593

Down

1. 859 −112 747
2. 985 −402 583
3. 887 −344 543
5. 789 −583 206
7. 699 −240 459
9. 589 −100 489
11. 767 −512 255
13. 497 −321 176
15. 259 −151 108
17. 974 −511 463
19. 689 −450 239
20. 797 −236 561

36

Subtracting Two-Digit Numbers
With Regrouping

Step 1: Decide whether to regroup. In the ones column, 3 is less than 9 so, regroup 4 tens 3 ones to 3 tens 13 ones.

4̸1̸3
− 1 9

Step 2: Subtract the ones.

3 13
4̸1̸3
− 1 9
4

Step 3: Subtract the tens.

3 13
4̸1̸3
− 1 9
2 4

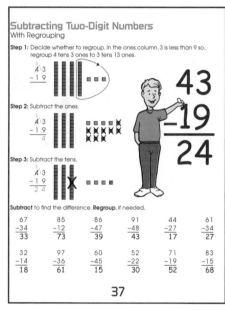

$$\begin{array}{r} 43 \\ -19 \\ \hline 24 \end{array}$$

Subtract to find the difference. **Regroup**, if needed.

| 67 −34 33 | 85 −12 73 | 86 −47 39 | 91 −48 43 | 44 −27 17 | 61 −34 27 |
| 32 −14 18 | 97 −36 61 | 60 −45 15 | 52 −22 30 | 71 −19 52 | 83 −15 68 |

37

Hats, Hats, Hats

Subtract to find the difference. If the bottom number is larger than the top number in a column, you will need to regroup from the column to the left.

Example:

2
7 3̸ 6
− 6 2 9
1 0 7

466 −327 139

837 −529 308

742 −428 314

784 −565 219

673 −458 215

648 −426 222

982 −665 317

947 −729 218

543 −426 117

928 −619 309

847 −628 219

427 −318 109

524 −318 206

245 −126 119

852 −328 524

545 −221 324

38

Soaring to the Stars

Connect the dots in order and form two stars. Begin one star with the subtraction problem whose difference is 100 and end with the problem whose difference is 109. Begin the other star with 110 and end with 120. Then, **color** the pictures.

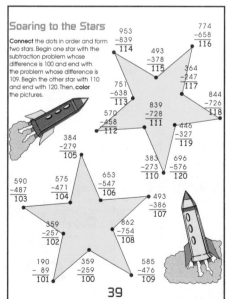

953 −839 114

774 −658 116

493 −378 115

364 −247 117

751 −638 113

844 −726 118

839 −728 111

570 −458 112

446 −327 119

384 −279 105

383 −273 110

696 −576 120

590 −487 103

575 −471 104

653 −547 106

493 −386 107

359 −257 102

862 −754 108

190 − 89 101

359 −259 100

585 −476 109

39

Dino-Code

How is a T-Rex like an explosion?
To find out, **solve** the following problems and **write** the matching letter above each answer on the blanks.

He's... F U L L   O F
        195 185 92 92   171 195

D I N O − M I G H T !
265 74 183 171   93 74 45 181 191

Remember to regroup when the bottom number is larger than the top number in a column.

F = 348 −153 195
L = 765 −673 92
G = 427 −382 45

T = 637 −446 191
H = 878 −697 181
U = 548 −363 185

O = 824 −653 171
N = 439 −256 183
I = 447 −373 74

M = 568 −475 93
D = 748 −483 265

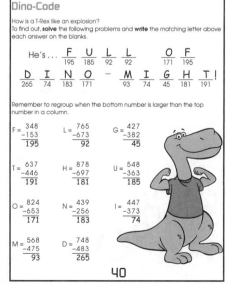

40

Paint by Number

Solve each problem. **Color** each shape according to the key below.

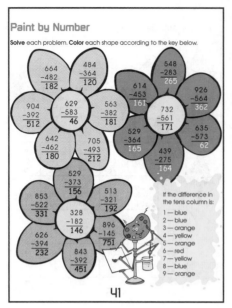

$$\begin{array}{r}664\\-482\\\hline 182\end{array}\quad\begin{array}{r}484\\-364\\\hline 120\end{array}\quad\begin{array}{r}548\\-283\\\hline 265\end{array}$$

$$\begin{array}{r}904\\-392\\\hline 512\end{array}\quad\begin{array}{r}629\\-583\\\hline 46\end{array}\quad\begin{array}{r}563\\-382\\\hline 181\end{array}\quad\begin{array}{r}614\\-453\\\hline 161\end{array}\quad\begin{array}{r}732\\-561\\\hline 171\end{array}\quad\begin{array}{r}926\\-564\\\hline 362\end{array}$$

$$\begin{array}{r}642\\-462\\\hline 180\end{array}\quad\begin{array}{r}705\\-493\\\hline 212\end{array}\quad\begin{array}{r}529\\-364\\\hline 165\end{array}\quad\begin{array}{r}635\\-573\\\hline 62\end{array}$$

$$\begin{array}{r}439\\-275\\\hline 164\end{array}$$

$$\begin{array}{r}529\\-373\\\hline 156\end{array}$$

$$\begin{array}{r}853\\-522\\\hline 331\end{array}\quad\begin{array}{r}513\\-321\\\hline 192\end{array}$$

$$\begin{array}{r}328\\-182\\\hline 146\end{array}$$

$$\begin{array}{r}626\\-394\\\hline 232\end{array}\quad\begin{array}{r}896\\-145\\\hline 751\end{array}$$

$$\begin{array}{r}843\\-392\\\hline 451\end{array}$$

If the difference in the tens column is:
1 — blue
2 — blue
3 — orange
4 — yellow
5 — orange
6 — red
7 — yellow
8 — blue
9 — orange

41

Sailing Through Subtraction

Subtract, regrouping when needed.

Example:
$$\begin{array}{r}7\;14\\8\;\cancel{8}\;\cancel{5}2\\-4\;6\;4\\\hline 3\;8\;8\end{array}$$

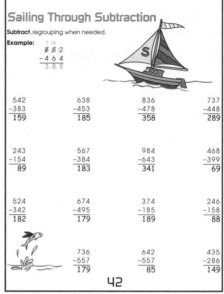

$$\begin{array}{r}542\\-383\\\hline 159\end{array}\quad\begin{array}{r}638\\-453\\\hline 185\end{array}\quad\begin{array}{r}836\\-478\\\hline 358\end{array}\quad\begin{array}{r}737\\-448\\\hline 289\end{array}$$

$$\begin{array}{r}243\\-154\\\hline 89\end{array}\quad\begin{array}{r}567\\-384\\\hline 183\end{array}\quad\begin{array}{r}984\\-643\\\hline 341\end{array}\quad\begin{array}{r}468\\-399\\\hline 69\end{array}$$

$$\begin{array}{r}524\\-342\\\hline 182\end{array}\quad\begin{array}{r}674\\-495\\\hline 179\end{array}\quad\begin{array}{r}374\\-185\\\hline 189\end{array}\quad\begin{array}{r}246\\-158\\\hline 88\end{array}$$

$$\begin{array}{r}736\\-557\\\hline 179\end{array}\quad\begin{array}{r}642\\-557\\\hline 85\end{array}\quad\begin{array}{r}435\\-286\\\hline 149\end{array}$$

42

Gobble, Gobble

Solve each problem. **Color** the picture according to the key below. If the answer has a **3** in it, color it orange, **4**—red, **5**—purple, **6**—brown, **7**—yellow, **8**—blue and **9**—green. Remember to regroup when needed.

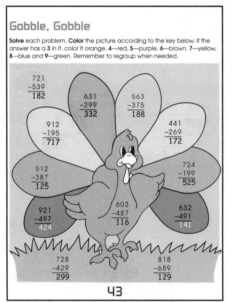

$$\begin{array}{r}721\\-539\\\hline 182\end{array}$$

$$\begin{array}{r}631\\-299\\\hline 332\end{array}\quad\begin{array}{r}563\\-375\\\hline 188\end{array}$$

$$\begin{array}{r}912\\-195\\\hline 717\end{array}\quad\begin{array}{r}441\\-269\\\hline 172\end{array}$$

$$\begin{array}{r}512\\-387\\\hline 125\end{array}\quad\begin{array}{r}724\\-199\\\hline 525\end{array}$$

$$\begin{array}{r}921\\-497\\\hline 424\end{array}\quad\begin{array}{r}603\\-487\\\hline 116\end{array}\quad\begin{array}{r}632\\-491\\\hline 141\end{array}$$

$$\begin{array}{r}728\\-429\\\hline 299\end{array}\quad\begin{array}{r}818\\-689\\\hline 129\end{array}$$

43

Round and Round She Goes

When regrouping with zeros follow these steps:

1. 7 is larger than 0. Go to the tens column to regroup. Since there is a 0 in that column, you can't regroup. Go to the hundreds column.

$$\begin{array}{r}8\,0\,0\\-1\,4\,7\end{array}$$

2. Take one hundred away. Move it to the tens column.

$$\begin{array}{r}{}^{7}\cancel{8}\,0\,0\\-1\,4\,7\end{array}$$

3. Regroup the tens column by subtracting one ten and adding that ten to the ones column.

$$\begin{array}{r}{}^{7\;9}\cancel{8}\,\cancel{0}\,0\\-1\,4\,7\end{array}$$

4. Now, subtract, starting at the ones column.

$$\begin{array}{r}{}^{7\;9}\cancel{8}\,\cancel{0}\,0\\-1\,4\,7\\\hline 1\,5\,3\end{array}$$

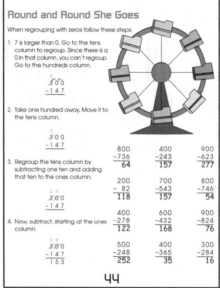

$$\begin{array}{r}800\\-736\\\hline 64\end{array}\quad\begin{array}{r}400\\-243\\\hline 157\end{array}\quad\begin{array}{r}900\\-623\\\hline 277\end{array}$$

$$\begin{array}{r}200\\-82\\\hline 118\end{array}\quad\begin{array}{r}700\\-543\\\hline 157\end{array}\quad\begin{array}{r}800\\-746\\\hline 54\end{array}$$

$$\begin{array}{r}400\\-278\\\hline 122\end{array}\quad\begin{array}{r}600\\-432\\\hline 168\end{array}\quad\begin{array}{r}900\\-824\\\hline 76\end{array}$$

$$\begin{array}{r}500\\-248\\\hline 252\end{array}\quad\begin{array}{r}400\\-365\\\hline 35\end{array}\quad\begin{array}{r}300\\-284\\\hline 16\end{array}$$

44

Jungle Math

Solve these problems.

Across

2. $\begin{array}{r}517\\-228\\\hline 289\end{array}$ 7. $\begin{array}{r}535\\-248\\\hline 287\end{array}$ 9. $\begin{array}{r}561\\-247\\\hline 314\end{array}$

3. $\begin{array}{r}428\\-249\\\hline 179\end{array}$ 8. $\begin{array}{r}857\\-389\\\hline 468\end{array}$

4. $\begin{array}{r}562\\-274\\\hline 288\end{array}$

5. $\begin{array}{r}924\\-348\\\hline 576\end{array}$

6. $\begin{array}{r}923\\-346\\\hline 577\end{array}$

Down

1. $\begin{array}{r}421\\-342\\\hline 79\end{array}$ 6. $\begin{array}{r}921\\-346\\\hline 575\end{array}$

2. $\begin{array}{r}627\\-348\\\hline 279\end{array}$ 7. $\begin{array}{r}926\\-718\\\hline 208\end{array}$

3. $\begin{array}{r}362\\-194\\\hline 168\end{array}$ 8. $\begin{array}{r}721\\-240\\\hline 481\end{array}$

4. $\begin{array}{r}582\\-346\\\hline 236\end{array}$ 10. $\begin{array}{r}768\\-292\\\hline 476\end{array}$

5. $\begin{array}{r}824\\-247\\\hline 577\end{array}$

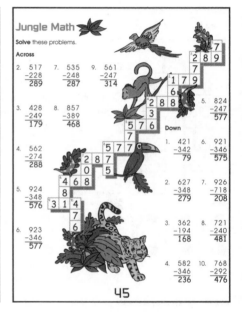

45

Timely Zeros

Subtract.

$$\begin{array}{r}300\\-189\\\hline 111\end{array}\quad\begin{array}{r}803\\-324\\\hline 479\end{array}\quad\begin{array}{r}504\\-362\\\hline 142\end{array}$$

$$\begin{array}{r}900\\-648\\\hline 252\end{array}\quad\begin{array}{r}800\\-724\\\hline 76\end{array}\quad\begin{array}{r}702\\-561\\\hline 141\end{array}$$

$$\begin{array}{r}200\\-149\\\hline 51\end{array}\quad\begin{array}{r}600\\-476\\\hline 124\end{array}\quad\begin{array}{r}500\\-362\\\hline 138\end{array}\quad\begin{array}{r}807\\-298\\\hline 509\end{array}\quad\begin{array}{r}406\\-328\\\hline 78\end{array}$$

$$\begin{array}{r}300\\-243\\\hline 57\end{array}\quad\begin{array}{r}600\\-421\\\hline 179\end{array}\quad\begin{array}{r}700\\-348\\\hline 352\end{array}\quad\begin{array}{r}308\\-189\\\hline 119\end{array}\quad\begin{array}{r}500\\-384\\\hline 116\end{array}$$

$$\begin{array}{r}302\\-195\\\hline 107\end{array}\quad\begin{array}{r}600\\-247\\\hline 353\end{array}\quad\begin{array}{r}400\\-108\\\hline 292\end{array}$$

$$\begin{array}{r}205\\-148\\\hline 57\end{array}\quad\begin{array}{r}308\\-189\\\hline 119\end{array}$$

46

Subtraction Maze

Solve the problems. Remember to regroup, when needed.

$$\begin{array}{r}4{,}172\\-1{,}536\\\hline 2{,}636\end{array}\quad\begin{array}{r}6{,}723\\-2{,}586\\\hline 4{,}137\end{array}\quad\begin{array}{r}547\\-259\\\hline 288\end{array}\quad\begin{array}{r}834\\-463\\\hline 371\end{array}\quad\begin{array}{r}562\\-325\\\hline 237\end{array}\quad\begin{array}{r}7{,}146\\-3{,}498\\\hline 3{,}648\end{array}$$

$$\begin{array}{r}9{,}427\\-6{,}648\\\hline 2{,}779\end{array}\quad\begin{array}{r}8{,}149\\-5{,}372\\\hline 2{,}777\end{array}\quad\begin{array}{r}5{,}389\\-1{,}652\\\hline 3{,}737\end{array}\quad\begin{array}{r}421\\-275\\\hline 146\end{array}\quad\begin{array}{r}7{,}456\\-3{,}724\\\hline 3{,}732\end{array}\quad\begin{array}{r}818\\-639\\\hline 179\end{array}$$

$$\begin{array}{r}772\\-586\\\hline 186\end{array}\quad\begin{array}{r}6{,}529\\-4{,}538\\\hline 1{,}991\end{array}\quad\begin{array}{r}5{,}379\\-2{,}835\\\hline 2{,}544\end{array}\quad\begin{array}{r}6{,}275\\-3{,}761\\\hline 2{,}514\end{array}\quad\begin{array}{r}5{,}612\\-1{,}505\\\hline 4{,}107\end{array}\quad\begin{array}{r}8{,}355\\-5{,}366\\\hline 2{,}989\end{array}$$

Shade in the answers from above to find the path.

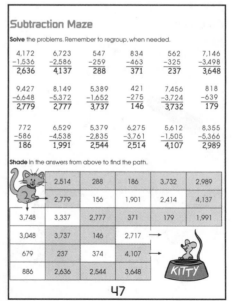

	2,514	288	186	3,732	2,989
	2,779	156	1,901	2,414	4,137
3,748	3,337	2,777	371	179	1,991
3,048	3,737	146	2,717		
679	237	374	4,107		
886	2,636	2,544	3,648	KITTY	

47

High Class Math

Solve these problems.

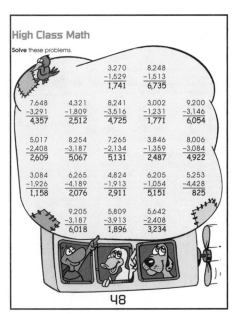

3,270 − 1,529 = 1,741	8,248 − 1,513 = 6,735

7,648 − 3,291 = 4,357	4,321 − 1,809 = 2,512	8,241 − 3,516 = 4,725	3,002 − 1,231 = 1,771	9,200 − 3,146 = 6,054
5,017 − 2,408 = 2,609	8,254 − 3,187 = 5,067	7,265 − 2,134 = 5,131	3,846 − 1,359 = 2,487	8,006 − 3,084 = 4,922
3,084 − 1,926 = 1,158	6,265 − 4,189 = 2,076	4,824 − 1,913 = 2,911	6,205 − 1,054 = 5,151	5,253 − 4,428 = 825
9,205 − 3,187 = 6,018	5,809 − 3,913 = 1,896	5,642 − 2,408 = 3,234		

48

Kite Craze!

Subtract.

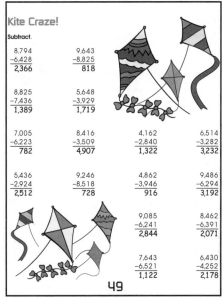

8,794 − 6,428 = 2,366	9,643 − 8,825 = 818		
8,825 − 7,436 = 1,389	5,648 − 3,929 = 1,719		
7,005 − 6,223 = 782	8,416 − 3,509 = 4,907	4,162 − 2,840 = 1,322	6,514 − 3,282 = 3,232
5,436 − 2,924 = 2,512	9,246 − 8,518 = 728	4,862 − 3,946 = 916	9,486 − 6,294 = 3,192
		9,085 − 6,241 = 2,844	8,462 − 6,391 = 2,071
		7,643 − 6,521 = 1,122	6,430 − 4,252 = 2,178

49

Subtraction on Stage!

Subtract.

5,648 − 2,425 = 3,223	2,148 − 825 = 1,323		
7,641 − 5,246 = 2,395	7,648 − 3,289 = 4,359	5,408 − 1,291 = 4,117	8,209 − 4,182 = 4,027
8,419 − 2,182 = 6,237	6,249 − 1,526 = 4,723	6,428 − 4,159 = 2,269	4,287 − 2,492 = 1,795
7,645 − 2,826 = 4,819	2,016 − 1,021 = 995	8,247 − 6,459 = 1,788	9,047 − 6,152 = 2,895
		5,231 − 1,642 = 3,589	
		7,689 − 2,845 = 4,844	

50

Subtraction Search

Solve each problem. **Find** the answer in the chart and **circle** it. The answers may go in any direction.

6,003 − 2,737 = 3,266	5,040 − 3,338 = 1,702	9,000 − 5,725 = 3,275
7,200 − 4,356 = 2,844	3,406 − 1,298 = 2,108	5,602 − 3,138 = 2,464
7,006 − 5,429 = 1,577	3,006 − 2,798 = 208	3,605 − 2,718 = 887
5,904 − 3,917 = 1,987	5,039 − 1,954 = 3,085	8,704 − 2,496 = 6,208
4,081 − 3,594 = 487	6,508 − 399 = 6,109	5,039 − 2,467 = 2,572
9,006 − 575 = 8,431	5,001 − 2,351 = 2,650	
8,002 − 5,686 = 2,316	6,058 − 2,175 = 3,883	9,504 − 7,368 = 2,136
7,290 − 1,801 = 5,489		

51

Skipping Through the Tens

Skip count by tens. Begin with the number on the first line. **Write** each number that follows.

0.	10	20	30	40	50	60	70	80	90	100
3.	13	23	33	43	53	63	73	83	93	103
1.	11	21	31	41	51	61	71	81	91	101
8.	18	28	38	48	58	68	78	88	98	108
6.	16	26	36	46	56	66	76	86	96	106
4.	14	24	34	44	54	64	74	84	94	104
2.	12	22	32	42	52	62	72	82	92	102
5.	15	25	35	45	55	65	75	85	95	105
7.	17	27	37	47	57	67	77	87	97	107
9.	19	29	39	49	59	69	79	89	99	109

What is ten more than . . . ?

26	36	29	39
44	54	77	87
53	63	91	101
24	34	49	59
66	76	35	45
54	64	82	92

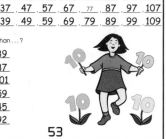

53

Counting to 100

Skip count to 100.

By twos:

2	4	6	8	10	12	14	16	18	20	22	24	26	28
30	32	34	36	38	40	42	44	46	48	50	52	54	56
58	60	62	64	66	68	70	72	74	76	78	80	82	84
86	88	90	92	94	96	98	100						

By threes:

3	6	9	12	15	18	21	24	27	30	33	36	39	42
45	48	51	54	57	60	63	66	69	72	75	78	81	84
87	90	93	96	99	102								

By fours:

4	8	12	16	20	24	28	32	36	40	44	48	52	56
60	64	68	72	76	80	84	88	92	96	100			

On another sheet of paper, count by fives to 100. Then, count by sixes.

54

Count the Legs!

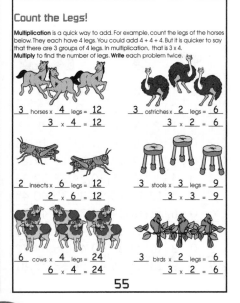

Multiplication is a quick way to add. For example, count the legs of the horses below. They each have 4 legs. You could add 4 + 4 + 4. But it is quicker to say that there are 3 groups of 4 legs. In multiplication, that is 3 x 4.
Multiply to find the number of legs. **Write** each problem twice.

3 horses x 4 legs = 12
3 x 4 = 12

3 ostriches x 2 legs = 6
3 x 2 = 6

2 insects x 6 legs = 12
2 x 6 = 12

3 stools x 3 legs = 9
3 x 3 = 9

6 cows x 4 legs = 24
6 x 4 = 24

3 birds x 2 legs = 6
3 x 2 = 6

55

Fact Snacks

Directions: Ask an adult for a paper plate and a couple of snacks, such as popcorn, pretzels, candy corn or chocolate-covered candies. Arrange the snacks into sets, such as five sets of 5 or nine sets of 3.

Now, **add** the sets together. **Write** the related fact. Use the snack manipulatives to **answer** the following multiplication problems. Group the snacks into sets with the number shown in each set.

4 x 2 = 4 sets with 2 in each set = 8

1. 3	2. 5	3. 1	4. 2	5. 6
x3	x3	x7	x9	x6
6	15	7	18	36

6. 7	7. 8	8. 3	9. 6	10. 10
x4	x5	x4	x7	x2
28	40	12	42	20

11. 1	12. 4	13. 9	14. 3	15. 5
x3	x8	x2	x3	x7
3	32	18	9	35

After you **answer** and **check** the problems, enjoy the tasty fact snacks.

56

Multiplying

Numbers to be multiplied together are called **factors**. The answer is the **product**.
Example: 3 x 6

1. The first factor tells how many groups there are. There are 3 groups.
2. The second factor tells how many are in each group. There are 6 in each group.

3 groups of 6 equal 18.
3 x 6 = 18

6 + 6 + 6 = 18

Some helpful hints to remember when multiplying:
- When you multiply by 0, the product is always 0. **Example:** 0 x 7 = 0
- When you multiply by 1, the product is always the factor being multiplied. **Example:** 1 x 12 = 12
- When multiplying by 2, double the factor other than 2. **Example:** 2 x 4 = 8
- The order doesn't matter when multiplying. **Example:** 5 x 3 = 15, 3 x 5 = 15
- When you multiply by 9, the digits in the product add up to 9 (until 9 x 11).
  Example: 7 x 9 = 63, 6 + 3 = 9
- When you multiply by 10, multiply by 1 and add 0 to the product. **Example:** 10 x 3 = 30
- When you multiply by 11, write the factor you are multiplying by twice (until 10).
  Example: 11 x 8 = 88

Multiply.

2	3	4	2	5	10	7	11	9
x9	x8	x9	x11	x9	x5	x6	x4	x7
18	24	36	22	45	50	42	44	63

8	7	8	10	4	5	8	3	7
x6	x12	x5	x10	x8	x5	x8	x6	x8
48	84	40	100	32	25	64	18	56

57

Factor Fun

When you change the order of the factors, you have the same product.

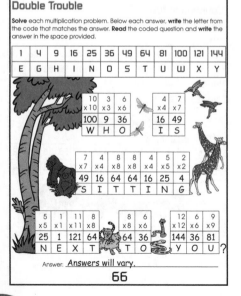

4 x3 = 12   3 x4 = 12

Multiply.

7	3	6	5	2	3
x3	x7	x5	x6	x3	x2
21	21	30	30	6	6

4	6	2	9	8	4
x6	x4	x9	x2	x4	x8
24	24	18	18	32	32

7	2	3	6	9	4
x2	x7	x6	x3	x4	x9
14	14	18	18	36	36

8	3	5	2	9	3
x3	x8	x2	x5	x3	x9
24	24	10	10	27	27

58

Racing to the Finish

Multiply.

5	4	4	9	7	3
x3	x8	x6	x3	x5	x9
15	16	24	27	35	27

4	6	4	0	3	7
x2	x2	x4	x6	x2	x2
8	12	16	0	6	14

6	3	8	4	5	7
x5	x4	x3	x5	x2	x4
30	12	24	20	10	28

6	4	2	8	3	5
x3	x8	x2	x5	x7	x5
18	32	4	40	21	25

5	9	4	9		
x9	x2	x6	x4		
45	18	24	36		

59

Climbing Granite Boulders!

Multiply.

9	6	3		2	8	7	8
x1	x1	x9		x9	x9	x8	x7
9	6	27		18	72	56	56

6	6				7	5	
x7	x6				x7	x9	
42	12				49	45	

8					5		
x8					x7		
64					35		

3 x 3 = ___9___
4 x 4 = ___16___
9 x 9 = ___81___
6 x 6 = ___36___
9 x 0 = ___0___

8 x 6 = ___48___   3 x 5 = ___15___
4 x 8 = ___32___   2 x 8 = ___16___
7 x 2 = ___14___   3 x 7 = ___21___
                      3 x 6 = ___18___
           6 x 6 = ___36___
           5 x 6 = ___30___   4 x 7 = ___28___
2 x 2 = ___4___   4 x 6 = ___24___
2 x 3 = ___6___   0 x 4 = ___0___
6 x 9 = ___54___   7 x 9 = ___63___
                        5 x 5 = ___25___

60

Time To Multiply

Complete the table. Try to do it in less than 3 minutes.

X	0	1	2	3	4	5	6	7	8	9
0	0	0	0	0	0	0	0	0	0	0
1	0	1	2	3	4	5	6	7	8	9
2	0	2	4	6	8	10	12	14	16	18
3	0	3	6	9	12	15	18	21	24	27
4	0	4	8	12	16	20	24	28	32	36
5	0	5	10	15	20	25	30	35	40	45
6	0	6	12	18	24	30	36	42	48	54
7	0	7	14	21	28	35	42	49	56	63
8	0	8	16	24	32	40	48	56	64	72
9	0	9	18	27	36	45	54	63	72	81

65

Double Trouble

Solve each multiplication problem. Below each answer, **write** the letter from the code that matches the answer. **Read** the coded question and **write** the answer in the space provided.

1	4	9	16	25	36	49	64	81	100	121	144
E	G	H	I	N	O	S	T	U	W	X	Y

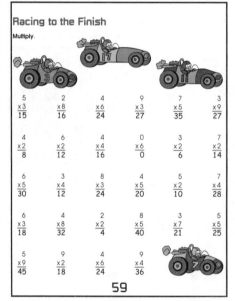

10	3	6		4	7
x10	x3	x6		x4	x7
100	9	36		16	49
W	H	O		I	S

7	4	8	8	4	5	2
x7	x4	x8	x8	x4	x5	x2
49	16	64	64	16	25	4
S	I	T	T	I	N	G

5	1	11	8		8	6		12	6	9
x5	x1	x11	x8		x8	x6		x12	x6	x9
25	1	121	64		64	36		144	36	81
N	E	X	T		T	O		Y	O	U ?

Answer: ___Answers will vary.___

66

Crossnumber Fun

Write the word form of each product in the puzzle.

Across
- 3. 9 x 4 = __36__
- 8. 10 x 5 = __50__
- 9. 2 x 9 = __18__
- 10. 3 x 12 = __36__
- 12. 7 x 11 = __77__
- 14. 4 x 10 = __40__
- 15. 6 x 5 = __30__
- 16. 0 x 7 = __0__

Down
- 1. 7 x 8 = __56__
- 2. 6 x 1 = __6__
- 4. 2 x 5 = __10__
- 5. 11 x 3 = __33__
- 6. 5 x 1 = __5__
- 7. 5 x 4 = __20__
- 11. 12 x 8 = __96__
- 13. 3 x 8 = __24__

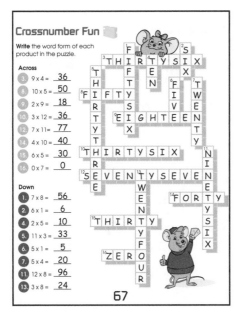

Crossword grid entries: THIRTYSIX, FIFTY, FIFTY, EIGHTEEN, THIRTYSIX, SEVENTYSEVEN, FORTY, THIRTY, ZERO, FIVE, TWENTY, NINETYSIX, SIX, THIRTYTHREE, TWENTYFOUR

67

Hmm, What Should I Do?

Example: 52 (+) 9 = 61

8 (X) 4 = 32

Write the correct symbols in the circles.

- 7 (X) 8 = 56
- 54 (÷) 9 = 6
- 36 (−) 5 = 31
- 12 (+) 6 = 18
- 72 (−) 7 = 65
- 0 (X) 1 = 0
- 9 (X) 1 = 9
- 45 (÷) 9 = 5

- 81 (−) 6 = 75
- 2 (X) 1 = 2
- 0 (+) 2 = 2
- 9 (X) 8 = 72

- 55 (−) 3 = 52
- 40 (−) 2 = 38
- 8 (X) 8 = 64
- 18 (+) 5 = 23
- 32 (+) 5 = 37
- 48 (÷) 6 = 8
- 32 (÷) 4 = 8
- 6 (X) 7 = 42

68

Wacky Waldo's Snow Show

Wacky Waldo's Snow Show is an exciting and fantastic sight. Waldo has trained whales and bears to skate together on the ice. There is a hockey game between a team of sharks and a pack of wolves. Elephants ride sleds down steep hills. Horses and buffaloes ski swiftly down mountains.

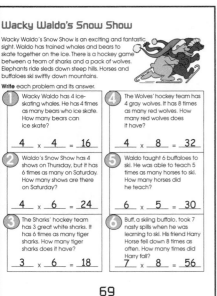

Write each problem and its answer.

1. Wacky Waldo has 4 ice-skating whales. He has 4 times as many bears who ice skate. How many bears can ice skate?

__4__ x __4__ = __16__

2. Waldo's Snow Show has 4 shows on Thursday, but it has 6 times as many on Saturday. How many shows are there on Saturday?

__4__ x __6__ = __24__

3. The Sharks' hockey team has 3 great white sharks. It has 6 times as many tiger sharks. How many tiger sharks does it have?

__3__ x __6__ = __18__

4. The Wolves' hockey team has 4 gray wolves. It has 8 times as many red wolves. How many red wolves does it have?

__4__ x __8__ = __32__

5. Waldo taught 6 buffaloes to ski. He was able to teach 5 times as many horses to ski. How many horses did he teach?

__6__ x __5__ = __30__

6. Buff, a skiing buffalo, took 7 nasty spills when he was learning to ski. His friend Harry Horse fell down 8 times as often. How many times did Harry fall?

__7__ x __8__ = __56__

69

Space Race

Complete the products. Begin by multiplying the ones place first, then the tens place. See the shading in the examples.

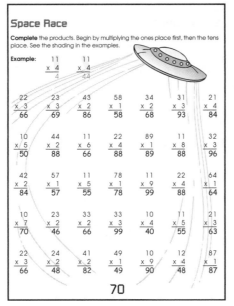

Example:
```
  11      11
 x 4     x 4
  4       44
```

```
 22     23     43     58     34     31     21
 x 3    x 3    x 2    x 1    x 2    x 3    x 4
 66     69     86     58     68     93     84

 10     44     11     22     89     11     32
 x 5    x 2    x 6    x 4    x 1    x 8    x 3
 50     88     66     88     89     88     96

 42     57     11     78     11     22     64
 x 2    x 1    x 5    x 1    x 9    x 4    x 1
 84     57     55     78     99     88     64

 10     23     33     33     10     11     21
 x 7    x 2    x 2    x 3    x 4    x 5    x 3
 70     46     66     99     40     55     63

 22     24     41     49     10     12     87
 x 3    x 2    x 2    x 1    x 9    x 4    x 1
 66     48     82     49     90     48     87
```

70

Multiplying and Regrouping

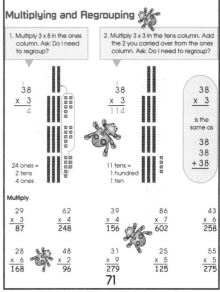

1. Multiply 3 x 8 in the ones column. Ask: Do I need to regroup?

2. Multiply 3 x 3 in the tens column. Add the 2 you carried over from the ones column. Ask: Do I need to regroup?

```
   2            2
  38           38          38
 x 3          x 3         x 3
  4           114

24 ones =     11 tens =
2 tens        1 hundred
4 ones        1 ten
```

is the same as
```
  38
  38
+ 38
```

Multiply.

```
 29     62     39     86     43
 x 3    x 4    x 4    x 7    x 6
 87    248    156    602    258

 28     48     31     25     55
 x 6    x 2    x 9    x 5    x 5
168     96    279    125    275
```

71

Multiplying Points

Multiply.

```
 12     22     32     19
 x 9    x 8    x 5    x 9
108    176    160    171

 22     33     27     14
 x 7    x 4    x 2    x 6
154    132     54     84

 38     25     15     16
 x 2    x 3    x 4    x 5
 76     75     60     80

 28     18     14     13     24     13     29
 x 3    x 5    x 7    x 5    x 4    x 6    x 2
 84     90     98     65     96     78     58

 17     36     29     14     18     19     28
 x 4    x 2    x 3    x 5    x 4    x 3    x 2
 68     72     87     70     72     57     56

 17     19     37     27     12     26     35
 x 5    x 4    x 2    x 3    x 8    x 3    x 5
 85     76     74     81     96     78    175

 48                                  27
 x 2                                x 4
 96                                108
```

72

Under the Big Top!

Complete this crossnumber puzzle.

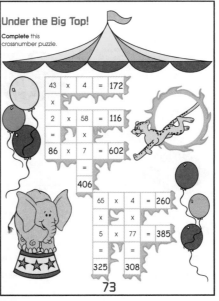

```
43  x  4  =  172
x
2   x  58 = 116
=          x
86  x  7  = 602
           =
          406
```

```
65  x  4  =  260
x
5   x  77 = 385
=          =
325        308
```

73

More Multiplication

Write the numbers given in the correct boxes to get the given answer.

```
 4 7 5      7 7 9      8 7 9      4 8 7      7 6 3
[5][4]      [9][7]     [7][9]     [8][4]     [7][3]
x  [7]      x  [7]     x  [8]     x  [7]     x  [6]
 3 7 8      6 7 9      6 3 2      5 8 8      4 3 8

 6 9 4      7 3 9      5 2 9      9 5 6      2 7 5
[9][4]      [3][7]     [9][2]     [6][9]     [2][5]
x  [6]      x  [9]     x  [5]     x  [5]     x  [7]
 5 6 4      3 3 3      4 6 0      3 4 5      1 7 5

 4 5 6      5 7 6      3 6 9      4 8 7      6 6 7
[5][6]      [7][6]     [3][9]     [4][8]     [6][7]
x  [4]      x  [5]     x  [6]     x  [7]     x  [6]
 2 2 4      3 8 0      2 3 4      3 3 6      4 0 2

 5 5 4      2 3 3      7 8 4      6 5 7      9 4 2
[5][4]      [3][2]     [7][4]     [7][6]     [4][9]
x  [5]      x  [3]     x  [8]     x  [5]     x  [2]
 2 7 0       9 6       5 9 2      3 8 0       9 8
```

77

Multiplying With Molly

Write the problem and the answer for each question.

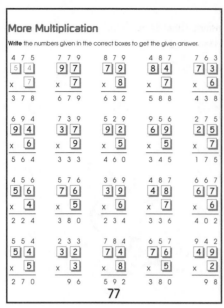

1. Molly is the toughest football player in her school. She ran for 23 yards on one play and went 3 times as far on the next play. How far did she run the second time?
```
 23
x 3
69 yards
```

2. Molly keeps a rock collection. She has 31 rocks in one sack. She has 7 times as many under her bed. How many rocks are under her bed?
```
 31
x 7
217 rocks
```

3. Molly had 42 marbles when she came to school. She went home with 4 times as many. How many did she go home with?
```
 42
x 4
168 marbles
```

4. Molly stuffed 21 sticks of gum in her mouth in the morning. In the afternoon, she crammed 9 times as many sticks into her mouth. How many sticks did she have in the afternoon?
```
 21
x 9
189 sticks
```

5. Molly did 51 multiplication problems in math last week. This week, she did 8 times as many. How many did she do this week?
```
 51
x 8
408 problems
```

6. Molly did 21 science experiments last year. This year, she did 7 times as many. How many experiments did she do this year?
```
 21
x 7
147 experiments
```

78

Three-Digit Regrouping

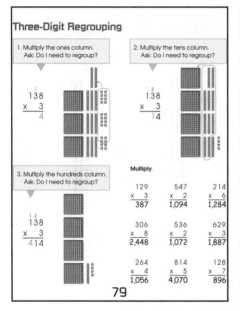

1. Multiply the ones column. Ask: Do I need to regroup?
```
  2
138
x 3
  4
```

2. Multiply the tens column. Ask: Do I need to regroup?
```
 1 2
138
x  3
 14
```

3. Multiply the hundreds column. Ask: Do I need to regroup?
```
 1 2
138
x  3
414
```

Multiply.
```
129      547      214
x 3      x 2      x 6
387    1,094    1,284

306      536      629
x 8      x 2      x 3
2,448  1,072    1,887

264      814      128
x 4      x 5      x 7
1,056  4,070      896
```

79

Space Math

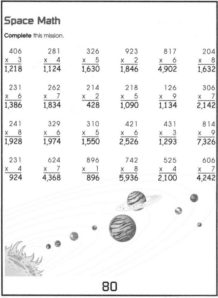

Complete this mission.
```
406      281      326      923      817      204
x 3      x 4      x 5      x 2      x 6      x 8
1,218  1,124    1,630    1,846    4,902    1,632

231      262      214      218      126      306
x 6      x 7      x 2      x 5      x 9      x 7
1,386  1,834      428    1,090    1,134    2,142

241      329      310      421      431      814
x 8      x 6      x 5      x 6      x 3      x 9
1,928  1,974    1,550    2,526    1,293    7,326

231      624      896      742      525      606
x 4      x 7      x 1      x 8      x 4      x 7
924    4,368      896    5,936    2,100    4,242
```

80

Solve It!

What set of ridges and loops are different on every person? To find out, solve the following problems and write the matching letter above each answer at the bottom of the page.

```
I.  303    303    303    R. 214    N. 413
    x 3    x 3    x 3       x 2       x 2
      9     09    909       428       826

N. 142         R. 211    F. 104
   x 2            x 4       x 2
   284            844       208

T. 131    P. 232         E. 301    I. 134
   x 2       x 3            x 2       x 1
   262       696            602       134

G. 244    S. 334
   x 2       x 2
   488       668
```

```
F  I  N  G  E  R  P  R  I  N  T  S
208 909 826 488 602 844 696 428 134 284 262 668
```

81

Four-Digit Regrouping

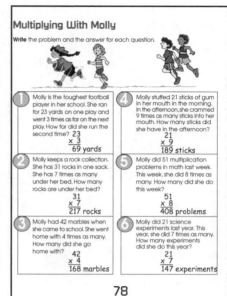

1. Multiply the ones column. Ask: Do I need to regroup?
```
    1
6,214
x   3
    2
12 ones =
1 ten 2 ones
```

2. Multiply the tens column. Ask: Do I need to regroup?
```
    1
6,214
x   3
   42
```

3. Multiply the hundreds column. Ask: Do I need to regroup?
```
    1
6,214
x   3
  642
```

4. Multiply the thousands column. Ask: Do I need to regroup?
```
    1
6,214
x   3
18,642
```

Multiply.
```
4,121     7,216     2,318     4,326     2,463
x   6     x   3     x   4     x   8     x   9
24,726   21,648     9,272   34,608   22,167

6,425     7,195     8,083     5,993     6,218
x   5     x   5     x   7     x   7     x   4
32,125   35,975   56,581   41,951   24,872
```

82

Amazing Arms

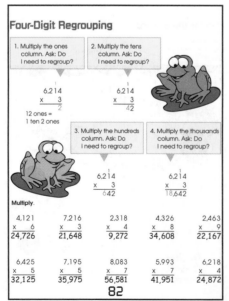
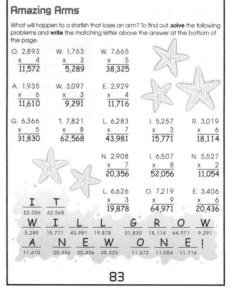

What will happen to a starfish that loses an arm? To find out, solve the following problems and write the matching letter above the answer at the bottom of the page.

```
O. 2,893    W. 1,763    W. 7,665
   x   4       x   3       x   5
   11,572      5,289      38,325

A. 1,935    W. 3,097    E. 2,929
   x   6       x   3       x   4
   11,610      9,291      11,716

G. 6,366    T. 7,821    L. 6,283    I. 5,257    R. 3,019
   x   5       x   8       x   7       x   3       x   6
   31,830     62,568     43,981     15,771     18,114

N. 2,908    I. 6,507    N. 5,527
   x   7       x   8       x   2
   20,356     52,056     11,054

L. 6,626    O. 7,219    E. 3,406
   x   3       x   9       x   6
   19,878     64,971     20,436
```

```
I  T
52,056 62,568

W  I  L  L     G  R  O  W
5,289 15,771 43,981 19,878  31,830 18,114 64,971 9,291

A  N  E  W  O  N  E !
11,610 20,356 20,436 38,325  11,716 11,572 11,716
```

83

Multiplying by a Two-Digit Number

1. Multiply by the ones place.
   3 x 2 = 6
   Ignore the 1 in the tens place.

   43
   x12
   6

Multiply.

19
x11
209

32
x31
992

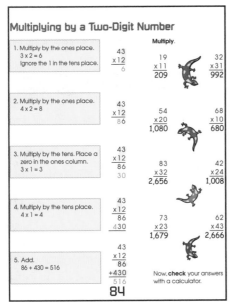

2. Multiply by the ones place.
   4 x 2 = 8

   43
   x12
   86

54
x20
1,080

68
x10
680

3. Multiply by the tens. Place a zero in the ones column.
   3 x 1 = 3

   43
   x12
   86
   30

83
x32
2,656

42
x24
1,008

4. Multiply by the tens place.
   4 x 1 = 4

   43
   x12
   86
   430

73
x23
1,679

62
x43
2,666

5. Add.
   86 + 430 = 516

   43
   x12
   86
   +430
   516

Now, **check** your answers with a calculator.

84

Multiplying by a Two-Digit Number
With Regrouping

1. Multiply by the ones.
   8 x 7 = 56 (Carry the 5.)

   ⁵
   67
   x38
   6

Multiply.

37
x24
888

77
x21
1,617

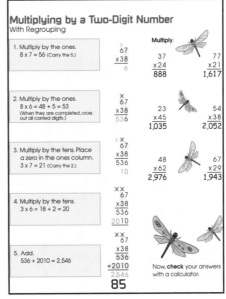

2. Multiply by the ones.
   8 x 6 = 48 + 5 = 53
   (When they are completed, cross out all carried digits.)

   x
   67
   x38
   536

23
x45
1,035

54
x38
2,052

3. Multiply by the tens. Place a zero in the ones column.
   3 x 7 = 21 (Carry the 2.)

   ²x
   67
   x38
   536
   10

48
x62
2,976

67
x29
1,943

4. Multiply by the tens.
   3 x 6 = 18 + 2 = 20

   xx
   67
   x38
   536
   2010

5. Add.
   536 + 2010 = 2,546

   xx
   67
   x38
   536
   +2010
   2,546

Now, **check** your answers with a calculator.

85

Multiplying by a Two-Digit Number

1. Multiply by the ones.
   6 x 3 = 18 (Carry the 1.)

   ¹
   43
   x26
   8

Multiply.

21
x54
1,134

52
x34
1,768

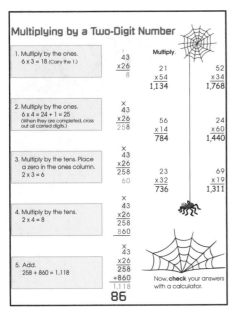

2. Multiply by the ones.
   6 x 4 = 24 + 1 = 25
   (When they are completed, cross out all carried digits.)

   x
   43
   x26
   258

56
x14
784

24
x60
1,440

3. Multiply by the tens. Place a zero in the ones column.
   2 x 3 = 6

   43
   x26
   258
   60

23
x32
736

69
x19
1,311

4. Multiply by the tens.
   2 x 4 = 8

   x
   43
   x26
   258
   860

5. Add.
   258 + 860 = 1,118

   x
   43
   x26
   258
   +860
   1,118

Now, **check** your answers with a calculator.

86

Elephant Escapades

Multiply.

56
x43
2,408

13
x24
312

24
x56
1,344

20
x93
1,860

23
x54
1,242

28
x43
1,204

21
x64
1,344

25
x34
850

13
x64
832

13
x82
1,066

34
x21
714

32
x55
1,760

42
x23
966

62
x31
1,922

51
x43
2,193

21
x64
1,344

10
x84
840

35
x24
840

24
x30
720

24
x53
1,272

81
x46
3,726

32
x27
864

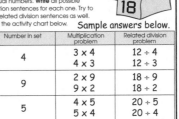

87

Multiplication Drill

Multiply. Color the picture below by matching each number with its paint brush.

134 x 22 = 2,948
48 x66 = 3,168
876 x 13 = 11,388
432 x 64 = 27,648

68 x11 = 748
5,478 x 8 = 43,824
248 x 61 = 15,128
6,897 x 6 = 41,382

82 x 4 = 328
6,798 x 5 = 33,990
79 x86 = 6,794
694 x 38 = 26,372

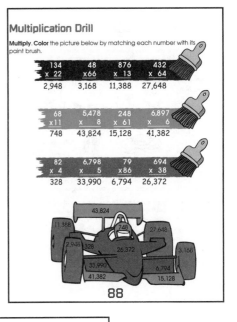

88

Step by Step

Read the problems below. **Write** each answer in the space provided.

1. One battalion of ants marches with 25 ants in a row. There are 35 rows of ants in each battalion. How many ants are in one battalion?

875 ants

2. The Ant Army finds a picnic! Now, they need to figure out how many ants should carry each piece of food. A team of 137 ants moves a celery stick. They need 150 ants to carry a carrot stick. A troop of 121 ants carries a very large radish. How many ants in all are needed to move the vegetables?

408 ants

Work space

3. Now, the real work begins—the big pieces of food that would feed their whole colony. It takes 1,259 ants to haul a peanut butter and jelly sandwich. It takes a whole battalion of 2,067 ants to lug the lemonade back, and it takes 1,099 ants to steal the pickle jar. How many soldiers carry these big items?

4,425 ants

4. Look-outs are posted all around the picnic blanket. It takes 53 soldiers to watch in front of the picnic basket. Another group of 69 ants watch out by the grill. Three groups of 77 watch the different trails in the park. How many ant-soldiers are on the look-out?

353 ants

89

Equally Alike

Label six shoe boxes with one of these numbers: 12, 18, 20, 24, 36 and 48. **Fill** each box with the number of objects on its label. For example, 12 game pieces may be in one box and 18 marbles in another.

Directions:
1. **Count** the number of objects in each box.
2. **Divide** the number of objects into different sets of equal numbers. **Write** all possible multiplication sentences for each one. Try to **write** the related division sentences as well.
3. **Complete** the activity chart below.

Sample answers below.

Box #	Number in set	Multiplication problem	Related division problem
12	4	3 x 4 4 x 3	12 ÷ 4 12 ÷ 3
18	9	2 x 9 9 x 2	18 ÷ 9 18 ÷ 2
20	5	4 x 5 5 x 4	20 ÷ 5 20 ÷ 4
24	3	3 x 8 8 x 3	24 ÷ 3 24 ÷ 8
36	4	4 x 9 9 x 4	36 ÷ 4 36 ÷ 9
48	6	6 x 8 8 x 6	48 ÷ 6 48 ÷ 8

90

Backward Multiplication

Division problems are like multiplication problems—just turned around.
As you solve 8 ÷ 4, think, "how many groups of 4 make 8?" or "what number 'times' 4 is eight?"

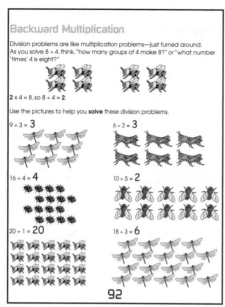

2 x 4 = 8, so 8 ÷ 4 = **2**.

Use the pictures to help you **solve** these division problems.

9 ÷ 3 = **3**   6 ÷ 2 = **3**

16 ÷ 4 = **4**   10 ÷ 5 = **2**

20 ÷ 1 = **20**   18 ÷ 3 = **6**

92

What Exactly Is Division?

In division, you begin with an amount of something (the dividend), separate it into small groups (the divisor), then find out how many groups are created (the quotient).

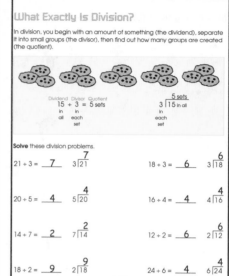

Dividend Divisor Quotient
15 ÷ 3 = 5 sets
in all   in each set

5 sets
3) 15 in all
in each set

Solve these division problems.

21 ÷ 3 = __7__ $\dfrac{7}{3\,)\,21}$ 18 ÷ 3 = __6__ $\dfrac{6}{3\,)\,18}$

20 ÷ 5 = __4__ $\dfrac{4}{5\,)\,20}$ 16 ÷ 4 = __4__ $\dfrac{4}{4\,)\,16}$

14 ÷ 7 = __2__ $\dfrac{2}{7\,)\,14}$ 12 ÷ 2 = __6__ $\dfrac{6}{2\,)\,12}$

18 ÷ 2 = __9__ $\dfrac{9}{2\,)\,18}$ 24 ÷ 6 = __4__ $\dfrac{4}{6\,)\,24}$

93

Sandwich Cookie

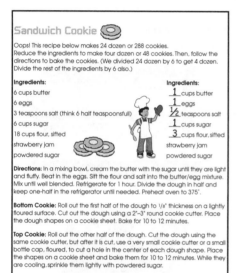

Oops! This recipe below makes 24 dozen or 288 cookies.
Reduce the ingredients to make four dozen or 48 cookies. Then, follow the directions to bake the cookies. (We divided 24 dozen by 6 to get 4 dozen. Divide the rest of the ingredients by 6 also.)

Ingredients:
6 cups butter
6 eggs
3 teaspoons salt (think 6 half teaspoonsfull)
6 cups sugar
18 cups flour, sifted
strawberry jam
powdered sugar

Ingredients:
__1__ cups butter
__1__ eggs
__1/2__ teaspoons salt
__1__ cups sugar
__3__ cups flour, sifted
strawberry jam
powdered sugar

Directions: In a mixing bowl, cream the butter with the sugar until they are light and fluffy. Beat in the eggs. Sift the flour and salt into the butter/egg mixture. Mix until well blended. Refrigerate for 1 hour. Divide the dough in half and keep one-half in the refrigerator until needed. Preheat oven to 375˚.

Bottom Cookie: Roll out the first half of the dough to 1/8" thickness on a lightly floured surface. Cut out the dough using a 2"–3" round cookie cutter. Place the dough shapes on a cookie sheet. Bake for 10 to 12 minutes.

Top Cookie: Roll out the other half of the dough. Cut the dough using the same cookie cutter, but after it is cut, use a very small cookie cutter or a small bottle cap, floured, to cut a hole in the center of each dough shape. Place the shapes on a cookie sheet and bake them for 10 to 12 minutes. While they are cooling, sprinkle them lightly with powdered sugar.

When both sets of cookies are cool, spread jam on the bottom cookie. Cover it with the top cookie.

94

Make It Fair

While your cookies are baking, practice fair sharing by completing these problems. **Circle** the objects and **write** two division problems to go with each picture.

There are six children. **Circle** the number of cookies each child will get if the cookies are divided equally.

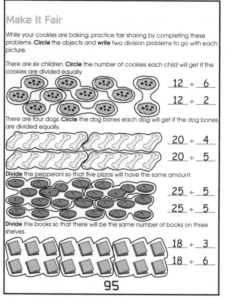

12 ÷ 6
12 ÷ 2

There are four dogs. **Circle** the dog bones each dog will get if the dog bones are divided equally.

20 ÷ 4
20 ÷ 5

Divide the pepperoni so that five pizzas will have the same amount.

25 ÷ 5
25 ÷ 5

Divide the books so that there will be the same number of books on three shelves.

18 ÷ 3
18 ÷ 6

95

Blastoff!

Divide.

$\dfrac{6}{1\,)\,6}$ $\dfrac{0}{20\,)\,0}$

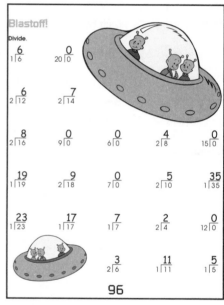

$\dfrac{6}{2\,)\,12}$ $\dfrac{7}{2\,)\,14}$

$\dfrac{8}{2\,)\,16}$ $\dfrac{0}{9\,)\,0}$ $\dfrac{0}{6\,)\,0}$ $\dfrac{4}{2\,)\,8}$ $\dfrac{0}{15\,)\,0}$

$\dfrac{19}{1\,)\,19}$ $\dfrac{9}{2\,)\,18}$ $\dfrac{0}{7\,)\,0}$ $\dfrac{5}{2\,)\,10}$ $\dfrac{35}{1\,)\,35}$

$\dfrac{23}{1\,)\,23}$ $\dfrac{17}{1\,)\,17}$ $\dfrac{7}{1\,)\,7}$ $\dfrac{2}{2\,)\,4}$ $\dfrac{0}{12\,)\,0}$

$\dfrac{3}{2\,)\,6}$ $\dfrac{11}{1\,)\,11}$ $\dfrac{5}{1\,)\,5}$

96

Carrier Math Messengers

Divide.

$\dfrac{4}{3\,)\,12}$ $\dfrac{6}{8\,)\,48}$ $\dfrac{9}{2\,)\,18}$

9) 72

$\dfrac{5}{5\,)\,25}$ $\dfrac{8}{9\,)\,72}$ $\dfrac{6}{4\,)\,24}$

$\dfrac{7}{6\,)\,42}$ $\dfrac{5}{8\,)\,40}$ $\dfrac{2}{2\,)\,4}$ $\dfrac{8}{7\,)\,56}$ $\dfrac{7}{9\,)\,63}$

$\dfrac{5}{9\,)\,45}$ $\dfrac{1}{7\,)\,7}$ $\dfrac{5}{3\,)\,15}$ $\dfrac{4}{2\,)\,8}$ $\dfrac{9}{7\,)\,63}$

$\dfrac{8}{3\,)\,24}$ $\dfrac{5}{6\,)\,30}$ $\dfrac{6}{9\,)\,54}$

8) 48

$\dfrac{9}{9\,)\,81}$ $\dfrac{4}{7\,)\,28}$ $\dfrac{8}{4\,)\,32}$

97

Bath Math!

Divide.

$\dfrac{4}{8\,)\,32}$ $\dfrac{6}{6\,)\,36}$ $\dfrac{1}{7\,)\,7}$

$\dfrac{5}{8\,)\,40}$ $\dfrac{8}{7\,)\,56}$ $\dfrac{8}{9\,)\,72}$

$\dfrac{7}{6\,)\,42}$ $\dfrac{2}{6\,)\,12}$ $\dfrac{8}{6\,)\,48}$ $\dfrac{3}{7\,)\,21}$ $\dfrac{4}{9\,)\,36}$

$\dfrac{2}{8\,)\,16}$ $\dfrac{7}{7\,)\,28}$ $\dfrac{3}{8\,)\,24}$

$\dfrac{1}{8\,)\,8}$ $\dfrac{9}{8\,)\,54}$ $\dfrac{9}{9\,)\,81}$ $\dfrac{3}{6\,)\,18}$

$\dfrac{2}{9\,)\,18}$ $\dfrac{4}{6\,)\,24}$ $\dfrac{5}{7\,)\,35}$ $\dfrac{6}{8\,)\,48}$

$\dfrac{5}{9\,)\,45}$

$\dfrac{7}{9\,)\,63}$ $\dfrac{3}{9\,)\,27}$

98

330

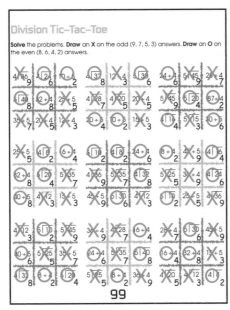

Division Tic-Tac-Toe

Solve the problems. **Draw** an **X** on the odd (9, 7, 5, 3) answers. **Draw** an **O** on the even (8, 6, 4, 2) answers.

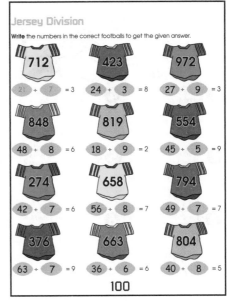

Jersey Division

Write the numbers in the correct footballs to get the given answer.

712   21 ÷ 7 = 3

423   24 ÷ 3 = 8

972   27 ÷ 9 = 3

848   48 ÷ 8 = 6

819   18 ÷ 9 = 2

554   45 ÷ 5 = 9

274   42 ÷ 7 = 6

658   56 ÷ 8 = 7

794   49 ÷ 7 = 7

376   63 ÷ 7 = 9

663   36 ÷ 6 = 6

804   40 ÷ 8 = 5

99

100

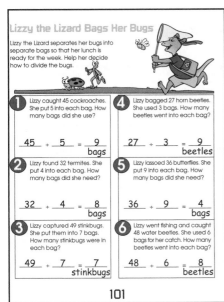

Lizzy the Lizard Bags Her Bugs

Lizzy the Lizard separates her bugs into separate bags so that her lunch is ready for the week. Help her decide how to divide the bugs.

1. Lizzy caught 45 cockroaches. She put 5 into each bag. How many bags did she use?

45 ÷ 5 = 9 bags

2. Lizzy found 32 termites. She put 4 into each bag. How many bags did she need?

32 ÷ 4 = 8 bags

3. Lizzy captured 49 stinkbugs. She put them into 7 bags. How many stinkbugs were in each bag?

49 ÷ 7 = 7 stinkbugs

4. Lizzy bagged 27 horn beetles. She used 3 bags. How many beetles went into each bag?

27 ÷ 3 = 9 beetles

5. Lizzy lassoed 36 butterflies. She put 9 into each bag. How many bags did she need?

36 ÷ 9 = 4 bags

6. Lizzy went fishing and caught 48 water beetles. She used 6 bags for her catch. How many beetles went into each bag?

48 ÷ 6 = 8 beetles

101

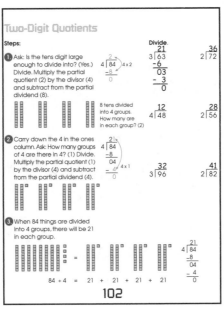

Two-Digit Quotients

Steps:

1. Ask: Is the tens digit large enough to divide into? (Yes.) Divide. Multiply the partial quotient (2) by the divisor (4) and subtract from the partial dividend (8).

8 tens divided into 4 groups. How many are in each group? (2)

2. Carry down the 4 in the ones column. Ask: How many groups of 4 are there in 4? (1) Divide. Multiply the partial quotient (1) by the divisor (4) and subtract from the partial dividend (4).

3. When 84 things are divided into 4 groups, there will be 21 in each group.

84 ÷ 4 = 21 + 21 + 21 + 21

Divide.

21 / 4)84
−8
03
−3
0

12 / 4)48

21 / 4)84
−8
04
−4
0

32 / 3)96

36 / 2)72

28 / 2)56

41 / 2)82

102

Snowball Bash

Divide this mound of giant snowballs!

12 / 7)84 (−7, 14, −14, 0)

15 / 5)75

15 / 3)45

11 / 9)99

22 / 4)88

16 / 5)80

16 / 4)64

19 / 3)57

26 / 3)78

24 / 3)72

12 / 8)96

43 / 2)86

19 / 2)38

11 / 6)66

13 / 5)65

13 / 4)52

17 / 4)68

13 / 6)78

13 / 7)91

21 / 2)42

12 / 6)72

103

Three-Digit Quotients

Steps:

1. Ask: Is the hundreds digit large enough to divide into? (Yes.) Divide. Multiply the partial quotient by the divisor and subtract from the partial dividend.

2. Ask: Can I divide the remaining 2 by 7? (No.) Bring down the 3 tens. 2 hundreds + 3 tens = 23 tens

3. Divide the 23 tens by 7. Multiply the partial quotient by the divisor and subtract.

4. Ask: Can I divide the remaining 2 by 7? (No.) Bring down 8 ones. 2 tens + 8 ones = 28 ones

5. Divide the 28 ones by 7. Multiply the partial quotient by the divisor and subtract.

Divide.

148 / 6)888 (−6, 28, −24, 48, −48, 0)

271 / 2)542

231 / 3)693

136 / 4)544

128 / 7)896

127 / 5)635

104

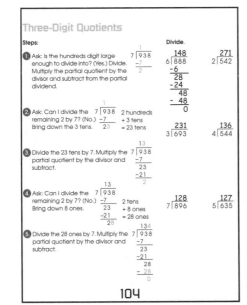

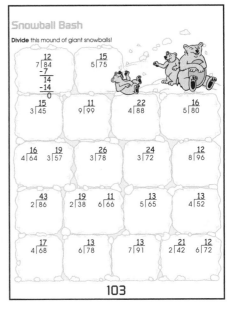

On-Stage Division

Divide.

148 / 6)888 (−6, 28, −24, 48, −48, 0)

478 / 2)956

356 / 2)712

215 / 4)860

169 / 5)845

125 / 6)750

111 / 9)999

121 / 8)968

258 / 3)774

147 / 5)735

115 / 8)920

123 / 8)984

125 / 4)500

423 / 2)846

178 / 4)712

105

Bargain Bonanza at Pat's Pet Place

Pat is having a gigantic sale. Help him divide his animals into groups for the sale.

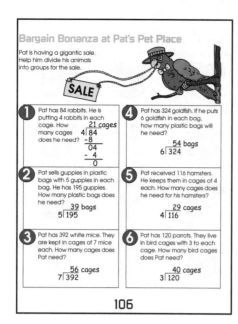

1 Pat has 84 rabbits. He is putting 4 rabbits in each cage. How many cages does he need?

```
    21 cages
  4 ) 84
    - 8
      04
    -  4
       0
```

2 Pat sells guppies in plastic bags with 5 guppies in each bag. He has 195 guppies. How many plastic bags does he need?

```
    39 bags
  5 ) 195
```

3 Pat has 392 white mice. They are kept in cages of 7 mice each. How many cages does Pat need?

```
    56 cages
  7 ) 392
```

4 Pat has 324 goldfish. If he puts 6 goldfish in each bag, how many plastic bags will he need?

```
    54 bags
  6 ) 324
```

5 Pat received 116 hamsters. He keeps them in cages of 4 each. How many cages does he need for his hamsters?

```
    29 cages
  4 ) 116
```

6 Pat has 120 parrots. They live in bird cages with 3 to each cage. How many bird cages does Pat need?

```
    40 cages
  3 ) 120
```

106

Zeros in the Quotient

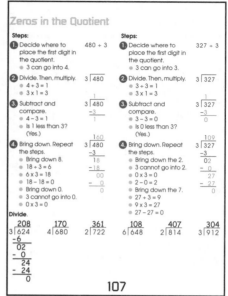

Steps:

1 Decide where to place the first digit in the quotient.　　480 ÷ 3
- 3 can go into 4.

2 Divide. Then, multiply.　　3) 480
- 4 ÷ 3 = 1
- 3 x 1 = 3

3 Subtract and compare.
- 4 − 3 = 1
- Is 1 less than 3? (Yes.)

```
    1
3 ) 480
  - 3
    1
```

4 Bring down. Repeat the steps.
- Bring down 8.
- 18 ÷ 3 = 6
- 6 x 3 = 18
- 18 − 18 = 0
- Bring down 0.
- 3 cannot go into 0.
- 0 x 3 = 0

```
    160
3 ) 480
  - 3
    18
  - 18
    00
  -  0
     0
```

Steps:

1 Decide where to place the first digit in the quotient.　　327 ÷ 3
- 3 can go into 3.

2 Divide. Then, multiply.　　3) 327
- 3 ÷ 3 = 1
- 3 x 1 = 3

3 Subtract and compare.
- 3 − 3 = 0
- Is 0 less than 3? (Yes.)

```
    1
3 ) 327
  - 3
    0
```

4 Bring down. Repeat the steps.
- Bring down the 2.
- 3 cannot go into 2.
- 0 x 3 = 0
- 2 − 0 = 2
- Bring down the 7.
- 27 ÷ 3 = 9
- 9 x 3 = 27
- 27 − 27 = 0

```
    109
3 ) 327
  - 3
    02
  - 0
    27
  - 27
     0
```

Divide.

```
    208          170      361       108      407      304
3 ) 624    4 ) 680   2 ) 722  6 ) 648  2 ) 814  3 ) 912
  - 6
    02
  - 0
    24
  - 24
     0
```

107

Marty's Mania

Help Marty Mouse eat all the cheese by traveling the route.

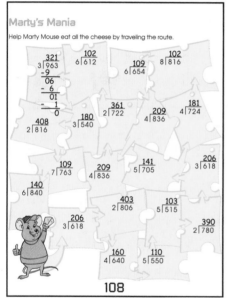

```
    321          102                102
3 ) 963    6 ) 612            8 ) 816
  - 9
    06
  - 6
    01
  - 1
    0
```

```
        109        361       209       181
      6 ) 654   2 ) 722   4 ) 836   4 ) 724
```

```
    408        180
2 ) 816    3 ) 540
```

```
    109        209       141       206
7 ) 763    4 ) 836   5 ) 705   3 ) 618
```

```
    140                  403       103
6 ) 840            2 ) 806   5 ) 515
```

```
        206                            390
      3 ) 618                       2 ) 780
```

```
    160        110
4 ) 640    5 ) 550
```

108

Yum! Yum!

What edible fungus is occasionally found on pizzas or in omelets? To find out, **solve** the following problems and **write** the matching letter above the answer at the bottom of the page.

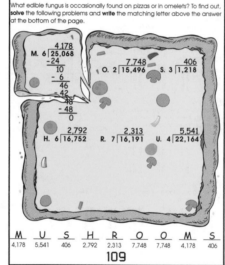

```
     4,178
M. 6 ) 25,068
   - 24
     10
   -  6
     46
   - 42
      48
    - 48
       0
```

```
      7,748            406
O. 2 ) 15,496   S. 3 ) 1,218
```

```
    2,792         2,313          5,541
H. 6 ) 16,752  R. 7 ) 16,191  U. 4 ) 22,164
```

M	U	S	H	R	O	O	M	S
4,178	5,541	406	2,792	2,313	7,748	7,748	4,178	406

109

Two-Digit Quotients
With Remainders

Steps:

1 Ask: Is the tens digit large enough to divide into? (Yes.) Divide. Multiply the partial quotient (1) by the divisor (3) and subtract from the partial dividend (4)

```
   1
3 ) 44    3 x 1
 - 3
   1
```

2 Ask: Can I divide the remaining 1 by 3? (No.) Bring down the 4. You now have 14 ones.

```
   1
3 ) 44
 - 3
   14
```
1 ten
+ 4 ones
= 14 ones

3 Divide the 14 ones by 3. Multiply the partial quotient by the divisor and subtract.

```
    14
3 ) 44
  - 3
    14
  - 12    3 x 4
     2
```

4 Ask: Can I divide the remaining 2 by 3? (No.) Make it a remainder.

```
    14 R 2
3 ) 44
  - 3
    14
  - 12
     2
```

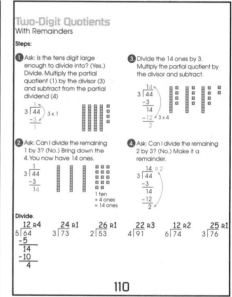

Divide.

```
    12 R4     24 R1    26 R1    22 R3    12 R2    25 R1
5 ) 64    3 ) 73   2 ) 53   4 ) 91   6 ) 74   3 ) 76
  - 5
    14
  - 10
     4
```

110

Mr. R Means Business

Solve the division problems below. **Write** the quotient and the remainder.

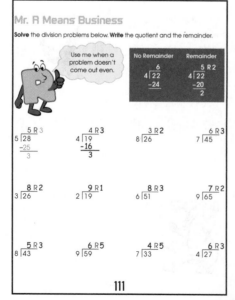

Use me when a problem doesn't come out even.

No Remainder	Remainder
6 4) 22 −24	5 R 2 4) 22 −20 　2

```
    5 R3        4 R3       3 R2       6 R3
5 ) 28     4 ) 19    8 ) 26    7 ) 45
 -25          -16
   3            3
```

```
    8 R2        9 R1       8 R3       7 R2
3 ) 26     2 ) 19    6 ) 51    9 ) 65
```

```
    5 R3        6 R5       4 R5       6 R3
8 ) 43     9 ) 59    7 ) 33    4 ) 27
```

111

Division Checklist

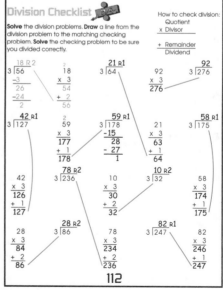

Solve the division problems. **Draw** a line from the division problem to the matching checking problem. **Solve** the checking problem to be sure you divided correctly.

How to check division:
```
   Quotient
 x Divisor

+ Remainder
  Dividend
```

```
   18 R2           2               21 R1              92
3 ) 56           18            3 ) 64           3 ) 276
 - 3            x 3                                x 3
   26            54                                276
 -24           + 2
   2            56
```

```
   42 R1           2               59 R1              21          58 R1
3 ) 127          59            3 ) 178             x 3        3 ) 175
                x 3             -15                 63
                177              63               + 1
               + 1            - 27                 64
                178              1
```

```
   42            78 R2           10             10 R2          58
  x 3          3 ) 236          x 3            3 ) 32         x 3
   126                           30                            174
  + 1                           + 2                           + 1
   127                           32                            175
```

```
   28            28 R2           78             82 R1          82
  x 3          3 ) 86           x 3            3 ) 247         x 3
   84                            234                           246
  + 2                           + 2                           + 1
   86                            236                           247
```

112

332

Looking to the Stars

Solve the problems. To find the path to the top, your answers should match the problem number. **Color** the path.

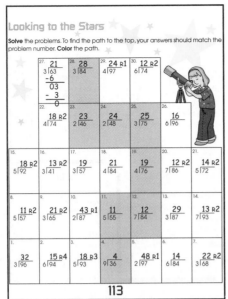

Three-Digit Quotients
With Remainders

Steps:

1. Ask: Is the hundreds digit large enough to divide into? (Yes.) Divide. Multiply the partial quotient by the divisor and subtract from the partial dividend.

2. Bring down the 5 tens. Ask: Can I divide 5 by 4? (Yes.) Multiply the partial quotient by the divisor and subtract.

3. Ask: Is the difference of 1 less than the divisor 4? (Yes.) Bring down the 4 ones.

   1 ten + 4 ones = 14 ones

4. Divide the 14 ones by 4. Multiply the partial quotient by the divisor and subtract.

5. Ask: Is the remaining difference of 2 less than the divisor? (Yes.) Make 2 a remainder.

Divide.

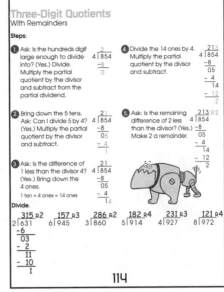

Puzzling Problems

Solve the following problems. **Write** the answers in the puzzle.

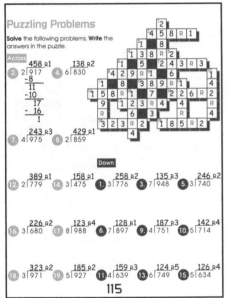

Four-Digit Quotients
With Remainders

Steps: $14{,}648 \div 6$

1. Decide where to place the first digit in the quotient.
   - 6 cannot go into 1.
   - 6 can go into 14.

2. Divide. Then, multiply.
   - $14 \div 6 = 2$
   - $6 \times 2 = 12$

3. Subtract and compare.
   - $14 - 12 = 2$
   - Is 2 less than 6? (Yes.)

4. Bring down. Repeat the steps.
   - Bring down the 6.
   - $26 \div 6 = 4$
   - $6 \times 4 = 24$
   - $26 - 24 = 2$
   - Is 2 less than 6? (Yes.)
   - Bring down the 4.
   - $24 \div 6 = 4$
   - $6 \times 4 = 24$
   - $24 - 24 = 0$
   - Is 0 less than 6? (Yes.)
   - Bring down the 8.
   - $8 \div 6 = 1$
   - $6 \times 1 = 6$
   - $8 - 6 = 2$
   - Is 2 less than 6? (Yes.)
   - No more numbers, so 2 is the remainder.

Divide.

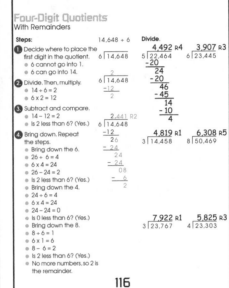

To Catch a Butterfly

Solve the problems. **Draw** a line to connect each net to the butterfly with the correct answer.

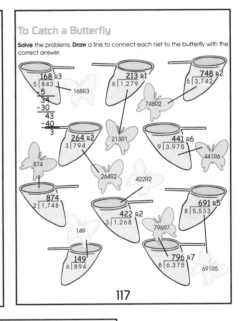

Two-Digit Divisors
With Remainders

Steps:

1. Decide where to place the first digit in the quotient. $240 \div 26$
   - 26 cannot go into 2.
   - 26 cannot go into 24.
   - 26 can go into 240.

2. Divide. Then, multiply.
   - $240 \div 26 = 9$
   - $9 \times 26 = 234$

3. Subtract and compare.
   - $240 - 234 = 6$
   - Is 6 less than 26? (Yes.)
   - No more numbers, so 6 is the remainder.

4. Check division with multiplication. Multiply the quotient by the divisor and add the remainder. If you divided correctly, your answer will be the dividend!

Steps:

1. Decide where to place the first digit in the quotient. $180 \div 25$
   - 25 cannot go into 1.
   - 25 cannot go into 18.
   - 25 can go into 180.

2. Divide. Then, multiply.
   - $180 \div 25 = 7$
   - $7 \times 25 = 175$

3. Subtract and compare.
   - $180 - 175 = 5$
   - Is 5 less than 25? (Yes.)
   - No more numbers, so 5 is the remainder.

4. Check.

Divide.

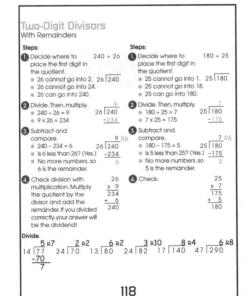

Hoppin' Division

Solve these division problems.

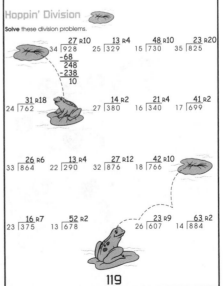

China's Dragon Kite

Solve the problems in this incredible dragon kite!

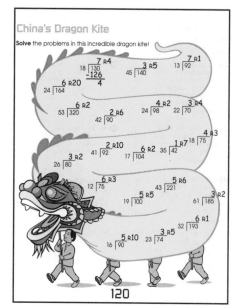

$$18\overline{)130} \quad 7\,R4$$
$$-126$$
$$\underline{4}$$
$$45\overline{)140} \quad 3\,R5 \qquad 13\overline{)92} \quad 7\,R1$$
$$24\overline{)164} \quad 6\,R20$$
$$53\overline{)320} \quad 6\,R2 \qquad 42\overline{)90} \quad 2\,R6 \qquad 24\overline{)98} \quad 4\,R2 \qquad 22\overline{)70} \quad 3\,R4$$
$$26\overline{)80} \quad 3\,R2 \qquad 41\overline{)92} \quad 2\,R10 \qquad 17\overline{)104} \quad 6\,R2 \qquad 35\overline{)42} \quad 1\,R7 \qquad 18\overline{)75} \quad 4\,R3$$
$$12\overline{)75} \quad 6\,R3 \qquad 19\overline{)100} \quad 5\,R5 \qquad 43\overline{)221} \quad 5\,R6 \qquad 61\overline{)185} \quad 3\,R2$$
$$16\overline{)90} \quad 5\,R10 \qquad 23\overline{)74} \quad 3\,R5 \qquad 32\overline{)193} \quad 6\,R1$$

120

Number Puzzles

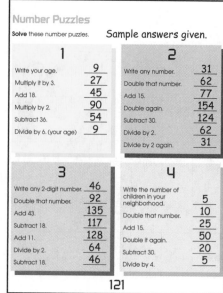

Solve these number puzzles.   *Sample answers given.*

1
Write your age.	9
Multiply it by 3.	27
Add 18.	45
Multiply by 2.	90
Subtract 36.	54
Divide by 6. (your age)	9

2
Write any number.	31
Double that number.	62
Add 15.	77
Double again.	154
Subtract 30.	124
Divide by 2.	62
Divide by 2 again.	31

3
Write any 2-digit number.	46
Double that number.	92
Add 43.	135
Subtract 18.	117
Add 11.	128
Divide by 2.	64
Subtract 18.	46

4
Write the number of children in your neighborhood.	5
Double that number.	10
Add 15.	25
Double it again.	50
Subtract 30.	20
Divide by 4.	5

121

Identifying Operations

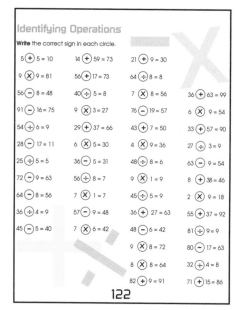

Write the correct sign in each circle.

5 (+) 5 = 10   14 (+) 59 = 73   21 (+) 9 = 30

9 (×) 9 = 81   56 (+) 17 = 73   64 (+) 8 = 8

56 (−) 8 = 48   40 (+) 5 = 8   7 (×) 8 = 56   36 (+) 63 = 99

91 (−) 16 = 75   9 (×) 3 = 27   76 (−) 19 = 57   6 (×) 9 = 54

54 (+) 6 = 9   29 (+) 37 = 66   43 (+) 7 = 50   33 (+) 57 = 90

28 (−) 17 = 11   6 (×) 5 = 30   4 (×) 9 = 36   27 (+) 3 = 9

25 (+) 5 = 5   36 (−) 5 = 31   48 (+) 8 = 6   63 (−) 9 = 54

72 (−) 9 = 63   56 (+) 8 = 7   9 (×) 1 = 9   8 (+) 38 = 46

64 (−) 8 = 56   7 (×) 1 = 7   45 (+) 5 = 9   2 (×) 9 = 18

36 (+) 4 = 9   57 (−) 9 = 48   36 (+) 27 = 63   55 (+) 37 = 92

45 (−) 5 = 40   7 (×) 6 = 42   48 (−) 6 = 42   81 (+) 9 = 9

9 (×) 8 = 72   80 (−) 17 = 63

8 (×) 8 = 64   32 (+) 4 = 8

82 (+) 9 = 91   71 (+) 15 = 86

122

Which Problem Is Correct?

Circle the equation on the left you should use to solve the problem. Then, **solve** the problem. Remember the decimal point in money questions.

1.
$$\begin{array}{c}56\\+17\\\hline73\end{array} \qquad \begin{array}{c}56\\-17\\\hline39\end{array}$$
Bill and his friends collect baseball cards. Bill has 17 fewer cards than Mack. Bill has 56 cards. How many baseball cards does Mack have?
73 cards

2.
$$\begin{array}{c}54\\\times\ 3\\\hline162\end{array} \qquad 3\overline{)54}$$
Amos bought 54 baseball cards. He already had 3 times as many. How many baseball cards did Amos have before his latest purchase?
162 cards

3.
$$\begin{array}{c}3.80\\+3.50\\\hline\end{array} \qquad \begin{array}{c}3.80\\-3.50\\\hline.30\end{array}$$
Joe paid $3.50 for a Mickey Mantle baseball card. Ted Williams cost him $3.80. How much more did he pay for Ted Williams than for Mickey Mantle?
$0.30 more

4.
$$\begin{array}{c}3.60\\\times\ 9\\\hline\end{array} \qquad 9\overline{)3.60}\ \ .40$$
Will bought 9 baseball cards for $3.60. How much did he pay per (for each) card?
$0.40 per card

5.
$$\begin{array}{c}8.00\\+\ .50\\\hline\end{array} \qquad \begin{array}{c}8.00\\-\ .50\\\hline7.50\end{array}$$
Babe Ruth baseball cards were selling for $8.00. Herb Score baseball cards sold for 50 cents. Herb Score sold for how much less than Babe Ruth cards?
$7.50 less

6.
$$\begin{array}{c}0.75\\\times\ 8\\\hline6.00\end{array} \qquad 8\overline{)0.75}$$
Andy bought 8 baseball cards at 75 cents each. How much did Andy pay in all?
$6.00 in all

123

Emery Prepares for His Party

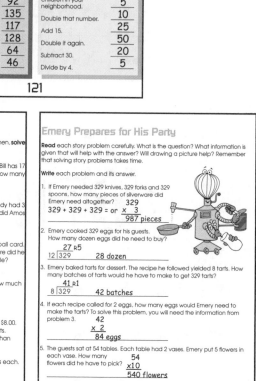

Read each story problem carefully. What is the question? What information is given that will help with the answer? Will drawing a picture help? Remember that solving story problems takes time.

Write each problem and its answer.

1. If Emery needed 329 knives, 329 forks and 329 spoons, how many pieces of silverware did Emery need altogether? 329
   329 + 329 + 329 = or $\begin{array}{c}329\\\times\ 3\\\hline\end{array}$ **987 pieces**

2. Emery cooked 329 eggs for his guests. How many dozen eggs did he need to buy?
   $12\overline{)329}\ \ 27\,R5$ **28 dozen**

3. Emery baked tarts for dessert. The recipe he followed yielded 8 tarts. How many batches of tarts would he have to make to get 329 tarts?
   $8\overline{)329}\ \ 41\,R1$ **42 batches**

4. If each recipe called for 2 eggs, how many eggs would Emery need to make the tarts? To solve this problem, you will need the information from problem 3.
   $\begin{array}{c}42\\\times\ 2\\\hline84\end{array}$ **84 eggs**

5. The guests sat at 54 tables. Each table had 2 vases. Emery put 5 flowers in each vase. How many flowers did he have to pick?
   $\begin{array}{c}54\\\times10\\\hline540\end{array}$ **540 flowers**

124

The Lion Dance

The Lion Dance, which started in China, became a Japanese folk dance. In this dance, many people line up under a long piece of colorful cloth. The person in front wears a mask of a lion's head. As a group, the line of people dances in the streets around the town.

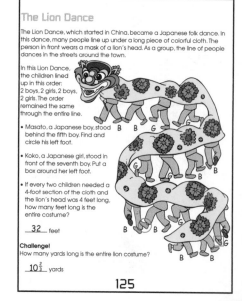

In this Lion Dance, the children lined up in this order: 2 boys, 2 girls, 2 boys, 2 girls. The order remained the same through the entire line.

- Masato, a Japanese boy, stood behind the fifth boy. Find and circle his left foot.

- Koko, a Japanese girl, stood in front of the seventh boy. Put a box around her left foot.

- If every two children needed a 4-foot section of the cloth and the lion's head was 4 feet long, how many feet long is the entire costume?

  32 feet

Challenge!
How many yards long is the entire lion costume?

  $10\frac{2}{3}$ yards

125

On the Average . . .

Division is good for finding averages. An **average** is a number that tells about how something is normally.

The children on the 6-on-6 basketball team made the following number of baskets:

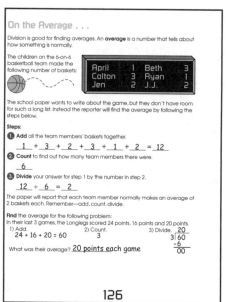

April	1	Beth	3
Colton	3	Ryan	1
Jen	2	J.J.	2

The school paper wants to write about the game, but they don't have room for such a long list. Instead the reporter will find the average by following the steps below.

Steps:

1. **Add** all the team members' baskets together.
   1 + 3 + 2 + 3 + 1 + 2 = 12

2. **Count** to find out how many team members there were.
   6

3. **Divide** your answer for step 1 by the number in step 2.
   12 ÷ 6 = 2

The paper will report that each team member normally makes an average of 2 baskets each. Remember—add, count, divide.

Find the average for the following problem:
In their last 3 games, the Longlegs scored 24 points, 16 points and 20 points.
1) Add.   24 + 16 + 20 = 60
2) Count.   3
3) Divide. $3\overline{)60}\ \ 20$
$$-6$$
$$\overline{00}$$

What was their average? **20 points each game**

126

Work It Out

The **average** is the result of dividing the **sum** of addends by the **number** of addends. **Match** the problem with its answer.

Add. $\begin{matrix}62\\79\\+87\end{matrix}\Big\}$ Count.   Divide. $3\overline{)228}\,^{76}$

228

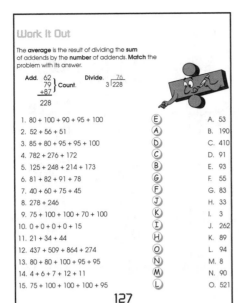

1. 80 + 100 + 90 + 95 + 100 — Ⓔ   A. 53
2. 52 + 56 + 51 — Ⓐ   B. 190
3. 85 + 80 + 95 + 95 + 100 — Ⓓ   C. 410
4. 782 + 276 + 172 — Ⓒ   D. 91
5. 125 + 248 + 214 + 173 — Ⓑ   E. 93
6. 81 + 82 + 91 + 78 — Ⓖ   F. 55
7. 40 + 60 + 75 + 45 — Ⓕ   G. 83
8. 278 + 246 — Ⓙ   H. 33
9. 75 + 100 + 100 + 70 + 100 — Ⓚ   I. 3
10. 0 + 0 + 0 + 0 + 15 — Ⓘ   J. 262
11. 21 + 34 + 44 — Ⓗ   K. 89
12. 437 + 509 + 864 + 274 — Ⓞ   L. 94
13. 80 + 80 + 100 + 95 + 95 — Ⓝ   M. 8
14. 4 + 6 + 7 + 12 + 11 — Ⓜ   N. 90
15. 75 + 100 + 100 + 100 + 95 — Ⓛ   O. 521

127

Story Problems

Solve the following problems.

Work Space

1. The daily temperatures for one week in May were 49°F, 51°F, 52°F, 69°F, 76°F, 77°F and 81°F. What was the average daily temperature for the entire week?
   65°F

2. Over a 5-day period, 255 cold lunches were brought to school. What was the average daily number of cold lunches brought to school over the 5-day period?
   51

3. Kayla scored 86%, 96%, 92%, 98%, 86% and 100% on her last six spelling tests. Based on these percentages, what is her average score?
   93%

4. Jonah practices basketball every night, and his goal is to practice an average of 60 minutes a night. He practiced 50 minutes on Monday, 68 minutes on Tuesday, 40 minutes on Wednesday, 40 minutes on Thursday and 72 minutes on Friday. What is the average amount of minutes per day Jonah practiced this past week? **54 min.**
   Did Jonah reach his goal? **No**

5. During the past soccer season, the Newhall Rovers had an average of 5 goals per game. If they play 25 games this coming season and score a total of 150 goals, will they achieve the same average number of goals?
   No (they will be better)

128

Geometry Match-Ups

A **polygon** is a closed shape with straight sides.

Directions: Cut out each polygon on the next page. To make them more durable, glue them onto cardboard or ooktag. Use the shapes to fill out the table below. (Keep the shapes for other activities as well.)

Game: Play this game with a partner. Put the shapes in a bag or cover them with a sheet of paper. Player One pulls out a shape and tells how many sides and angles it has. Without showing the shape, he/she puts the polygon back. Player Two should name the shape. Then, Player Two puts his/her hand in the bag and, without looking, tries to find the polygon from the description. Then, switch roles. Continue the game until all the polygons have been identified.

When you finish playing, **complete** the chart below.

Drawing of the shape (or polygon)	Shape name	Number of sides	Number of angles (or corners)
△	triangle	3	3
□	square	4	4
⬠	pentagon	5	5
▭	rectangle	4	4
⬡	hexagon	6	6

130

Triangle Puzzle

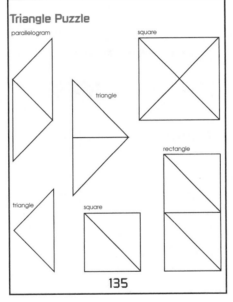

parallelogram   square   triangle   rectangle   triangle   square

135

Triangle Puzzle

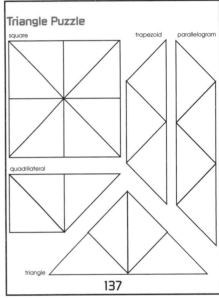

square   trapezoid   parallelogram   quadrilateral   triangle

137

A Native American Wall Hanging

Congruent figures have the same size and shape. They do not have to be the same color or in the same position.

Congruent figures   Not congruent figures

Directions: Draw two congruent figures to create a new shape. You can use triangles, squares, rectangles, pentagons, hexagons, octagons, semicircles, quarter-circles or trapezoids to make the shape. Use the new shape to create a wall hanging design. Connect the two congruent figures at one side. Color each part of the congruent pairs. Display your hanging on a wall of your house.

Patterns will vary.

139

Perimeter Problems

The **perimeter** is the distance around the outside of a shape. **Find** the perimeters for the figures below by adding the lengths of all the sides.

Example:

Rectangle: 5, 4, 5, + 4 = 18 → **18**

Triangle: 6, 6, + 5 = 17 → **17**

Hexagon: 3, 3, 3, 3, 3, + 3 = 18 → **18**

Figures (answers): **20**, **26**, **26**, **26**, **26**, **36**

142

Figuring Distance

Find the perimeter of each figure.

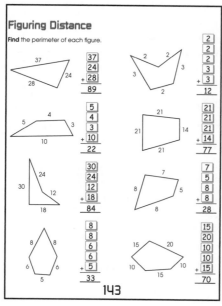

$$\begin{array}{r} 37 \\ 24 \\ +28 \\ \hline 89 \end{array}$$

$$\begin{array}{r} 2 \\ 2 \\ 2 \\ 3 \\ +3 \\ \hline 12 \end{array}$$

$$\begin{array}{r} 5 \\ 4 \\ 3 \\ +10 \\ \hline 22 \end{array}$$

$$\begin{array}{r} 21 \\ 21 \\ 21 \\ +14 \\ \hline 77 \end{array}$$

$$\begin{array}{r} 30 \\ 24 \\ 12 \\ +18 \\ \hline 84 \end{array}$$

$$\begin{array}{r} 7 \\ 5 \\ 8 \\ +8 \\ \hline 28 \end{array}$$

$$\begin{array}{r} 8 \\ 8 \\ 6 \\ 6 \\ +5 \\ \hline 33 \end{array}$$

$$\begin{array}{r} 15 \\ 20 \\ 10 \\ 10 \\ +15 \\ \hline 70 \end{array}$$

143

Silhouette Shapes

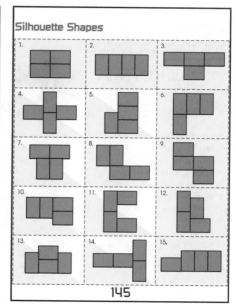

145

A Square Activity

The **area** is the number of square units covering a flat surface. **Find** the area by counting the square units.

Example: 2 squares x 5 squares = 10 squares

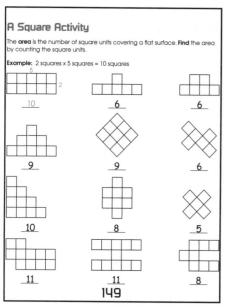

10

6 — 6

9 — 9 — 6

10 — 8 — 5

11 — 11 — 8

149

Quilt Math

The area of a rectangle is calculated by multiplying the length of one side by the width of another side. **Find** the perimeter and area of each quilt.

1. perimeter __30__ area __14__

2. perimeter __18__ area __18__

3. perimeter __14__ area __10__

4. perimeter __16__ area __7__

5. perimeter __16__ area __12__

6. perimeter __16__ area __16__

7. perimeter __16__ area __15__

8. What did you notice about the perimeter in problems 4, 5, 6 and 7?
They are all the same length.

9. On another sheet of paper, lay out, then sketch a quilt that has 30 blocks in it. **Answers will vary.**

10. On another sheet of paper, lay out, then sketch a quilt that has a perimeter of 14 units. **Answers will vary.**

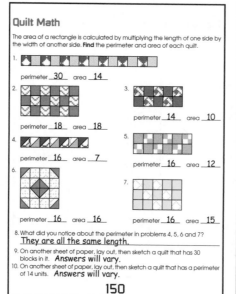

150

The Way Around Polygons

Use the cut-out shapes from pages 131–137. **Write** the name of each shape in the shape column. **Measure** the sides of each polygon and **record** its measurements. Then, **calculate** the perimeter of the polygon in the perimeter column. **Find** the area of every square and rectangle.
Sample answers given.

Shape	Each Side's Measurement	Perimeter side + side + side + side	Area 1 side x 1 side
square	4"	4 + 4 + 4 + 4 = 16 in.	4 x 4 = 16 sq. in.
triangle	4" – 4" – 5.5"	4 + 4 + 5.5 = 13.5 in. or $13\frac{1}{2}$"	
rectangle	$4\frac{1}{4}$" – 2" $4\frac{1}{4}$" – 2"	$4\frac{1}{4} + 4\frac{1}{4} + 2 + 2 = 12\frac{2}{4}$ or $12\frac{1}{2}$ in.	4.25 x 2 = 8.5 or $8\frac{1}{2}$ sq. in.
hexagon	$1\frac{1}{2}$" all six sides	$1\frac{1}{2} + 1\frac{1}{2} + 1\frac{1}{2} + 1\frac{1}{2} + 1\frac{1}{2} + 1\frac{1}{2} = 9$ in.	
pentagon	2" all five sides	2 + 2 + 2 + 2 + 2 = 10 in.	
quadrilateral	4" – 2" 2" – 3"	4 + 2 + 2 + 3 = 11 in.	
trapezoid	3" – 2" 2" – $5\frac{1}{2}$"	3 + 2 + 2 + $5\frac{1}{2}$ = $12\frac{1}{2}$ in.	
parallelogram	6" – 6" 2" – 2"	6 + 6 + 2 + 2 = 16 in.	

151

Suzy Spider, Interior Decorator

Suzy Spider is decorating her house. She is a very clever decorator, but she needs your help **calculating** the area and perimeter. **Draw** a picture to help.

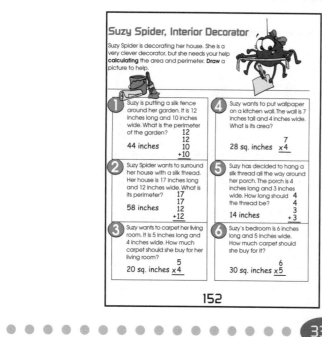

1 Suzy is putting a silk fence around her garden. It is 12 inches long and 10 inches wide. What is the perimeter of the garden?
44 inches
$$\begin{array}{r} 12 \\ 12 \\ 10 \\ +10 \\ \hline \end{array}$$

2 Suzy Spider wants to surround her house with a silk thread. Her house is 17 inches long and 12 inches wide. What is its perimeter?
58 inches
$$\begin{array}{r} 17 \\ 17 \\ 12 \\ +12 \\ \hline \end{array}$$

3 Suzy wants to carpet her living room. It is 5 inches long and 4 inches wide. How much carpet should she buy for her living room?
20 sq. inches $\times 4$, 5

4 Suzy wants to put wallpaper on a kitchen wall. The wall is 7 inches tall and 4 inches wide. What is its area?
28 sq. inches $\begin{array}{r} 7 \\ \times 4 \end{array}$

5 Suzy has decided to hang a silk thread all the way around her porch. The porch is 4 inches long and 3 inches wide. How long should the thread be?
14 inches
$$\begin{array}{r} 4 \\ 4 \\ 3 \\ +3 \\ \hline \end{array}$$

6 Suzy's bedroom is 6 inches long and 5 inches wide. How much carpet should she buy for it?
30 sq. inches $\begin{array}{r} 6 \\ \times 5 \end{array}$

152

"State"istics

Choose ten states. Then, **research** their "lengths" and "heights" and **multiply** them to find their areas.
Sample answers given. Numbers are approximate.

State Name	Approximate Miles E–W	Approximate Miles N–S	Area in Square Miles
Montana			147,000
Nebraska			77,000
Nevada			110,000
New Hampshire			9,000
New Jersey			8,000
New Mexico			122,000
New York			49,000
North Carolina			53,000
North Dakota			70,000
Ohio			41,000

153

Turn Up the Volume

The **volume** is the measure of the inside of a shape. **Find** the volume of these shapes by counting the boxes. You might not be able to see all the boxes, but you can tell that they are there.

Example:

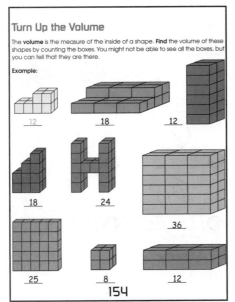

12   18   12

18   24

36

25   8   12

154

How Much Can a Container Contain?

To find volume: Multiply length x width x height

1. Select four food boxes and draw and color one in each box below.
2. Measure the width, length and height (the sides) of each box and record it next to its picture.
3. Find the volume of each box and record it next to its picture.

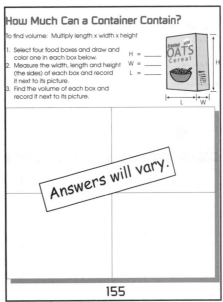

H = _____
W = _____
L = _____

Answers will vary.

155

Going in Circles

A **circle** is a round, closed figure. It is named by its center. A **radius** is a line segment from the center to any point on the circle. A **diameter** is a line segment with both points on the circle. The diameter always passes through the center of the circle.

Name the radius, diameter and circle.

Example:

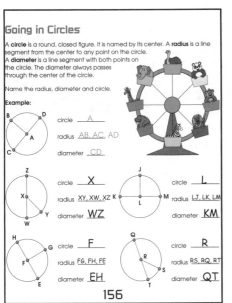

circle   A
radius   AB, AC, AD
diameter   CD

circle   X
radius   XY, XW, XZ
diameter   WZ

circle   L
radius   LJ, LK, LM
diameter   KM

circle   F
radius   FG, FH, FE
diameter   EH

circle   R
radius   RS, RQ, RT
diameter   QT

156

Perfect Symmetry

A figure that can be separated into two matching parts is **symmetric**. The **line of symmetry** is the line that divides the shape in half.

Is the dotted line shown a line of symmetry?

Line of Symmetry

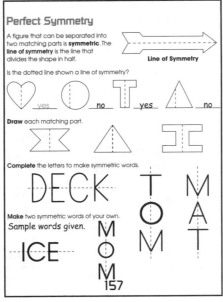

yes   no   yes   no

Draw each matching part.

Complete the letters to make symmetric words.

DECK

Make two symmetric words of your own.
Sample words given.

ICE

TOM
MAT
MOM

157

Look at the World From a Different Angle

Lines come together in many different ways. The point where two lines meet is called an **angle**. You may have to look at the things around you in a different way to find these angles.

Use the table below to **record** your observations from around the house. Look for objects that illustrate each category on the chart. **Draw** a sketch of each object and **label** it. **Find** as many objects for each category as possible.

Challenge: Look around the house and find one object that illustrates all five geometric categories. Sketch the object and label the various types of angles, lines or shapes that it has.   Sample answers given.

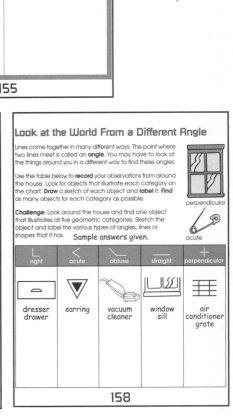

perpendicular

acute

L right	< acute	∟ obtuse	⌐ straight	+ perpendicular
dresser drawer	earring	vacuum cleaner	window sill	air conditioner grate

158

Graham Cracker Denominator

Find a cracker. If possible, use one that has four pieces. Break your cracker into as many or as few pieces as desired but make each piece the same size.

With fractions, the number of pieces into which an object is broken is how the bottom number, the **denominator**, obtains its numerical value. Remember that you started with one cracker that is in pieces now. **Write** the number of pieces as a denominator.

$\frac{4}{4}$ ← numerator

denominator → 4

To determine the top number, the **numerator**, eat part of the cracker. In the diagram at the right, cross out the part you ate. This is the numerator.

Write two fractions—a fraction to show what is left and a fraction to show what was eaten.

numerator 3 of the cracker is left   numerator 1 of the cracker is gone
denominator 4   denominator 4

Eat another piece of the cracker. **Cross out** the part you ate in the diagram. Now, **write** how much is left.

numerator 2 of the cracker is left   numerator 2 of the cracker is gone
denominator 4   denominator 4

Eat another piece of the cracker. **Cross out** the part you ate in the diagram. Now, **write** how much is left.

numerator 1 of the cracker is left   numerator 3 of the cracker is gone
denominator 4   denominator 4

Which part changes, the numerator or the denominator?

160

Fraction Fun

4 gloves are shaded. 9 gloves in all.

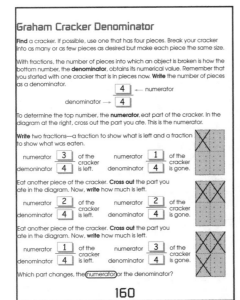

$\frac{4}{9}$ of the gloves are shaded.

TOYS

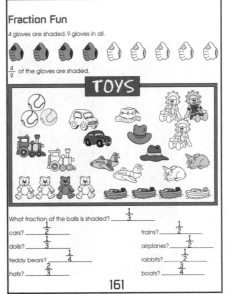

What fraction of the balls is shaded? $\frac{1}{3}$

cars? $\frac{1}{2}$ trains? $\frac{1}{2}$
dolls? $\frac{1}{3}$ airplanes? $\frac{1}{2}$
teddy bears? $\frac{1}{4}$ rabbits? $\frac{1}{2}$
hats? $\frac{2}{3}$ boats? $\frac{3}{4}$

161

337

Button Collection

Preparation: Use the boxes from **Equally Alike Boxes** on page 90 or collect sets of buttons. Count the number of buttons in each box or container. Create a response sheet like the one on the bottom of this page. You can choose how to group each of your objects. Those become the categories you write at the top of the response sheet.

Remember: A fraction has two numbers with a horizontal line drawn between them. The bottom number is called the **denominator**. The denominator tells how many equal parts or total pieces are in the whole. The top number is called the **numerator**. The numerator tells how many parts of the whole there are.

Example: $\frac{2}{5}$ the part of the total buttons with 2 holes / total number of buttons in the set

Sample: What is the fraction of buttons in this set with 2 holes?

Response Sheet

Box #	# of buttons in box	Buttons with 2 holes	Buttons with 4 holes	White buttons	Gold buttons	Black buttons	Brown buttons
1	8	$\frac{2}{8}$	$\frac{6}{8}$	$\frac{4}{8}$	$\frac{2}{8}$	$\frac{1}{8}$	$\frac{1}{8}$
2	6	$\frac{1}{6}$	$\frac{5}{6}$	$\frac{2}{6}$	$\frac{5}{6}$	$\frac{1}{6}$	$\frac{0}{6}$
3	3	$\frac{1}{3}$	$\frac{2}{3}$	$\frac{1}{3}$	$\frac{1}{3}$	$\frac{1}{3}$	$\frac{0}{3}$
4	9	$\frac{4}{9}$	$\frac{5}{9}$	$\frac{4}{9}$	$\frac{3}{9}$	$\frac{1}{9}$	$\frac{1}{9}$
5	10	$\frac{6}{10}$	$\frac{4}{10}$	$\frac{5}{10}$	$\frac{2}{10}$	$\frac{2}{10}$	$\frac{1}{10}$
6	5	$\frac{3}{5}$	$\frac{2}{5}$	$\frac{4}{5}$	$\frac{0}{5}$	$\frac{0}{5}$	$\frac{1}{5}$
7	4	$\frac{1}{7}$	$\frac{6}{7}$	$\frac{3}{7}$	$\frac{2}{7}$	$\frac{0}{7}$	$\frac{2}{7}$

162

The Mystery of the Missing Sweets

Some mysterious person is sneaking away with pieces of desserts from Sam Sillicook's Diner. Help him figure out how much is missing.

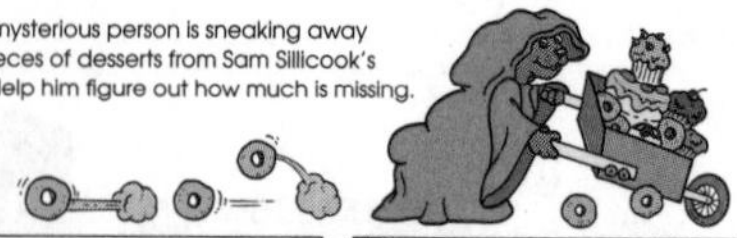

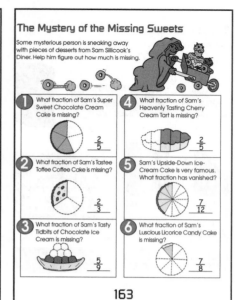

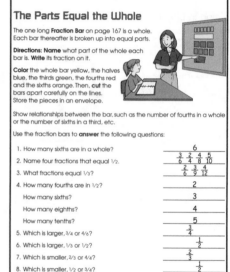

1. What fraction of Sam's Super Sweet Chocolate Cream Cake is missing? $\frac{2}{5}$
2. What fraction of Sam's Tastee Toffee Coffee Cake is missing? $\frac{2}{3}$
3. What fraction of Sam's Tasty Tidbits of Chocolate Ice Cream is missing? $\frac{5}{9}$
4. What fraction of Sam's Heavenly Tasting Cherry Cream Tart is missing? $\frac{2}{5}$
5. Sam's Upside-Down Ice-Cream Cake is very famous. What fraction has vanished? $\frac{7}{12}$
6. What fraction of Sam's Luscious Licorice Candy Cake is missing? $\frac{7}{8}$

163

Star Gazing

To find 1/2 of the stars, **divide** by 2.

Example:

$\frac{1}{2}$ of 10 = 5

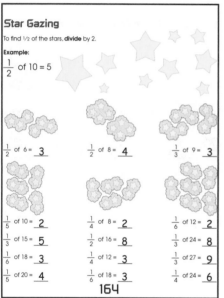

$\frac{1}{2}$ of 6 = 3 | $\frac{1}{2}$ of 8 = 4 | $\frac{1}{3}$ of 9 = 3

$\frac{1}{5}$ of 10 = 2 | $\frac{1}{4}$ of 8 = 2 | $\frac{1}{6}$ of 12 = 2

$\frac{1}{3}$ of 15 = 5 | $\frac{1}{2}$ of 16 = 8 | $\frac{1}{3}$ of 24 = 8

$\frac{1}{6}$ of 18 = 3 | $\frac{1}{4}$ of 12 = 3 | $\frac{1}{3}$ of 27 = 9

$\frac{1}{5}$ of 20 = 4 | $\frac{1}{6}$ of 18 = 3 | $\frac{1}{4}$ of 24 = 6

164

What Fraction Am I?

Identify the fraction for each shaded section.

Example: There are 5 sections on this figure. 2 sections are shaded. 2/5 of the sections are shaded. 3 sections are not shaded. 3/5 of the sections are not shaded.

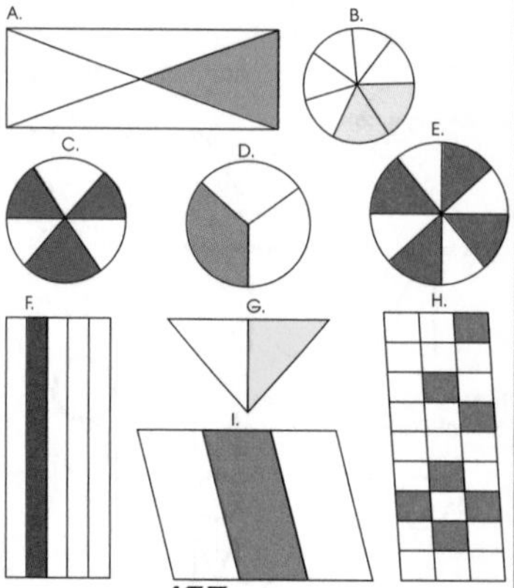

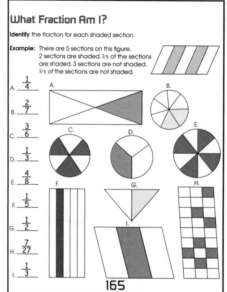

A. $\frac{1}{4}$
B. $\frac{2}{7}$
C. $\frac{3}{6}$
D. $\frac{1}{3}$
E. $\frac{4}{8}$
F. $\frac{1}{5}$
G. $\frac{1}{2}$
H. $\frac{7}{27}$
I. $\frac{1}{3}$

165

The Parts Equal the Whole

The one long **Fraction Bar** on page 167 is a whole. Each bar thereafter is broken up into equal parts.

Directions: Name what part of the whole each bar is. **Write** its fraction on it.

Color the whole bar yellow, the halves blue, the thirds green, the fourths red and the sixths orange. Then, **cut** the bars apart carefully on the lines. Store the pieces in an envelope.

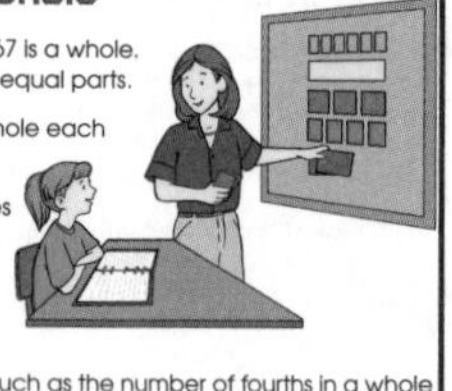

Show relationships between the bar, such as the number of fourths in a whole or the number of sixths in a third, etc.

Use the fraction bars to **answer** the following questions:

1. How many sixths are in a whole? 6
2. Name four fractions that equal 1/2. $\frac{3}{6}$ $\frac{2}{4}$ $\frac{4}{8}$ $\frac{5}{10}$
3. What fractions equal 1/3? $\frac{2}{6}$ $\frac{3}{9}$ $\frac{4}{12}$
4. How many fourths are in 1/2? 2
   How many sixths? 3
   How many eighths? 4
   How many tenths? 5
5. Which is larger, 3/4 or 4/6? $\frac{3}{4}$
6. Which is larger, 1/3 or 1/2? $\frac{1}{2}$
7. Which is smaller, 2/3 or 4/4? $\frac{2}{3}$
8. Which is smaller, 1/2 or 3/4? $\frac{1}{2}$

166

Fraction Bars

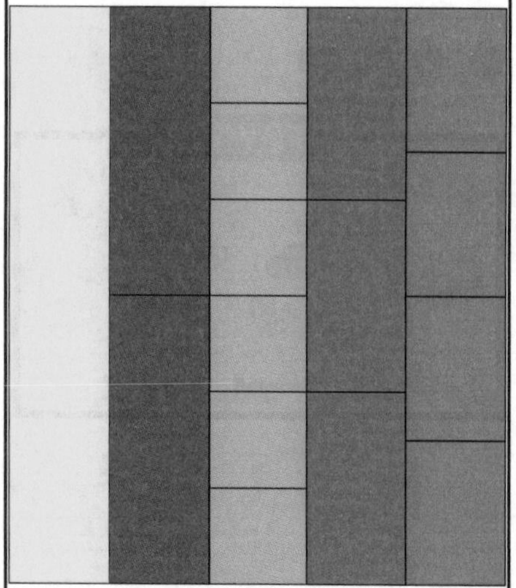

167

Working With Fractions

Use the fraction bars to help you **find** the smallest fraction in each row. **Circle** it.

1. $\frac{1}{2}$ $\frac{2}{3}$ ($\frac{1}{6}$) $\frac{1}{3}$
2. $\frac{2}{3}$ ($\frac{2}{6}$) $\frac{3}{3}$ $\frac{3}{6}$
3. $\frac{2}{2}$ $\frac{3}{6}$ $\frac{2}{3}$ ($\frac{1}{3}$)
4. $\frac{5}{6}$ $\frac{4}{6}$ ($\frac{1}{2}$) $\frac{2}{3}$
5. $\frac{6}{6}$ ($\frac{2}{3}$) $\frac{5}{6}$ $\frac{2}{2}$

1 Whole					
$\frac{1}{2}$			$\frac{2}{2}$		
$\frac{1}{3}$		$\frac{2}{3}$		$\frac{3}{3}$	
$\frac{1}{6}$	$\frac{2}{6}$	$\frac{3}{6}$	$\frac{4}{6}$	$\frac{5}{6}$	$\frac{6}{6}$

Use the fraction bars to help you **find** the greatest fraction in each row. **Circle** it.

1 Whole							
$\frac{1}{2}$				$\frac{2}{2}$			
$\frac{1}{4}$		$\frac{2}{4}$		$\frac{3}{4}$		$\frac{4}{4}$	
$\frac{1}{8}$	$\frac{2}{8}$	$\frac{3}{8}$	$\frac{4}{8}$	$\frac{5}{8}$	$\frac{6}{8}$	$\frac{7}{8}$	$\frac{8}{8}$

1. $\frac{1}{2}$ $\frac{3}{4}$ $\frac{6}{8}$ ($\frac{8}{8}$)
2. $\frac{1}{4}$ $\frac{1}{8}$ ($\frac{7}{8}$) $\frac{1}{2}$
3. $\frac{1}{8}$ ($\frac{1}{2}$) $\frac{1}{4}$ $\frac{2}{8}$
4. $\frac{1}{4}$ $\frac{3}{8}$ $\frac{5}{8}$ ($\frac{3}{4}$)
5. $\frac{2}{8}$ $\frac{1}{8}$ $\frac{1}{4}$ ($\frac{6}{8}$)

170

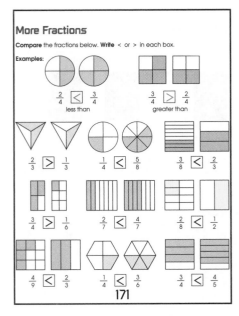

More Fractions

Compare the fractions below. **Write** < or > in each box.

Examples:

$\frac{2}{4}$ **<** $\frac{3}{4}$
less than

$\frac{3}{4}$ **>** $\frac{2}{4}$
greater than

$\frac{2}{3}$ **>** $\frac{1}{3}$ $\frac{1}{4}$ **<** $\frac{5}{8}$ $\frac{3}{8}$ **<** $\frac{2}{3}$

$\frac{3}{4}$ **>** $\frac{1}{6}$ $\frac{2}{7}$ **<** $\frac{4}{7}$ $\frac{2}{8}$ **<** $\frac{1}{2}$

$\frac{4}{9}$ **<** $\frac{2}{3}$ $\frac{1}{4}$ **<** $\frac{3}{6}$ $\frac{3}{4}$ **<** $\frac{4}{5}$

171

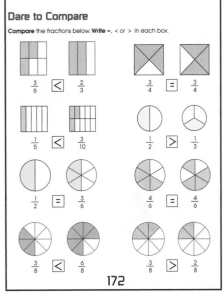

Dare to Compare

Compare the fractions below. **Write** =, < or > in each box.

$\frac{3}{6}$ **<** $\frac{2}{3}$ $\frac{3}{4}$ **=** $\frac{3}{4}$

$\frac{1}{5}$ **<** $\frac{3}{10}$ $\frac{1}{2}$ **>** $\frac{1}{3}$

$\frac{1}{2}$ **=** $\frac{3}{6}$ $\frac{4}{6}$ **=** $\frac{4}{6}$

$\frac{3}{8}$ **<** $\frac{6}{8}$ $\frac{3}{8}$ **>** $\frac{2}{8}$

172

Exploring Equivalent Fractions

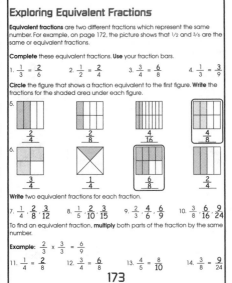

Equivalent fractions are two different fractions which represent the same number. For example, on page 172, the picture shows that ½ and ³⁄₆ are the same or equivalent fractions.

Complete these equivalent fractions. **Use** your fraction bars.

1. $\frac{1}{3} = \frac{2}{6}$ 2. $\frac{1}{2} = \frac{2}{4}$ 3. $\frac{3}{4} = \frac{6}{8}$ 4. $\frac{1}{3} = \frac{3}{9}$

Circle the figure that shows a fraction equivalent to the first figure. **Write** the fractions for the shaded area under each figure.

5. $\frac{2}{4}$ $\frac{2}{8}$ $\frac{4}{16}$ $\frac{4}{8}$

6. $\frac{3}{4}$ $\frac{1}{4}$ $\frac{6}{8}$ $\frac{2}{4}$

Write two equivalent fractions for each fraction.

7. $\frac{1}{4}, \frac{2}{8}, \frac{3}{12}$ 8. $\frac{1}{5}, \frac{2}{10}, \frac{3}{15}$ 9. $\frac{2}{3}, \frac{4}{6}, \frac{6}{9}$ 10. $\frac{3}{8}, \frac{6}{16}, \frac{9}{24}$

To find an equivalent fraction, **multiply** both parts of the fraction by the same number.

Example: $\frac{2}{3} \times \frac{3}{3} = \frac{6}{9}$

11. $\frac{1}{4} = \frac{2}{8}$ 12. $\frac{3}{4} = \frac{6}{8}$ 13. $\frac{4}{5} = \frac{8}{10}$ 14. $\frac{3}{8} = \frac{9}{24}$

173

Match the Fractions

Above each bar, **write** a fraction for the shaded part. Then, **match** each fraction on the left with its equivalent fraction on the right.

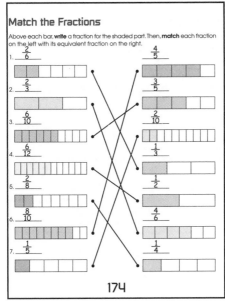

174

Fraction Patterns

Each row contains equivalent fractions except for one. **Find** which three fractions are equivalent for each row.
Draw an **X** on the fraction that is not equivalent. On the line, **write** a fraction that could be in the set. If necessary, **draw** a picture to help.

| Example: | $\frac{1}{2}$ | $\frac{2}{4}$ | $\frac{3}{5}$ | $\frac{4}{8}$ | Numerator (N) x 2 / Denominator (D) x 2 | New Fraction $\frac{8}{16}$ |

Sample answers given.

					New Fraction
1.	$\frac{1}{2}$	$\frac{2}{16}$	$\frac{3}{24}$	$\frac{4}{32}$	$\frac{3}{24}$
2.	$\frac{3}{4}$	$\frac{6}{8}$	$\frac{12}{16}$	$\frac{20}{30}$	$\frac{9}{12}$
3.	$\frac{3}{10}$	$\frac{9}{30}$	$\frac{27}{90}$	$\frac{36}{180}$	$\frac{6}{20}$
4.	$\frac{1}{5}$	$\frac{2}{15}$	$\frac{3}{15}$	$\frac{4}{20}$	$\frac{5}{25}$
5.	$\frac{3}{7}$	$\frac{6}{14}$	$\frac{8}{14}$	$\frac{12}{28}$	$\frac{9}{21}$
6.	$\frac{1}{2}$	$\frac{4}{32}$	$\frac{16}{32}$	$\frac{8}{128}$	$\frac{5}{10}$
7.	$\frac{5}{8}$	$\frac{7}{12}$	$\frac{15}{24}$	$\frac{20}{32}$	$\frac{10}{16}$

Write a rule to find equivalent fractions.
Multiply the denominator and numerator by one common number.

175

Alligator Problems

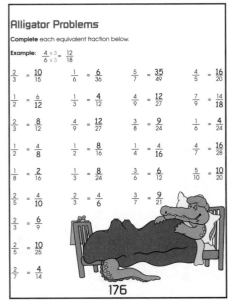

Complete each equivalent fraction below.

Example: $\frac{4 \times 3}{6 \times 3} = \frac{12}{18}$

$\frac{2}{3} = \frac{10}{15}$ $\frac{1}{6} = \frac{6}{36}$ $\frac{5}{7} = \frac{35}{49}$ $\frac{4}{5} = \frac{16}{20}$

$\frac{1}{2} = \frac{6}{12}$ $\frac{1}{3} = \frac{4}{12}$ $\frac{4}{9} = \frac{12}{27}$ $\frac{7}{9} = \frac{14}{18}$

$\frac{2}{3} = \frac{8}{12}$ $\frac{4}{9} = \frac{12}{27}$ $\frac{3}{8} = \frac{9}{24}$ $\frac{1}{6} = \frac{4}{24}$

$\frac{1}{2} = \frac{4}{8}$ $\frac{1}{2} = \frac{8}{16}$ $\frac{1}{4} = \frac{4}{16}$ $\frac{4}{7} = \frac{16}{28}$

$\frac{1}{8} = \frac{2}{16}$ $\frac{1}{3} = \frac{8}{24}$ $\frac{3}{6} = \frac{6}{12}$ $\frac{5}{10} = \frac{10}{20}$

$\frac{2}{5} = \frac{4}{10}$ $\frac{2}{3} = \frac{4}{6}$ $\frac{3}{7} = \frac{9}{21}$

$\frac{2}{3} = \frac{6}{9}$

$\frac{2}{5} = \frac{10}{25}$

$\frac{2}{7} = \frac{4}{14}$

176

More Than Peanuts

Write <, >, or = to compare the fractions below. **Draw** pictures or **write** equivalent fractions, if needed.

$\frac{3}{8}$ **>** $\frac{2}{8}$ $\frac{2}{3}$ **>** $\frac{3}{6}$ $\frac{3}{6}$ **=** $\frac{1}{2}$

$\frac{4}{7}$ **>** $\frac{4}{14}$ $\frac{1}{3}$ **<** $\frac{6}{7}$ $\frac{7}{10}$ **>** $\frac{2}{5}$

$\frac{8}{12}$ **>** $\frac{3}{6}$ $\frac{7}{14}$ **=** $\frac{1}{2}$ $\frac{4}{7}$ **>** $\frac{3}{7}$ $\frac{4}{8}$ **=** $\frac{8}{16}$

$\frac{1}{3}$ **=** $\frac{2}{6}$ $\frac{2}{8}$ **<** $\frac{1}{2}$ $\frac{1}{5}$ **<** $\frac{3}{10}$ $\frac{6}{11}$ **>** $\frac{5}{11}$

$\frac{6}{12}$ **=** $\frac{1}{2}$ $\frac{2}{3}$ **>** $\frac{2}{5}$ $\frac{7}{12}$ **>** $\frac{5}{12}$ $\frac{5}{6}$ **>** $\frac{1}{3}$

$\frac{7}{10}$ **>** $\frac{3}{10}$ $\frac{1}{2}$ **<** $\frac{8}{12}$ $\frac{1}{5}$ **<** $\frac{6}{10}$ $\frac{3}{4}$ **>** $\frac{2}{4}$

$\frac{3}{8}$ **>** $\frac{1}{4}$ $\frac{2}{5}$ **<** $\frac{5}{10}$

$\frac{5}{6}$ **>** $\frac{2}{3}$ $\frac{6}{10}$ **>** $\frac{2}{5}$

$\frac{6}{10}$ **>** $\frac{3}{10}$ $\frac{3}{6}$ **=** $\frac{6}{12}$

$\frac{1}{8}$ **<** $\frac{1}{4}$ $\frac{1}{2}$ **>** $\frac{1}{4}$

177

Catch It If You Can

For each fraction below, determine if the fraction equals more or less than 1/2. For each fraction, **cross out** the ball that does not describe the fraction. Then, **fill in** the blanks with the letters left to solve the riddle at the bottom of the page.

		Less than	More than
1.	$\frac{3}{8}$	Y	✗
2.	$\frac{4}{5}$	✗	O
3.	$\frac{1}{3}$	U	✗
4.	$\frac{4}{6}$	✗	R
5.	$\frac{1}{4}$	B	✗

		Less than	More than
6.	$\frac{2}{3}$	✗	R
7.	$\frac{5}{8}$	✗	E
8.	$\frac{7}{8}$	✗	A
9.	$\frac{1}{8}$	T	✗
10.	$\frac{1}{6}$	H	✗

What is harder to catch the faster you run?

Y O U R   B R E A T H

178

Reduce, Reduce

To reduce a fraction, **divide** each number in the fraction by a common factor. A fraction is reduced when the numerator and the denominator have only a common factor of 1. This is called a fraction's **lowest terms**.

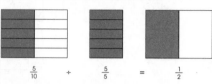

$$\frac{5}{10} \quad + \quad \frac{5}{5} \quad = \quad \frac{1}{2}$$

5 is a common factor of 5 and 10. (It can be divided into groups of five.) Is there another number these both can be divided by? (Only the number 1.)

Example: $\frac{16}{20} \div \frac{2}{2} = \frac{8}{10}$ **Ask:** Is this the lowest? Is there another number these both can be divided by? (Yes, 2.)

$\frac{8}{10} \div \frac{2}{2} = \frac{4}{5}$ Can this still divided by a common number? (No.)

Reduce these fractions.

$\frac{9}{12} = \frac{3}{4}$ $\frac{3}{15} = \frac{1}{5}$ $\frac{12}{16} = \frac{3}{4}$ $\frac{4}{5} = \frac{4}{5}$ $\frac{2}{8} = \frac{1}{4}$

$\frac{1}{8} = \frac{1}{8}$ $\frac{4}{6} = \frac{2}{3}$ $\frac{3}{9} = \frac{1}{3}$ $\frac{7}{14} = \frac{1}{2}$ $\frac{18}{24} = \frac{3}{4}$

179

Reduce the Fat

Reduce each fraction to its lowest terms.

Example: $\frac{5 \div 5}{25 \div 5} = \frac{1}{5}$ common factors

$\frac{8}{16} = \frac{1}{2}$ $\frac{12}{18} = \frac{2}{3}$

$\frac{10}{25} = \frac{2}{5}$ $\frac{12}{30} = \frac{2}{5}$ $\frac{3}{30} = \frac{1}{10}$ $\frac{6}{30} = \frac{1}{5}$

$\frac{12}{20} = \frac{3}{5}$ $\frac{3}{18} = \frac{1}{6}$ $\frac{3}{9} = \frac{1}{3}$ $\frac{4}{26} = \frac{2}{13}$

$\frac{4}{28} = \frac{1}{7}$ $\frac{7}{21} = \frac{1}{3}$ $\frac{16}{20} = \frac{4}{5}$ $\frac{2}{10} = \frac{1}{5}$

$\frac{3}{27} = \frac{1}{9}$ $\frac{5}{60} = \frac{1}{12}$ $\frac{21}{35} = \frac{3}{5}$ $\frac{3}{12} = \frac{1}{4}$

$\frac{9}{36} = \frac{1}{4}$ $\frac{24}{40} = \frac{3}{5}$ $\frac{8}{24} = \frac{1}{3}$

$\frac{16}{40} = \frac{2}{5}$

180

Mix 'Em Up

A **mixed number** is a whole number with a fraction.

Example: $1\frac{2}{3}$

An **improper fraction** is a fraction representing a whole and a fraction. The numerator is larger than the denominator.

Example: $\frac{16}{3}$

To change a mixed number to an improper fraction, **multiply** the whole number by the denominator.

Example: $2\frac{3}{4}$ $2 \times 4 = 8$ (How many fourths?)

Add the numerator to that number. 8 + 3 = 11

Write the fraction with the resulting number as numerator over the original denominator. $\frac{11}{4}$

$1\frac{1}{3} = \frac{4}{3}$ $3\frac{2}{5} = \frac{17}{5}$ $4\frac{3}{4} = \frac{19}{4}$ $2\frac{2}{7} = \frac{16}{7}$

To change an improper fraction to a mixed number, **divide** the numerator by the denominator. $\frac{10}{3}$

(How many wholes can be made?) $3\overline{)10}$ → $3\frac{R1}{}$

Write the quotient as the whole number and **write** any remainder as a fraction (with the denominator from the original problem).

$3\frac{1}{3}$

$\frac{5}{2} = 2\frac{1}{2}$ $\frac{7}{6} = 1\frac{1}{6}$ $\frac{4}{3} = 1\frac{1}{3}$ $\frac{10}{4} = 2\frac{2}{4}$

181

Oh, My!

When the numerator is greater than the denominator (an improper fraction), write a mixed number or divide to write a whole number. A mixed number is made up of a whole number and a fraction. **Example:** $2\frac{1}{2}$

Draw the correct mouths on the animals by finding the whole or mixed number for each.

Example:

$\frac{11}{2} =$ $\frac{20}{3} = 6\frac{2}{3}$ $\frac{21}{7} = 3$ $\frac{24}{2} = 12$

11 ÷ 2 = 5 R 1 = $5\frac{1}{2}$

$\frac{16}{2} = 8$ $\frac{49}{7} = 7$ $\frac{16}{16} = 1$ $\frac{16}{6} = 2\frac{4}{6}$

7 ⊘ $5\frac{1}{2}$ ⊘ $2\frac{4}{6}$ ⊘ $6\frac{2}{3}$ ⊘

3   8   1   12

182

Figure It Out

Solve the problems. Then, **connect** the dots in the same order as the answers appear.

1. $3\frac{3}{4} = \frac{15}{4}$ 2. $\frac{30}{11} = 2\frac{8}{11}$ 3. $\frac{10}{6} = 1\frac{4}{6}$ 4. $4\frac{1}{5} = \frac{21}{5}$

5. $\frac{13}{7} = 1\frac{6}{7}$ 6. $1\frac{5}{6} = \frac{11}{6}$ 7. $4\frac{1}{3} = \frac{13}{3}$ 8. $2\frac{2}{5} = \frac{12}{5}$

9. $1\frac{1}{9} = \frac{10}{9}$ 10. $1\frac{2}{5} = \frac{7}{5}$ 11. $\frac{9}{2} = 4\frac{1}{2}$ 12. $8\frac{1}{2} = \frac{17}{2}$

13. $4\frac{3}{8} = \frac{35}{8}$ 14. $\frac{11}{3} = 3\frac{2}{3}$ 15. $3\frac{5}{6} = \frac{23}{6}$ 16. $\frac{13}{5} = 2\frac{3}{5}$

17. $\frac{12}{7} = 1\frac{5}{7}$ 18. $6\frac{2}{5} = \frac{32}{5}$ 19. $\frac{13}{8} = 1\frac{5}{8}$ 20. $1\frac{1}{8} = \frac{9}{8}$

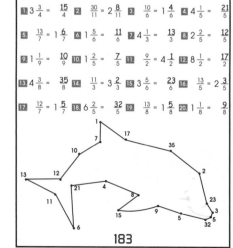

183

The Ultimate Adding Machine

Find the sum for each problem. **Reduce** it to the lowest terms.

$\frac{7}{9} + \frac{1}{9} = \frac{8}{9}$ $\frac{4}{12} + \frac{3}{12} = \frac{7}{12}$ $\frac{3}{6} + \frac{2}{6} = \frac{5}{6}$

$\frac{1}{9} + \frac{3}{9} = \frac{4}{9}$ $\frac{4}{10} + \frac{4}{10} = \frac{8}{10} = \frac{4}{5}$ $\frac{3}{6} + \frac{1}{6} = \frac{4}{6} = \frac{2}{3}$

$\frac{5}{9} + \frac{3}{9} = \frac{8}{9}$ $\frac{2}{5} + \frac{1}{5} = \frac{3}{5}$ $\frac{5}{11} + \frac{5}{11} = \frac{10}{11}$

$\frac{3}{7} + \frac{2}{7} = \frac{5}{7}$ $\frac{4}{8} + \frac{1}{8} = \frac{5}{8}$ $\frac{4}{12} + \frac{1}{12} = \frac{5}{12}$

$\frac{5}{8} + \frac{2}{8} = \frac{7}{8}$ $\frac{6}{12} + \frac{4}{12} = \frac{10}{12} = \frac{5}{6}$ $\frac{4}{6} + \frac{1}{6} = \frac{5}{6}$

$\frac{4}{11} + \frac{4}{11} = \frac{8}{11}$ $\frac{2}{5} + \frac{2}{5} = \frac{4}{5}$

$\frac{5}{8} + \frac{5}{8} = \frac{10}{8} = 1\frac{2}{8} = 1\frac{1}{4}$ $\frac{1}{9} + \frac{2}{9} = \frac{3}{9} = \frac{1}{3}$

$\frac{7}{10} + \frac{2}{10} = \frac{9}{10}$

7+9+6+

184

Sea Math

Reduce each sum to a whole number or a mixed number in the lowest terms.

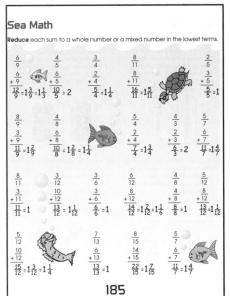

$\frac{6}{9} + \frac{6}{9} = \frac{12}{9} = 1\frac{3}{9} = 1\frac{1}{3}$ $\frac{4}{5} + \frac{6}{5} = \frac{10}{5} = 2$ $\frac{3}{4} + \frac{2}{4} = \frac{5}{4} = 1\frac{1}{4}$ $\frac{8}{11} + \frac{8}{11} = \frac{16}{11} = 1\frac{5}{11}$ $\frac{2}{5} + \frac{5}{5} = \frac{5}{5} = 1$

$\frac{8}{9} + \frac{3}{9} = \frac{11}{9} = 1\frac{2}{9}$ $\frac{4}{8} + \frac{6}{8} = \frac{10}{8} = 1\frac{2}{8} = 1\frac{1}{4}$ $\frac{5}{4} + \frac{2}{4} = \frac{7}{4} = 1\frac{3}{4}$ $\frac{4}{3} + \frac{2}{3} = \frac{6}{3} = 2$ $\frac{5}{7} + \frac{6}{7} = \frac{11}{7} = 1\frac{4}{7}$

$\frac{8}{11} + \frac{3}{11} = \frac{11}{11} = 1$ $\frac{3}{12} + \frac{10}{12} = \frac{13}{12} = 1\frac{1}{12}$ $\frac{6}{6} + \frac{6}{6} = \frac{6}{6} = 1$ $\frac{6}{12} + \frac{8}{12} = \frac{14}{12} = 1\frac{2}{12} = 1\frac{1}{6}$ $\frac{4}{8} + \frac{8}{8} = \frac{13}{8} = 1\frac{1}{8}$

$\frac{5}{12} + \frac{10}{12} = \frac{15}{12} = 1\frac{3}{12} = 1\frac{1}{4}$ $\frac{7}{13} + \frac{6}{13} = \frac{13}{13} = 1$ $\frac{8}{15} + \frac{14}{15} = \frac{22}{15} = 1\frac{7}{15}$ $\frac{5}{7} + \frac{6}{7} = \frac{11}{7} = 1\frac{4}{7}$

185

Soaring Subtraction

Solve each subtraction problem. Reduce each difference to the lowest terms.

$\frac{7}{10} - \frac{3}{10} = \frac{4}{10} = \frac{2}{5}$ $\frac{14}{16} - \frac{7}{16} = \frac{7}{16}$ $\frac{7}{7} - \frac{3}{7} = \frac{4}{7}$

$\frac{6}{8} - \frac{2}{8} = \frac{4}{8} = \frac{1}{2}$ $\frac{9}{11} - \frac{7}{11} = \frac{2}{11}$ $\frac{16}{21} - \frac{9}{21} = \frac{7}{21} = \frac{1}{3}$ $\frac{9}{10} - \frac{6}{10} = \frac{3}{10}$ $\frac{17}{18} - \frac{6}{18} = \frac{11}{18}$ $\frac{9}{12} - \frac{7}{12} = \frac{2}{12} = \frac{1}{6}$

$\frac{15}{18} - \frac{7}{18} = \frac{8}{18} = \frac{4}{9}$ $\frac{11}{14} - \frac{8}{14} = \frac{3}{14}$ $\frac{17}{17} - \frac{8}{17} = \frac{9}{17}$ $\frac{14}{15} - \frac{8}{15} = \frac{6}{15} = \frac{2}{5}$ $\frac{11}{12} - \frac{2}{12} = \frac{9}{12} = \frac{3}{4}$ $\frac{12}{10} - \frac{2}{10} = \frac{10}{10} = \frac{2}{5}$

$\frac{8}{9} - \frac{7}{9} = \frac{1}{9}$ $\frac{8}{10} - \frac{4}{10} = \frac{4}{10} = \frac{2}{5}$ $\frac{2}{3} - \frac{1}{3} = \frac{1}{3}$ $\frac{4}{9} - \frac{1}{9} = \frac{3}{9} = \frac{1}{3}$

186

Take a Closer Look

What is a stamp collector called?

To find out, **solve** the following subtraction problems and reduce to the lowest terms. Then, **write** the letter above its matching answer at the bottom of the page.

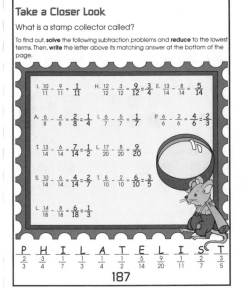

I. $\frac{10}{11} - \frac{9}{11} = \frac{1}{11}$ H. $\frac{12}{12} - \frac{3}{12} = \frac{9}{12} = \frac{3}{4}$ E. $\frac{13}{14} - \frac{8}{14} = \frac{5}{14}$

A. $\frac{6}{8} - \frac{4}{8} = \frac{2}{8} = \frac{1}{4}$ I. $\frac{6}{7} - \frac{5}{7} = \frac{1}{7}$ P. $\frac{6}{6} - \frac{2}{6} = \frac{4}{6} = \frac{2}{3}$

T. $\frac{13}{14} - \frac{6}{14} = \frac{7}{14} = \frac{1}{2}$ L. $\frac{17}{20} - \frac{8}{20} = \frac{9}{20}$

S. $\frac{10}{14} - \frac{6}{14} = \frac{4}{14} = \frac{2}{7}$ T. $\frac{8}{10} - \frac{2}{10} = \frac{6}{10} = \frac{3}{5}$

L. $\frac{14}{18} - \frac{8}{18} = \frac{6}{18} = \frac{1}{3}$

$\underset{\frac{2}{3}}{P}\ \underset{\frac{3}{4}}{H}\ \underset{\frac{1}{7}}{I}\ \underset{\frac{1}{4}}{L}\ \underset{\frac{1}{4}}{A}\ \underset{\frac{1}{2}}{T}\ \underset{\frac{5}{14}}{E}\ \underset{\frac{9}{20}}{L}\ \underset{\frac{1}{11}}{I}\ \underset{\frac{2}{7}}{S}\ \underset{\frac{3}{5}}{T}$

187

Finding a Common Denominator

When adding or subtracting fractions with different denominators, find a common denominator first. A **common denominator** is a common multiple of two or more denominators.

Cut a paper plate in half. **Cut** another paper plate into eighths. Use these models to help **solve** the following addition and subtraction problems.

$\frac{1}{2} + \frac{2}{8}$ = The common denominator is 8 because 2 x 4 = 8; 8 x 1 = 8.

$\frac{1}{2} \times \frac{4}{4} = \frac{4}{8}$ $\frac{4}{8} + \frac{2}{8} = \frac{6}{8}$

$\frac{7}{8} - \frac{1}{2}$ = The common denominator is 8 because 1 x 4 = 8; 2 x 4 = 8.

$\frac{7}{8} - \frac{4}{8} = \frac{3}{8}$

To find a common denominator of two or more fractions, follow these steps:

1. Write equivalent fractions so that the fractions have the same denominator.
2. Write the fractions with the same denominator.

Example: Step 1   Step 2

$\frac{1}{2} + \frac{2}{6}$ = $\frac{1}{2} \times \frac{3}{3} = \frac{3}{6}$ $\frac{3}{6} + \frac{2}{6} = \frac{5}{6}$

Follow the steps above. Then, **add**. Reduce the answer to its lowest terms.

$\frac{5}{9} + \frac{1}{3} = \frac{8}{9}$ $\frac{3}{8} - \frac{1}{4} = \frac{1}{8}$

$\frac{1}{3} + \frac{5}{12} = \frac{9}{12} = \frac{3}{4}$ $\frac{5}{12} - \frac{1}{6} = \frac{3}{12} = \frac{1}{4}$

188

Bug Me!

Solve the puzzle.

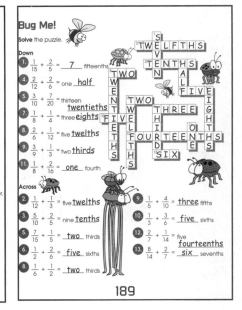

Down

1. $\frac{1}{15} + \frac{2}{5} = \_\_ 7 \_\_$ fifteenths
4. $\frac{2}{6} + \frac{2}{12} = \_\_$ one _half_
5. $\frac{3}{10} + \frac{7}{20} = \_\_$ thirteen _twentieths_
7. $\frac{1}{8} + \frac{1}{4} = \_\_$ three _eights_
8. $\frac{2}{6} + \frac{1}{12} = \_\_$ five _twelths_
9. $\frac{3}{9} + \frac{1}{3} = \_\_$ two _thirds_
11. $\frac{1}{8} + \frac{2}{16} = \_\_$ one _fourth_

Across

2. $\frac{1}{12} + \frac{1}{3} = \_\_$ five _twelths_
5. $\frac{5}{10} + \frac{2}{5} = \_\_$ nine _tenths_
5. $\frac{7}{15} + \frac{1}{5} = \_\_$ two _thirds_
6. $\frac{1}{2} + \frac{1}{3} = \_\_$ five _sixths_
8. $\frac{1}{6} + \frac{1}{2} = \_\_$ two _thirds_
9. $\frac{1}{5} + \frac{4}{10} = \_\_$ three _fifths_
10. $\frac{1}{3} + \frac{3}{6} = \_\_$ five _sixths_
12. $\frac{2}{7} + \frac{1}{14} = \_\_$ five _fourteenths_
13. $\frac{8}{14} + \frac{2}{7} = \_\_$ six _sevenths_

189

Numeral Nibblers

Complete these equations. Use another sheet of paper to solve the problems, if needed.

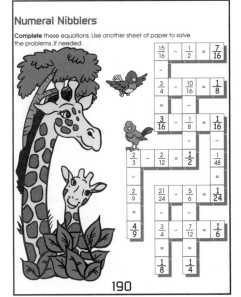

$\frac{15}{16} - \frac{1}{2} = \frac{7}{16}$

$\frac{3}{4} - \frac{10}{16} = \frac{1}{8}$

$\frac{3}{16} - \frac{1}{8} = \frac{1}{16}$

$\frac{2}{3} - \frac{2}{12} = \frac{1}{2}$ $\frac{1}{48}$

$\frac{2}{9} - \frac{21}{24} - \frac{5}{6} = \frac{1}{24}$

$\frac{4}{9} - \frac{3}{4} - \frac{7}{12} = \frac{1}{6}$

$\frac{1}{8}$ $\frac{1}{4}$

190

Make a Wish

Solve these problems.

Example: $\frac{2}{9}$ of 27 = 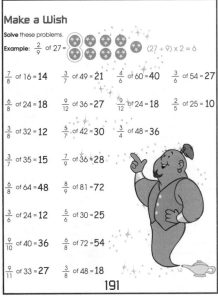   (27 ÷ 9) x 2 = 6

$\frac{7}{8}$ of 16 = **14** $\frac{3}{7}$ of 49 = **21** $\frac{4}{6}$ of 60 = **40** $\frac{3}{6}$ of 54 = **27**

$\frac{6}{8}$ of 24 = **18** $\frac{9}{12}$ of 36 = **27** $\frac{9}{12}$ of 24 = **18** $\frac{2}{5}$ of 25 = **10**

$\frac{3}{8}$ of 32 = **12** $\frac{5}{7}$ of 42 = **30** $\frac{3}{4}$ of 48 = **36**

$\frac{3}{7}$ of 35 = **15** $\frac{7}{9}$ of 36 = **28**

$\frac{6}{8}$ of 64 = **48** $\frac{8}{9}$ of 81 = **72**

$\frac{3}{6}$ of 24 = **12** $\frac{5}{6}$ of 30 = **25**

$\frac{9}{10}$ of 40 = **36** $\frac{6}{8}$ of 72 = **54**

$\frac{9}{11}$ of 33 = **27** $\frac{3}{8}$ of 48 = **18**

191

Make the Move

Complete the puzzle by writing the answers in words.

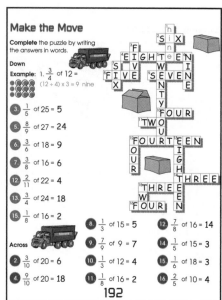

Down

Example: 1. $\frac{3}{4}$ of 12 =

$(12 \div 4) \times 3 = 9$ nine

3. $\frac{1}{5}$ of 25 = **5**

5. $\frac{8}{9}$ of 27 = **24**

6. $\frac{3}{6}$ of 18 = **9**

7. $\frac{3}{8}$ of 16 = **6**

12. $\frac{2}{11}$ of 22 = **4**

13. $\frac{3}{4}$ of 24 = **18**

15. $\frac{1}{8}$ of 16 = **2**

Across

2. $\frac{3}{10}$ of 20 = **6**

4. $\frac{9}{10}$ of 20 = **18**

8. $\frac{1}{3}$ of 15 = **5**

9. $\frac{7}{9}$ of 9 = **7**

10. $\frac{1}{3}$ of 12 = **4**

11. $\frac{1}{8}$ of 16 = **2**

12. $\frac{7}{8}$ of 16 = **14**

14. $\frac{1}{5}$ of 15 = **3**

15. $\frac{1}{6}$ of 18 = **3**

16. $\frac{2}{5}$ of 10 = **4**

192

Picture the Problem

Use the picture to **solve** each problem.

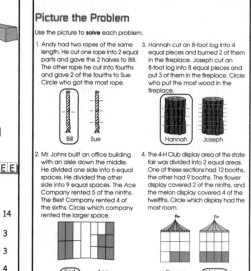

1. Andy had two ropes of the same length. He cut one rope into 2 equal parts and gave the 2 halves to Bill. The other rope he cut into fourths and gave 2 of the fourths to Sue. Circle who got the most rope.

2. Mr. Johns built an office building with an aisle down the middle. He divided one side into 6 equal spaces. He divided the other side into 9 equal spaces. The Ace Company rented 5 of the ninths. The Best Company rented 4 of the sixths. Circle which company rented the larger space.

3. Hannah cut an 8-foot log into 4 equal pieces and burned 2 of them in the fireplace. Joseph cut an 8-foot log into 8 equal pieces and put 3 of them in the fireplace. Circle who put the most wood in the fireplace.

4. The 4-H Club display area at the state fair was divided into 2 equal areas. One of these sections had 12 booths, the other had 9 booths. The flower display covered 2 of the ninths, and the melon display covered 4 of the twelfths. Circle which display had the most room.

195

Doing Decimals

Just as a fraction stands for part of a whole number, a decimal also shows part of a whole number. And with decimals, the number is always broken into ten or a power of ten (hundred, thousand, etc.) parts. These place values are named tenths, hundredths, thousandths, etc.

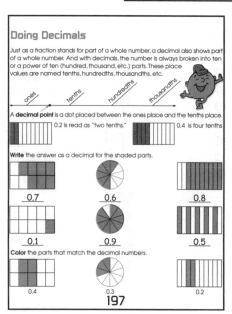

A **decimal point** is a dot placed between the ones place and the tenths place.

0.2 is read as "two tenths."   0.4 is four tenths

Write the answer as a decimal for the shaded parts.

0.7   **0.6**   **0.8**

0.1   **0.9**   **0.5**

Color the parts that match the decimal numbers.

0.4   0.3   0.2

197

Hundredth Picture Grid

Pictures will vary.

199

Decimal Divisions

Decimals are often used with whole numbers.

Examples: 2.8   3.5

Write the decimal for each picture.

1.2   **5.7**   **2.4**

Shade in the picture to show the decimal number.

1.9   3.5   0.4   4.1

When reading decimals with whole numbers, say "point" or "and" for the decimal point.

Write the word names for each decimal from above.

1.9 <u>one and nine tenths</u>   0.4 <u>four tenths or point four</u>

3.5 <u>three and five tenths</u>   4.1 <u>four and one tenth or four point one</u>

200

How Hot Are You?

Write the number for each word name. **Cross off** the number in the cloud. The number that is left is your body temperature. **Hint:** Remember to add a zero to hold any place value not given.

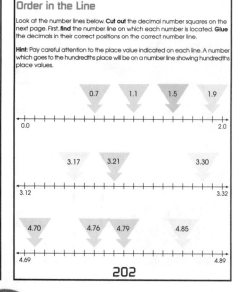

1. six and eight tenths	6.8
2. four and nine tenths	4.9
3. thirteen and seven tenths	13.7
4. twenty-one and one tenth	21.1
5. five and fifteen hundredths	5.15
6. nine and sixty-two hundredths	9.62
7. fifteen and four hundredths	15.04
8. fifty-seven and eighty-two hundredths	57.82
9. three and seven tenths	3.7
10. sixty and forty-three hundredths	60.43
11. ninety and seven hundredths	90.07
12. fourteen and two hundredths	14.02
13. five and seven hundredths	5.07
14. ten and one tenth	10.1
15. thirty and twenty hundredths	30.20
Your body temperature is:	98.6

201

Order in the Line

Look at the number lines below. **Cut out** the decimal number squares on the next page. First, **find** the number line on which each number is located. **Glue** the decimals in their correct positions on the correct number line.

Hint: Pay careful attention to the place value indicated on each line. A number which goes to the hundredths place will be on a number line showing hundredths place values.

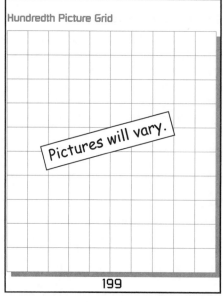

0.7   1.1   1.5   1.9

0.0   2.0

3.17   3.21   3.30

3.12   3.32

4.70   4.76   4.79   4.85

4.69   4.89

202

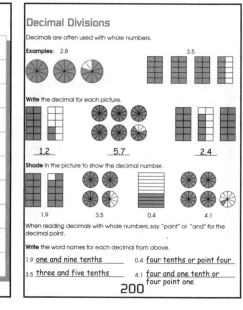

Order in the Line

0.12   0.18   0.24

0.09 ———————————————— 0.29

6.75   6.80   6.85   6.88

6.70 ———————————————— 6.90

203

Get the Point

When you add or subtract decimals, remember to include the decimal point.

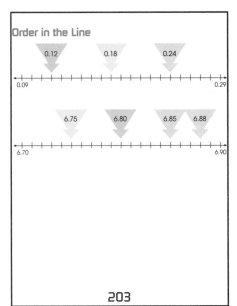

Add. 3.6
      +3.3
      6.9

Subtract. 6.8
          −2.6
          4.2

Solve these problems.

4.2 +5.2 **9.4**	6.4 +1.4 **7.8**	3.1 +7.8 **10.9**	4.7 +3.2 **7.9**	4.9 +2.0 **6.9**	4.2 7 +5.5 2 **9.79**
5.9 −3.2 **2.7**	6.7 −5.6 **1.1**	7.8 −2.5 **5.3**	5.8 −3.3 **2.5**	3.9 −1.5 **2.4**	4.8 6 −1.7 6 **3.10**
0.2 3 +0.2 5 **0.48**	0.4 3 +0.1 6 **0.59**	0.2 6 +0.4 2 **0.68**	0.6 4 +0.1 5 **0.79**	0.6 8 +0.3 1 **0.99**	6.7 3 +1.1 5 **7.88**
0.8 7 −0.4 2 **0.45**	0.9 8 −0.3 5 **0.63**	0.7 9 −0.1 5 **0.64**	0.8 7 −0.6 7 **0.20**	0.8 3 −0.1 2 **0.71**	5.8 6 −3.8 3 **2.03**
3.1 3 +2.2 6 **5.39**	4.7 2 +1.1 5 **5.87**	6.8 7 +2.1 1 **8.98**	4.9 8 −2.3 2 **2.66**	5.9 7 −2.5 4 **3.43**	6.9 8 −1.4 5 **5.53**

205

Animal Trivia

1 An earthworm is 14.9 cm long. A grasshopper is 8.7 cm long. What is the difference?

6.2 cm

2 A pocket gopher has a hind foot 3.5 cm long. A ground squirrel's hind foot is 6.4 cm long. How much longer is the ground squirrel's hind foot?

2.9 cm

3 A porcupine has a tail 30.0 cm long. An opossum has a tail 53.5 cm long. How much longer is the opossum's tail?

23.5 cm

4 A wood rat has a tail which is 23.6 cm long. A deer mouse has a tail 12.2 cm long. What is the difference between the two?

11.4 cm

5 A cottontail rabbit has ears which are 6.8 cm long. A jackrabbit has ears 12.9 cm long. How much shorter is the cottontail's ear?

6.1 cm

6 The hind foot of a river otter is 14.6 cm long. The hind foot of a hog-nosed skunk is 9.0 cm long. What is the difference?

5.6 cm

7 A rock mouse is 26.1 cm long. His tail adds another 14.4 cm. What is his total length from his nose to the tip of his tail?

40.5 cm

206

Subtraction Cards

1.0 4 0 −0.2 1 6 **0.824**	5.5 −3.2 **2.3**
0.3 5 0 −0.1 2 8 **0.222**	8.6 −4.8 **3.8**
0.6 0 9 −0.3 1 7 **0.292**	1.3 0 −0.1 7 **1.13**
0.8 7 −0.4 9 **0.38**	0.9 4 −0.5 3 **0.41**
0.7 0 4 −0.3 2 6 **0.378**	2.3 −1.4 **0.9**

211

Rounding Cards

3.5̲35 **3.54** Round to the underlined number.	9̲.7 **10.0** Round to the underlined number.
0.3̲34 **0.3** Round to the underlined number.	2.0̲9 **2.0** Round to the underlined number.
5.4̲8 **5.0** Round to the underlined number.	6.8̲3 **6.8** Round to the underlined number.
0.6̲12 **0.61** Round to the underlined number.	0.0̲51 **0.1** Round to the underlined number.
7.7̲17 **7.72** Round to the underlined number.	1̲.842 **2.0** Round to the underlined number.

213

Comparison Cards

7.2 **<** 7.5 < or >	0.3 **<** 3.0 < or >
4.9 **>** 4.8 < or >	1.5 **<** 1.7 < or >
3.23 **<** 3.32 < or >	6.19 **<** 6.2 < or >
2.08 **<** 2.40 < or >	0.86 **<** 0.88 < or >
5.61 **<** 5.62 < or >	8.3 **>** 8.06 < or >

215

Addition Cards

0.3 0 7 +0.9 0 0 **1.207**	0.6 4 +0.3 3 **0.97**
0.7 8 +0.2 1 **0.99**	0.6 5 +0.6 5 **1.30**
1.2 9 +4.5 0 **5.79**	0.4 4 2 +0.7 8 4 **1.226**
0.7 0 4 +0.1 2 7 **0.831**	0.9 4 6 +0.0 3 5 **0.981**
4.7 6 +2.2 5 **7.01**	2.1 2 +3.7 9 **5.91**

217

Decimal Riddles

Read the clues to **write** the numbers.

1. Numbers: 4, 8, 2, 2
   Clues:
   ● The numbers in the tens place and the tenths place are the same.
   ● The greatest number is in the hundredths place.

   `2 4 . 2 8`

2. Numbers: 1, 2, 3, 8
   Clues:
   ● The number in the tens place is 5 less than the number in the hundredths place.
   ● The number in the tenths place is twice the number in the ones place.

   `3 1 . 2 8`

3. Numbers: 3, 5, 8, 9
   Clues:
   ● The greatest number is in the hundredths place.
   ● The number in the tenths place is 2 less than the number in the tens place.

   `5 8 . 3 9`

4. Numbers: 2, 3, 4, 6
   Clues:
   ● The 3 is in the tenths place.
   ● The number in the hundreds place is half the number in the tens place.
   ● The number in the ones place is the sum of the numbers in the hundreds place and the tens place.

   `2 4 6 . 3`

5. Numbers: 0, 5, 6, 7, 8
   Clues:
   ● The number in the hundredths place is 8 more than the number in the tenths place.
   ● The 6 is in the tens place.
   ● The number in the hundreds place is greater than the number in the ones place.

   `7 6 5 . 0 8`

6. Numbers: 2, 4, 6, 7, 8
   Clues:
   ● The number in the hundredths place is twice the number in the tenths place.
   ● The 7 is in the ones place.
   ● The number in the hundreds place is three times the number in the tens place.

   `6 2 7 . 4 8`

221

Flower Graph

A **pictograph** is a graph using pictures to give information. **Cut out** the flowers and **glue** them onto the pictograph.

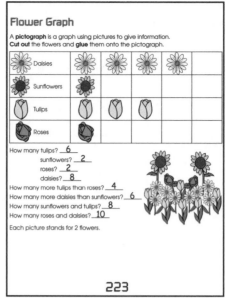

How many tulips? __6__
   sunflowers? __2__
   roses? __2__
   daisies? __8__
How many more tulips than roses? __4__
How many more daisies than sunflowers? __6__
How many sunflowers and tulips? __8__
How many roses and daisies? __10__

Each picture stands for 2 flowers.

223

Frog Bubbles

Complete the line graph to show how many bubbles each frog blew.

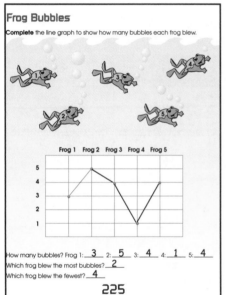

How many bubbles? Frog 1: __3__ 2: __5__ 3: __4__ 4: __1__ 5: __4__
Which frog blew the most bubbles? __2__
Which frog blew the fewest? __4__

225

Potato Face

Read the line graphs to **draw** the potato faces.

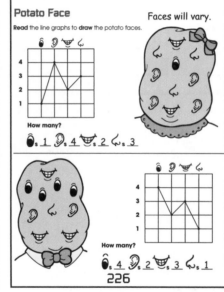

Faces will vary.

How many?

👁s __1__ 👃s __4__ 👄s __2__ 👂s __3__

How many?

👁s __4__ 👂s __2__ 👄s __3__ 👃s __1__

226

Vote for Me!

Middletown school had an election to choose the new members of the Student Council. Grace, Bernie, Laurie, Sherry and Sam all ran for the office of president. On the chart below are the five students' names with the number of the votes each received.

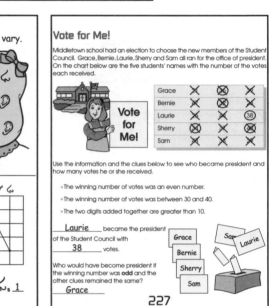

Grace	✗	⊗	✗
Bernie	✗	⊗	✗
Laurie	✗	✗	㉚
Sherry	⊗	✗	⊗
Sam	✗	✗	✗

Use the information and the clues below to see who became president and how many votes he or she received.

● The winning number of votes was an even number.
● The winning number of votes was between 30 and 40.
● The two digits added together are greater than 10.

__Laurie__ became the president of the Student Council with __38__ votes.

Who would have become president if the winning number was **odd** and the other clues remained the same?
__Grace__

227

School Statistics

Read each graph and follow the directions.

List the names of the students from the shortest to the tallest.

1. __Tiffany__   4. __Louis__
2. __Michele__   5. __Jessie__
3. __Andy__   6. __Stephie__

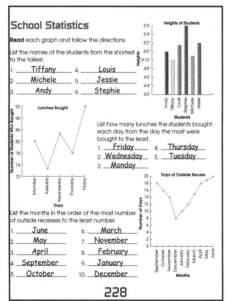

List how many lunches the students bought each day, from the day the most were bought to the least.

1. __Friday__   4. __Thursday__
2. __Wednesday__   5. __Tuesday__
3. __Monday__

List the months in the order of the most number of outside recesses to the least number.

1. __June__   6. __March__
2. __May__   7. __November__
3. __April__   8. __February__
4. __September__   9. __January__
5. __October__   10. __December__

228

Candy Sales

Every year the students at Lincoln Elementary sell candy as a fund-raising project. These are the results of the sales for this year.

Grade Level	Number of Sales
Kindergarten	40
First	70
Second	50
Third	80
Fourth	85
Fifth	75

Color the bar graph to show the number of sales made at each grade level.

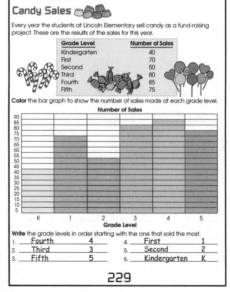

Write the grade levels in order starting with the one that sold the most.

1. __Fourth__   4   4. __First__   1
2. __Third__   3   5. __Second__   2
3. __Fifth__   5   6. __Kindergarten__   K

229

344

Hot Lunch Favorites

The cooks in the cafeteria asked each third- and fourth-grade class to rate the hot lunches. They wanted to know which food the children liked the best.

The table shows how the students rated the lunches.
Key: Each 🧍 equals 2 students.

Food	Number of students who liked it best	
hamburgers	🧍🧍🧍🧍🧍🧍	12
hot dogs	🧍🧍🧍🧍🧍🧍🧍	14
tacos	🧍🧍🧍🧍🧍	10
chili		0
soup and sandwiches	🧍	2
spaghetti	🧍🧍	4
fried chicken	🧍🧍🧍🧍	8
fish sticks	🧍🧍🧍	6

Color the bar graph to show the information on the table. Remember that each 🧍 equals 2 people. The first one is done for you.

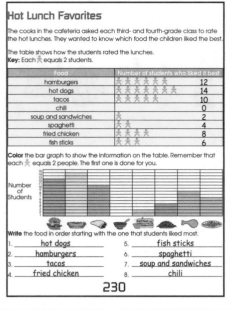

Write the food in order starting with the one that students liked most.

1. ____hot dogs____   5. ____fish sticks____
2. ____hamburgers____   6. ____spaghetti____
3. ____tacos____   7. ____soup and sandwiches____
4. ____fried chicken____   8. ____chili____

230

Gliding Graphics

Draw the lines as directed from point to point for each graph.

Draw a line from:
- F,7 to D,1
- D,1 to I,6
- I,6 to N,8
- N,8 to M,3
- M,3 to F,1
- F,1 to G,4
- G,4 to E,4
- E,4 to B,1
- B,1 to A,8
- A,8 to D,11
- D,11 to F,9
- F,9 to F,7
- F,7 to I,9
- I,9 to I,6
- I,6 to F,7

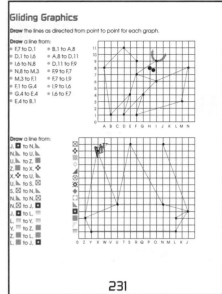

Draw a line from:
- J,■ to N,■
- N,▲ to U,▲
- U,▲ to Z,■
- Z,■ to X,✤
- X,✤ to U,▲
- U,▲ to S,◙
- S,◙ to N,▲
- N,▲ to N,◙
- N,◙ to J,■
- J,■ to L,▒
- L,▒ to Y,▥
- Y,▥ to Z,▒
- Z,▒ to L,▒
- L,▒ to J,■

231

Tally Ho!

A **tally mark** is a line to represent one. The fifth tally mark is written diagonally over the first four marks for easy reading of the results. (**Example:** 🜂 = 5.)

Use the **Die Pattern** on page 233 to **make** two dice.

Roll the dice 10 times. **Record** the sum rolled each time by making a tally mark in the chart.

Sample answers given.

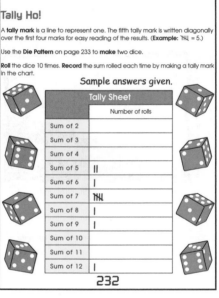

Tally Sheet	
	Number of rolls
Sum of 2	
Sum of 3	
Sum of 4	
Sum of 5	II
Sum of 6	I
Sum of 7	🜂
Sum of 8	I
Sum of 9	I
Sum of 10	
Sum of 11	
Sum of 12	I

232

Roll 'Em!

Roll the die 20 times in a row. **Use** the following tally sheet to keep track of the number you roll each time.

Sample answers given. Tally Sheet

Number rolled	Number of rolls
Number 1 ⚀	I
Number 2 ⚁	II
Number 3 ⚂	🜂
Number 4 ⚃	IIII
Number 5 ⚄	🜂 I
Number 6 ⚅	II

Answer the following questions about the tally sheet.
1. Which number was rolled most frequently? ____5____
2. Which number was rolled least frequently? ____1____
3. Were any numbers rolled the same number of times? ____yes____
   Which ones? ____2 and 6____   Sample answers given.
   Why do you think this happened? ____They had equal changes.____

Extension:

Do this exercise again and compare the first results with the second results.

Why did the results turn out the way they did? _____

Was there anything that could have been done to change the results?

_____

Predict what would happen if the die were rolled 40 times? _____

235

Pie Graph Survey

Step 1: Conducting a Survey
A **survey** is a mini-interview of many people to find out what they like or do not like. Possible topics might be a favorite television show, a food or a career choice. Choose a survey topic to create the survey table.

Directions: Create a title for the survey. Write it across the top of the chart below. Next, provide several choices for the survey. For example, if the title of the survey is "Favorite Subject," you would choose some popular subjects and write them vertically along the left margin of the chart. Next, you will survey sixteen people.

You may want to discuss the sample population and perhaps set limits. Will you survey a group of people that are all the same? Will you survey only friends your age? The first sixteen people you see on the street? Relatives?

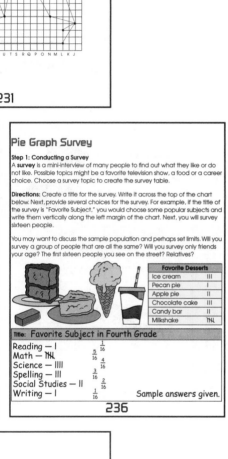

Favorite Desserts	
Ice cream	III
Pecan pie	I
Apple pie	II
Chocolate cake	III
Candy bar	II
Milkshake	🜂

Title: Favorite Subject in Fourth Grade

Reading — I		$\frac{1}{16}$
Math — 🜂		$\frac{5}{16}$
Science — IIII		$\frac{4}{16}$
Spelling — III		$\frac{3}{16}$
Social Studies — II		$\frac{2}{16}$
Writing — I		$\frac{1}{16}$

Sample answers given.

236

Pie Graph Survey

Step 2: Creating Fractions
Directions: Convert the results of your survey into fractions. The denominator will be 16, because that is the number of people who make up the whole survey. Determine the numerator by counting the number of people who chose an item. (For example, if four people chose math as their favorite subject, the fraction would be 4/16.) When all tallied results have been converted into fractions, you are ready to create the pie graph.

Chocolate cake = 3/16 means three children out of sixteen picked the cake as their favorite dessert.

Step 3: Creating the Pie Graph
Directions: Shade in the number of sections that each numerator indicates, using a different color for each numerator, or choice from the survey. Write the choice, fraction and the color in the key. Now, copy your pie graph and key, cut them out, mount them and share them with the people you surveyed.

Key:
Pecan pie 1/16
Apple pie 2/16
Chocolate cake 3/16
Candy bar 2/16
Milkshake 5/16
Ice cream 3/16

Sample answer given.

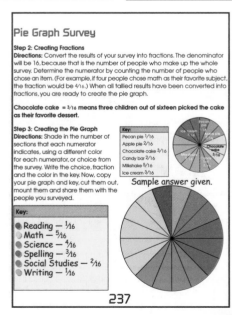

Key:
- ● Reading — ¹⁄₁₆
- ● Math — ⁵⁄₁₆
- ● Science — ⁴⁄₁₆
- ● Spelling — ³⁄₁₆
- ● Social Studies — ²⁄₁₆
- ● Writing — ¹⁄₁₆

237

Guess the Color

Probability shows the chance that a given event will happen. To show probability, write a fraction. The number of different possibilities is the denominator. The number of times the event could happen is the numerator. (Remember to reduce fractions to the lowest terms.)

Look at the spinner. What is the probability that the arrow will land on . . .

1. red? $\frac{3}{8}$
2. blue? $\frac{2}{8} = \frac{1}{4}$
3. yellow? $\frac{1}{8}$
4. green? $\frac{1}{8}$
5. orange? $\frac{1}{8}$

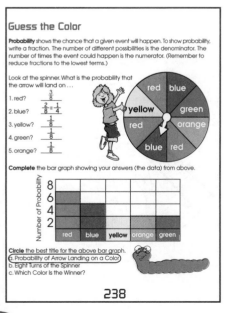

Complete the bar graph showing your answers (the data) from above.

| red | blue | yellow | orange | green |

Circle the best title for the above bar graph.
a. Probability of Arrow Landing on a Color
b. Eight Turns of the Spinner
c. Which Color Is the Winner?

238

Trees

Possible combinations of two events can be organized on trees. **Use** the spinners from page 239.

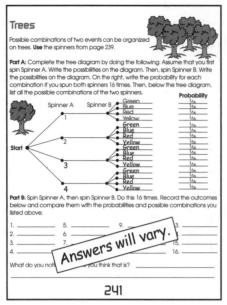

Part A: Complete the tree diagram by doing the following: Assume that you first spin Spinner A. Write the possibilities on the diagram. Then, spin Spinner B. Write the possibilities on the diagram. On the right, write the probability for each combination if you spun both spinners 16 times. Then, below the tree diagram, list all the possible combinations of the two spinners.

Spinner A   Spinner B   **Probability**

Start

1 — Green, Blue, Red, Yellow — 1/16 each
2 — Green, Blue, Red, Yellow — 1/16 each
3 — Green, Blue, Red, Yellow — 1/16 each
4 — Green, Blue, Red, Yellow — 1/16 each

Part B: Spin Spinner A, then spin Spinner B. Do this 16 times. Record the outcomes below and compare them with the probabilities and possible combinations you listed above.

1. ___ 5. ___ 9. ___ 13. ___
2. ___ 6. ___ 10. ___ 14. ___
3. ___ 7. ___ 11. ___ 15. ___
4. ___ 8. ___ 12. ___ 16. ___

Answers will vary.

What do you notice? ___ Why do you think that is? ___

241

How Many Outfits?

Suppose you had two pairs of jeans (one blue and the other gray) and three shirts (orange, red and green). How many different outfits could you wear? **Use** a tree to help you with the answer.

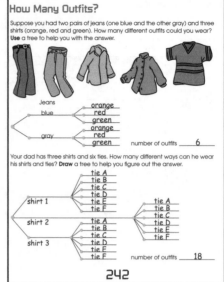

Jeans
blue — orange, red, green
gray — orange, red, green

number of outfits ___6___

Your dad has three shirts and six ties. How many different ways can he wear his shirts and ties? **Draw** a tree to help you figure out the answer.

shirt 1 — tie A, tie B, tie C, tie D, tie E, tie F
shirt 2 — tie A, tie B, tie C, tie D, tie E, tie F
shirt 3 — tie A, tie B, tie C, tie D, tie E, tie F

number of outfits ___18___

242

Keep Your Heads Up!

Collect 21 pennies. **Predict** the numbers of heads and tails that will turn up before you toss the pennies. Then, **toss** the coins ten times.

Does anything change about your predictions the more you guess?
___

Toss	Guess Heads	Guess Tails	Actual Heads	Actual Tails
1				
2				
3				
4				
5				
6				
7				
8				
9				
10				

Answers will vary.

243

How Does Your Home Measure Up?

Directions: Take a "measuring journey" through your house. To begin, brainstorm a list of various destinations around your house. Then, **list** five objects found in each room and **write** them on the left-hand side of a sheet of paper.

Example:

Kitchen	Bathroom	Bedroom
stove	toothbrush	books
teaspoon	hairbrush	desk/table
cookbook	soap	pillow
can opener	mirror	clock
box of cereal	bandage	hanger

Read through the objects on the list and **write** estimations of their measurements. Decide on a unit of measurement to use and whether to measure length, width or both. Then, **measure** the objects. (A tape measure or string may be used to measure the size or circumference of any oddly shaped objects.) Finally, compare your estimations with the actual measurements.

Sample answers given.

Object	Estimate	Actual
box of cereal	12 in. by 6 in.	11 in. by 8 in.
soap	2 in. by 3 in.	3 in. by 4 in.
pillow	24 in. by 18 in.	26 in. by 20 in.
foot stool	24 in. by 18 in.	27 in. by 24 in.
table top	40 in. by 28 in.	42 in. by 30 in.

247

Growing String Beans
Bar Graph

Sample graph given.

String Bean Plant Growth

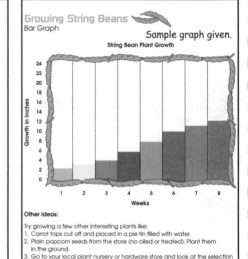

Growth in Inches (y-axis: 0–24)
Weeks (x-axis: 1–8)

Other Ideas:
Try growing a few other interesting plants like:
1. Carrot tops cut off and placed in a pie tin filled with water.
2. Plain popcorn seeds from the store (no oiled or treated). Plant them in the ground.
3. Go to your local plant nursery or hardware store and look at the selection of plant seeds available.
4. Plant a young tree in your yard and measure its growth each year.

249

Hand—Foot—Ruler

Directions:
1. Measure the span of your hand by stretching your thumb and little finger as far apart as possible. Lay your hand on a ruler to find out this length (span). Record the inches (") of the span on the record sheet below.

2. Measure the length of your pace by taking one step forward and holding it. Have someone put the edge of a yardstick next to the heel of your back foot and measure to the back of the heel on your forward foot. Record the pace distance in inches on the record sheet.

3. Using a ruler or yardstick, measure the distances listed on the record sheet. Record all findings in feet and/or inches.

Sample answers given.

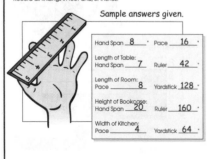

Hand Span ___8___ "   Pace ___16___
Length of Table:
Hand Span ___7___   Ruler ___42___
Length of Room:
Pace ___8___   Yardstick ___128___
Height of Bookcase:
Hand Span ___20___   Ruler ___160___
Width of Kitchen:
Pace ___4___   Yardstick ___64___

250

A Measurement of Our Own

Create your own new system of measurement. Brainstorm ideas on what and how you should base the new unit. For example, you may use the length of your finger, the length of a juice box, the length of your backpack, etc. as a base.
Next, **create** a ruler using your new unit of measurement. A foot is made of inches and a meter is made of centimeters. Break your standard unit into smaller units and **add** these to the ruler. When the ruler is complete, fill out the form below.

Answer the questions below.

1. What is the name of your unit of measurement? ___

2. What would your unit of measurement be best suited for measuring—long distances or microscopic organisms? ___
   Why? ___

3. Would you rather use ___ measurement versus the standard unit? ___ not?

4. Measure an object using your new ruler. What did it measure? ___
   If you were to tell someone that the object you measured was that long, do you think that person would be able to picture its length? ___
   Why or why not? ___

5. Why do you think everyone in the entire country uses the exact same unit of measurement? ___

Answers will vary.

251

346

Krab E. Krabby

Krab E. Krabby carries a yardstick with him everywhere he goes and he measures everything he can.

Key:
12 inches = 1 foot
36 inches = 3 feet = 1 yard

1 Krab E. Krabby wanted to measure the length of a grasshopper. Would he use a ruler or a yardstick?

ruler

2 Krab E. measured a garter snake that was 44 inches long. How many yards and inches is this?

1 yard **8** inches

3 Krab E. measured a monarch butterfly that was 4 inches wide. How many inches less than a foot is the butterfly?

8 inches

4 Krab E. Krabby scolded Rollo Rattlesnake because Rollo wouldn't straighten out and cooperate. Should Krab E. use a ruler or a yardstick to measure Rollo?

yardstick

5 Krab E. measured a tomato hornworm that was 5 inches long. How many inches less than a foot is this?

7 inches

6 Krab E. measured a lazy tuna that was 1 foot 11 inches long. How many total inches is the tuna?

23 inches

252

Calculating Lengths

Use your yardstick to **calculate** and **write** the following lengths. Remember to write feet or yards. Some lengths may not be exactly in feet or yards, so be sure to write the inches too. Have a friend or parent help you **measure** these lengths.

Sample answers given. Answers will vary.

1. How long is the biggest step you can take? **1 yd. 2 in.**
2. How far can a paper airplane fly? **100 ft.**
3. From start to finish, how much distance do you cover when you do a somersault? **5 ft.**
4. How far can you throw a feather? **6 in.**
5. How wide is your driveway? **6 ft.**
6. How far can you walk balancing a book on your head? **7 ft.**
7. How high can you stack wooden blocks before they fall? **2 ft.**
8. How high can you jump? (Measure from where your finger touches to the floor.) **9 in.**
9. How far can you jump? (Begin with your feet together.) **12 in.**
10. How much distance is covered if you skip 10 times? **10 ft.**
11. What is the distance you can hit a softball with your bat before it hits the ground? **40 ft.**
12. What is the distance you can throw a baseball? **30 ft.**
13. How far away were you when you caught your friend's throw? **20 ft.**
14. How far can you spit a seed? **8 ft.**
15. How much distance do you cover when you sprint for 3 seconds? **30 ft.**

253

Animal Math

The chart below lists some of the body statistics of 15 endangered animals. Use these measurements to **solve** the problems below the chart.

Animal	Height	Weight	Length
Mountain gorilla	6 feet	450 pounds	
Black rhinoceros	5.5 feet	4,000 pounds	12 feet
Cheetah	2.5 feet	100 pounds	5 feet
Leopard	2 feet	150 pounds	4.5 feet
Spectacled bear	2.5 feet	300 pounds	5 feet
Giant armadillo		100 pounds	4 feet
Vicuna	2.5 feet	100 pounds	
Siberian tiger	38 inches	600 pounds	6 feet
Orangutan	4.5 feet	200 pounds	
Giant panda		300 pounds	6 feet
Polar bear		1,600 pounds	8 feet
Yak	5.5 feet	1,200 pounds	

1. What is the total height of a mountain gorilla, a vicuna and a yak? **14 ft.**
2. What is the total weight of a leopard, a cheetah and a polar bear? **1,850 lbs.**
3. What is the total weight of a giant panda and a giant armadillo? **400 lbs.**
4. Add the lengths of a black rhinoceros, a spectacled bear and a Siberian tiger. **23 ft.**
5. Add the heights of two leopards, three yaks and four orangutans. **38.5 ft.**
6. Subtract the height of a vicuna from the height of a cheetah. **0**
7. Add the weights of all the animals. **9,100 lbs.**
8. Write the lengths of the animals from longest to shortest.
   12 ft. (black rhino)   8 ft. (polar bear)   6 ft. (panda & tiger)
   5 ft. (cheetah & spectacled bear)   4.5 ft. (leopard)
   4 ft. (armadillo)

254

Finding Weight Equivalents

In the United States, we use a standard weight system that includes ounces (oz.), pounds (lb.) and tons (tn.). Develop your own standard weight system below.

You will need: marbles, paper clips, ice-cream sticks, crayons, pencils, spoons, etc. (anything that has weight and can be counted), a scale or balance

Directions: Your standard weight is _____.

Now, use your scale to find out how much different objects weigh.

1. Place the object to be weighed on one side of the scale.
2. Find out, for example, how many of your standard weight it takes to equal the object being weighed.
3. When the scale is level, you have found your equivalent weight.
4. Weigh different objects and record the results below.

Example: bottle of glue   weight: 16 crayons

object: _____   weight: _____
object: _____   weight: _____
object: _____   weight: _____
object: _____   weight: _____
object: _____   weight: _____
object: _____   weight: _____
object: _____   weight: _____
object: _____   weight: _____
object: _____   weight: _____
object: _____   weight: _____
object: _____   weight: _____

Answers will vary.

255

Discovering Capacity   Sample answers given.

Capacity measures how much can fit inside an object.

You will need:
measuring cup (2 cup capacity)   tablespoon
pie tin   cake pan
1 cup of salt   1 cup of ice
bathroom sink   baking pan
1 gallon plastic jug   1 gallon freezer bag
2 liter plastic jug

Complete the tasks below to discover the capacity of objects around your house.

1. How many cups of water are there in a 1-gallon plastic jug? **16 cups**
2. How many tablespoons of salt does it take to fill up 1 cup? **16 T**
   How many tablespoons of water does it take to fill up ½ cup? **8 T**
3. Plug your bathroom sink. How many cups of water will it hold? **18 cups**
   How many gallons is that? **1½ gal.**
5. How many cups of water does it take to fill a pie tin? **4 cups**
6. Does a gallon-size plastic freezer bag really hold a gallon of something?
   No Count how many cups of water you can fit inside one. **14 cups**
   No Is that a gallon?
7. Fill a cake pan with water. Count how many cups it takes. **6 cups**
   If 2 cups = 1 pint, how many pints does it hold? **3 pints**
   If 2 pints = 1 quart, what is the quart capacity of your cake pan? **1½ qt.**

256

Discovering Capacity Equivalents
Sample answers given.

Gallons, quarts, cups and pints are used for measuring capacity in the U.S.A. You use them every day, but you probably don't measure them every time. When you pour milk on your cereal in the morning, you are estimating how much milk you will need to cover your breakfast. We are always making estimates.

You will need:
1 cup capacity measuring cup, pint, quart and half gallon containers, two 1-gallon capacity plastic jugs, water

Directions:
Set the two 1-gallon jugs beside each other. Fill one with water. Then, fill the measuring cups with water from the jug to determine the number of cups, pints, quarts and gallons of water it will take to fill the other jug.

1 cup — How many cups do you think it will take to fill
1 gallon? **16 cups**
The actual amount **15 cups**

1 pint (2 cups) — How many pints do you think it will take to fill
1 gallon? **8 pints**
The actual amount **7½ pints**

1 quart (2 pints) — How many quarts do you think it will take to fill
1 gallon? **4 quarts**
The actual amount **4 quarts**

1 half gallon (2 quarts) — How many half gallons do you think it will take to fill
1 gallon? **2 half gallons**
The actual amount **2 half gallons**

257

Comparing Temperatures   Sample answers vary.

Temperatures tell how warm or cold something is.
You will need: Fahrenheit thermometer
measuring cup (1 or 2 cup capacity)

Measure and **record** the temperatures of:
70° 1. Water from the tap
40° 2. The dairy section at the grocery store (Call or visit store to ask.)
102° 3. A pet's body temperature (Call or visit veterinarian.)
0° 4. Your freezer (Have your parents help you.)
100° 5. Bathtub water (Fill a cup from the bathtub and place the thermometer in it.)
85° 6. A cup of water outside in the sun
   • Place a cup of water in a safe place with the thermometer resting inside.
   • Let it set until the temperature stops rising.
   • Record the temperature.
   Is it the same as the temperature outside? **NO**
32° 7. A cup of ice water
98.6° 8. Your body temperature

Now, **compare.**

1. How many degrees warmer is the bathtub water than the tap water?
   30°
2. How many degrees difference is a pet's body temperature than yours?
   2.2° Who is warmer? **pet**
3. What is the difference between your freezer's temperature and the temperature in the dairy section of your grocery store? **40°**
4. What is the difference in temperature between a cup of water that has set out in the sun and a cup of ice water? **22°**

258

Weather Page

Examine the weather page from the newspaper for two or more consecutive days (preferably the two days prior to this activity).

Look for the following information:
time of sunrise and sunset for each day,
low temperature for each day,
high temperature for each day,
high and low tides (if applicable.)

How accurate was the forecast for:
time of sunrise and sunset for each day?
low temperature for each day?
high temperature for each day?
high and low tides?

time of sunrise	
time of sunset	
low temperature	
high tem...	
times...	
times of low tides	

Answers will vary.

259

Today's Temperature

Record the indoor and outdoor temperatures in degrees Celsius and Fahrenheit. Post the daily temperature on poster paper on your refrigerator. If desired, use an almanac or newspaper to share record high and low temperatures for each day.

Indoor temperature
(8 A.M. and 3 P.M.)

Outdoor temperature
(8 A.M. and 3 P.M.)

Extension: Create ongoing line graphs to show temperature differences. Each day, plot the temperatures. Display them near the daily temperature recordings.

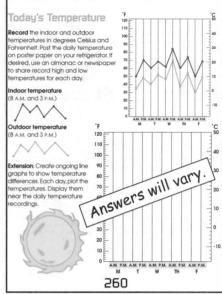

Answers will vary.

260

Super Shadows

Go outside to **measure** your shadow every hour on a sunny day. Have someone help you by **drawing** around your shadow with colored chalk. **Record** the time and length on your chart. Stand in the same place each time. Predict what will be different.
Were your predictions accurate? <u>Answers</u> will vary.

8 A.M. Shadows
Everyone's shadow is taller than really,
The shadows of giants are taller than trees.
The shadows of children are big as their parents,
And shadows of trotting dogs bend at the knees.
Everyone's shadow is taller than really,
Everyone's shadow is thinner than thin,
8 A.M. shadows are long at the dawning,
Pulling the night away,
Coaxing the light to say:
"Welcome, all shadows,
Day, please begin!"
Patricia Hubbel

Sample answers given.

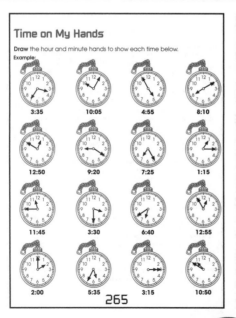

Time	Length of shadow
9:00 A.M.	8 ft.
10:00 A.M.	5 ft.
11:00 A.M.	13 in.
12:00 A.M.	1 in.
1:00 A.M.	12 in.
2:00 A.M.	4 ft.
3:00 A.M.	6 ft.

261

My Schedule

Keep track of what you do all day for a week on several copies of this page. **Write** the day and date at the start of the day. Then, **write** what you do and the time you do it. Each time you change activities, you should **write** a new time entry. At the end of the day, **add** how much time was spent in each type of activity. Some activities can be grouped together (i.e., breakfast, lunch, dinner = eating; social studies, language, math = school subjects; etc.). Tally up your activities on Friday.

Extension: Use the information collected to plot a pie graph, bar graph, line graph or pictograph.

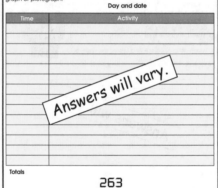

	Day and date
Time	Activity
Totals	

Answers will vary.

263

Timely Fun   Sample answers given.

Predict how many times you can do each activity in 1 minute. Then, **time** yourself and see how accurate your predictions were.

Say the alphabet.

Estimate: 20   Actual: 14

Clap your hands.

Estimate: 60   Actual: 42

Do 20 jumping jacks.

Estimate: 20   Actual: 15

Count to 20.

Estimate: 10   Actual: 8

Hop on one foot.

Estimate: 25   Actual: 20

Count backward from 20 to 1.

Estimate: 10   Actual: 8

264

Time on My Hands

Draw the hour and minute hands to show each time below.
Example:

3:35   10:05   4:55   8:10

12:50   9:20   7:25   1:15

11:45   3:30   6:40   12:55

2:00   5:35   3:15   10:50

265

Minute Men

Draw the hour and minute hands on these clocks.
Example:

4:42   9:03   6:51

1:24   7:33   10:11

3:58   12:01   2:49

4:17   5:36   8:23

266

Take Time for These

Write the time shown on these clocks.

Example:

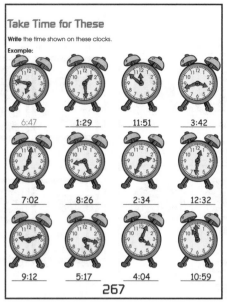

6:47	1:29	11:51	3:42
7:02	8:26	2:34	12:32
9:12	5:17	4:04	10:59

267

Father Time Teasers

Write the times below.

Example:

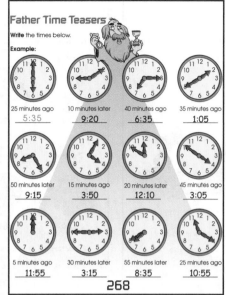

25 minutes ago	10 minutes later	40 minutes ago	35 minutes ago
5:35	9:20	6:35	1:05
50 minutes later	15 minutes ago	20 minutes later	45 minutes ago
9:15	3:50	12:10	3:05
5 minutes ago	30 minutes later	55 minutes later	25 minutes ago
11:55	3:15	8:35	10:55

268

Time "Tables"

Draw the hands on these clocks.

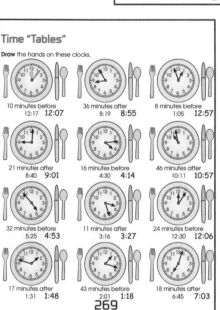

10 minutes before	36 minutes after	8 minutes before
12:17 12:07	8:19 8:55	1:05 12:57
21 minutes after	16 minutes before	46 minutes after
8:40 9:01	4:30 4:14	10:11 10:57
32 minutes before	11 minutes after	24 minutes before
5:25 4:53	3:16 3:27	12:30 12:06
17 minutes after	43 minutes before	18 minutes after
1:31 1:48	2:01 1:18	6:45 7:03

269

Feeding Time

The abbreviations **A.M.** and **P.M.** help tell the time of day. At midnight, A.M. begins. At noon, P.M. begins. Ken and Angie enjoy watching the animals being fed at the zoo. However, when they arrived, they were a little confused by the signs. Help them figure out the feeding time for each kind of animal. Be sure to include if it's A.M. or P.M.

Zebras: Feeding time is 2 hours after the monkeys.
2:00 P.M.

Tigers: Feeding time is 2 hours after 9:00 A.M.
11:00 A.M.

Elephants: Feeding time is 1:00 P.M.

Giraffes: Feeding time is 1 hour before the lions.
3:00 P.M.

Monkeys: Feeding time is 3 hours before the giraffes.
12:00 P.M.

Lions: Feeding time is 3 hours after the elephants.
4:00 P.M.

Now, **trace** the path in the zoo that Ken and Angie would take so that they could see all the animals being fed.

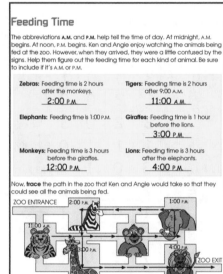

270

Monkeying Around

Nat can't tell time. He needs your help to **solve** these problems.

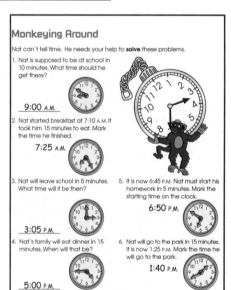

1. Nat is supposed to be at school in 10 minutes. What time should he get there?
   9:00 A.M.

2. Nat started breakfast at 7:10 A.M. It took him 15 minutes to eat. Mark the time he finished.
   7:25 A.M.

3. Nat will leave school in 5 minutes. What time will it be then?
   3:05 P.M.

4. Nat's family will eat dinner in 15 minutes. When will that be?
   5:00 P.M.

5. It is now 6:45 P.M. Nat must start his homework in 5 minutes. Mark the starting time on the clock.
   6:50 P.M.

6. Nat will go to the park in 15 minutes. It is now 1:25 P.M. Mark the time he will go to the park.
   1:40 P.M.

271

How Far Is It?

Drawing pictures can be a good problem-solving strategy. **Draw** pictures to help you **solve** the problems below. Each problem requires three answers.

1. Jimmy has to walk 12 blocks to get to the park where he likes to play ball. It takes him 3 minutes to walk one block. How many minutes will it take him to walk to the park? Sample diagram: J ―3―6―9―12―15―18―21―24―27―30―33―36― P
   Distance **12 blocks**   Speed **3 min. per block**   Time **36 min.**

2. An airplane leaves the airport at 9:00 A.M. It flies at 200 miles per hour. When it lands at 11:00 A.M., how far will it have gone?
   Distance **400 miles**   Speed **200 mph.**   Time **2 hrs.**

3. It is 50 miles between Dakota City and Blue Falls. It takes Mr. Oliver 1 hour to make the drive. How fast does he drive?
   Distance **50 miles**   Speed **50 mph.**   Time **1 hr.**

4. Tad rides his bike to his grandmother's house. It takes him 45 minutes to ride there. She lives 5 miles from his house. How many minutes does it take him to ride 1 mile?
   Distance **1 mile**   Speed **6.7 mph.**   Time **9 min.**

5. Rachel loves to visit her grandparents who live 150 miles from her house. When they make the trip, her dad drives. He averages 50 miles an hour. How many hours will the trip take?
   Distance **150 miles**   Speed **50 mph.**   Time **3 hrs.**

277

Time Problems

Draw the hands on the clocks to show the starting time and the ending time. Then, **write** the answer to the question.

1. The bike race started at 2:55 P.M. and lasted 2 hours and 10 minutes. What time did the race end?

   5:05 P.M.

4. Sherry walked in the 12-mile Hunger Walk. She started at 12:30 P.M. and finished at 4:50 P.M. How long did she walk?

   4 hrs. 20 min.

2. The 500-mile auto race started at 11:00 A.M. and lasted 2 hours and 25 minutes. What time did the race end?

   1:25 P.M.

5. The chili cook-off started at 10:00 A.M., and all the chili was cooked by 4:30 P.M. How long did it take to cook the chili?

   6½ hrs.

3. The train left Indianapolis at 7:25 A.M. and arrived in Chicago at 10:50 A.M. How long did the trip take?

   3 hrs. 25 min.

6. The chili judging began at 4:30 P.M. After 3 hours and 45 minutes the chili had all been eaten. At what time was the chili judging finished?

   8:15 P.M.

278

Racing Chimps

One chimpanzee in the forest always likes to brag that it can get more fruit than any other animal in the forest. So an older and wiser chimpanzee decided to challenge him to a race.

"Let us see who can bring back more bananas in 1 hour," said the older chimp. The race began.

Quickly, the younger chimp picked a bunch of five bananas and carried it back. He continued doing this every 5 minutes.

The older chimp was not quite as fast. Every 10 minutes he carried back eight bananas.

After 45 minutes, the young chimp decided to stop and eat one of his bananas before continuing. By the time he finished, the hour was over and the older chimp called out, "The race is over. Whose pile of bananas is bigger?"

Using the information above, figure out how many bananas were in each pile and which chimp won the race.

The younger chimp had __44__ bananas in his pile.

The older chimp had __48__ bananas in his pile.

The winner was the __older__ chimp!

285

Garage Sale

Use the fewest number of coins possible to equal the amount shown in each box. **Write** or **draw** the coins you would use in each box.

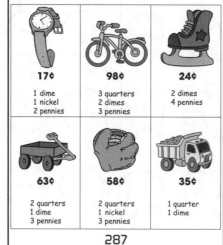

17¢ 1 dime 1 nickel 2 pennies	**98¢** 3 quarters 2 dimes 3 pennies	**24¢** 2 dimes 4 pennies
63¢ 2 quarters 1 dime 3 pennies	**58¢** 2 quarters 1 nickel 3 pennies	**35¢** 1 quarter 1 dime

287

Your Answer's Safe With Me

Find the right "combination" to open each safe. **Draw** the bills and coins needed to make each amount.

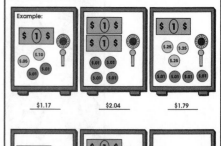

Example:

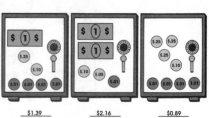

\$1.17	\$2.04	\$1.79

\$1.39	\$2.16	\$0.89

288

Easy Street

What is each house worth? **Count** the money in each house on Easy Street. **Write** the amount on the line below it.

Example:

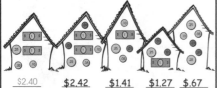

\$2.40   \$2.42   \$1.41   \$1.27   \$.67

\$1.51   \$1.57   \$1.31   \$2.01   \$2.07

289

A Collection of Coins

Write the number of coins needed to make the amount shown.

Money	Quarters	Dimes	Nickels	Pennies
76¢	3	0	0	1
45¢	1	2	0	0
98¢	3	2	0	3
40¢	1	1	1	0
84¢	3	0	1	4
62¢	2	1	0	2
31¢	1	0	1	1
\$1.42	5	1	1	2
\$1.98	7	2	0	3

290

Monetary Message

What's the smartest thing to do with your money? To find out, **solve** the following problems and **write** the matching letter above the answer.

$$\underset{\$42.71}{S} \ \underset{\$33.94}{A} \ \underset{\$50.42}{V} \ \underset{\$100.73}{E} \quad \underset{\$45.70}{I} \ \underset{\$2.39}{T},$$

$$\underset{\$33.94}{A} \ \underset{\$26.13}{N} \ \underset{\$88.02}{D} \quad \underset{\$45.70}{I} \ \underset{\$2.39}{T} \quad \underset{\$51.12}{W} \ \underset{\$45.70}{I} \ \underset{\$11.01}{L} \ \underset{\$11.01}{L}$$

$$\underset{\$33.94}{A} \ \underset{\$88.02}{D} \ \underset{\$88.02}{D} \quad \underset{\$55.76}{U} \ \underset{\$42.79}{P}!$$

$$V = \begin{array}{r} \$42.13 \\ + \ 8.29 \\ \hline \$50.42 \end{array} \quad A = \begin{array}{r} \$ 4.56 \\ + 29.38 \\ \hline \$33.94 \end{array} \quad N = \begin{array}{r} \$ 4.65 \\ + 21.48 \\ \hline \$26.13 \end{array} \quad S = \begin{array}{r} \$23.46 \\ + 19.25 \\ \hline \$42.71 \end{array}$$

$$P = \begin{array}{r} \$ 9.31 \\ + 33.48 \\ \hline \$42.79 \end{array} \quad L = \begin{array}{r} \$ 6.73 \\ + 4.28 \\ \hline \$11.01 \end{array} \quad E = \begin{array}{r} \$81.49 \\ + 19.24 \\ \hline \$100.73 \end{array} \quad T = \begin{array}{r} \$ .42 \\ 1.94 \\ + .03 \\ \hline \$2.39 \end{array}$$

$$U = \begin{array}{r} \$50.84 \\ + 4.92 \\ \hline \$55.76 \end{array} \quad I = \begin{array}{r} \$ 7.49 \\ + 38.21 \\ \hline \$45.70 \end{array}$$

$$D = \begin{array}{r} \$ 3.04 \\ + 84.98 \\ \hline \$88.02 \end{array} \quad W = \begin{array}{r} \$ 1.89 \\ + 49.23 \\ \hline \$51.12 \end{array}$$

291

Add 'Em Up!

Write the prices, then **add**. **Regroup**, when needed.

Prices: \$29.32, \$0.69, \$0.84, \$2.41, \$34.99, \$3.84, \$3.84, \$8.43, \$43.09, \$29.32, \$3.09, \$4.37

1. $\begin{array}{r} \$29.32 \text{ skateboard} \\ + \ 2.41 \text{ hat} \\ \hline \$31.73 \end{array}$

2. $\begin{array}{r} \$8.43 \text{ dictionary} \\ + 43.09 \text{ radio} \\ \hline \$51.52 \end{array}$

3. $\begin{array}{r} \$3.09 \text{ wallet} \\ + \ .84 \text{ goldfish} \\ \hline \$3.93 \end{array}$

4. $\begin{array}{r} \$ .69 \text{ hot dog} \\ + \ 4.37 \text{ watch} \\ \hline \$5.06 \end{array}$

5. $\begin{array}{r} \$8.43 \text{ dictionary} \\ + \ 3.84 \text{ kite} \\ \hline \$12.27 \end{array}$

6. $\begin{array}{r} \$29.32 \text{ in-line skates} \\ + 34.99 \text{ trumpet} \\ \hline \$64.31 \end{array}$

7. $\begin{array}{r} \$ .69 \text{ hot dog} \\ + \ 3.84 \text{ rocket} \\ \hline \$4.53 \end{array}$

8. $\begin{array}{r} \$29.32 \text{ skateboard} \\ + \ .84 \text{ goldfish} \\ \hline \$30.16 \end{array}$

9. $\begin{array}{r} \$ 2.41 \text{ hat} \\ + \ 3.84 \text{ kite} \\ \hline \$6.25 \end{array}$

10. $\begin{array}{r} \$43.09 \text{ radio} \\ + 34.99 \text{ trumpet} \\ \hline \$78.08 \end{array}$

11. $\begin{array}{r} \$ 3.84 \text{ rocket} \\ + \ .84 \text{ goldfish} \\ \hline \$4.68 \end{array}$

12. $\begin{array}{r} \$29.32 \text{ skateboard} \\ + 29.32 \text{ in-line skates} \\ \hline \$58.64 \end{array}$

292

Making Change

When you do not have the exact change to buy something at a store, the clerk must give you change. The first amount of money is what you give the clerk. The second amount is what the item costs. In the box, **list** the fewest number of coins and bills you will receive in change.

	Amount I Have	Cost of Item	Change
1	\$3.75	\$3.54	2 dimes, 1 penny
2	\$10.00	\$5.63	four 1 dollar bills, 1 quarter, 1 dime, 2 pennies
3	\$7.00	\$6.05	3 quarters, 2 dimes
4	\$7.25	\$6.50	3 quarters
5	\$7.50	\$6.13	1 dollar bill, 1 quarter, 1 dime, 2 pennies
6	\$0.75	\$0.37	1 quarter, 1 dime, 3 pennies
7	\$7.00	\$6.99	1 penny
8	\$15.00	\$12.75	two 1 dollar bills, 1 quarter

293

Super Savers!

Add to find the amounts of money each person saved.

Sam's Account	Debbie's Account	Sarah's Account	Roberto's Account
\$8.03 0.84 + 5.47 **\$14.34**	\$45.32 2.41 + 34.28 **\$82.01**	\$85.42 12.58 + 2.21 **\$100.21**	\$41.46 + 8.89 **\$50.35**

Alex's Account	Eva's Account	Bill's Account	Monica's Account
\$ 4.06 81.23 + 2.84 **\$88.13**	\$89.42 3.06 + 0.94 **\$93.42**	\$62.41 3.84 + 64.21 **\$130.46**	\$20.04 3.42 + 25.81 **\$49.27**

Tom's Account	Andy's Account	Earl's Account	Mark's Account
\$ 8.05 21.21 + 0.98 **\$30.24**	\$ 0.47 31.24 + 2.38 **\$34.09**	\$50.42 3.84 + 0.98 **\$55.24**	\$21.46 20.00 + 5.58 **\$47.04**

Katelyn's Account	Kimberly's Account	
\$ 0.42 0.59 + 3.42 **\$4.43**	\$ 5.42 40.64 + 3.89 **\$49.95**	Whose account is the largest? __Bill's__ Whose is the smallest? __Katelyn's__ Whose is closest to \$50? __Kimberly's__

299

350

Fast Food

Mealwormy is the latest restaurant of that famous fast food creator, Buggs I. Lyke. His Mealwormy Burger costs $1.69. An order of Roasted Roaches cost $0.59 for the regular size and $0.79 for the larger size. A Cricket Cola is $0.89.

1. You buy a Mealwormy Burger and a regular order of Roasted Roaches. What is the total? $1.69 + .59 = $2.28
2. Your teacher buys a Cricket Cola and a regular order of Roasted Roaches. What does it cost her? $ .89 + .59 = $1.48
3. Your mom goes to Mealwormy to buy your dinner. She spends $3.37. How much change does she get from a $5.00 bill? $5.00 − 3.37 = $1.63
4. Your best friend orders a Mealwormy Burger, a large order of Roasted Roaches and Cricket Cola. How much will it cost you? $1.69 + .79 + .89 = $3.37
5. The principal is very hungry, so his bill comes to $14.37. How much change will he get from $20.00? $20.00 − 14.37 = $ 5.63
6. You have $1.17 in your bank. How much more do you need to pay for a Mealwormy Burger? $1.69 − 1.17 = $ .52

300

Spending Spree

Use the clues to figure out what each person bought. Then, **subtract** to find out how much change each had left.

		Clue:	
1. David began with:	$40.25 − 9.31 = $30.94	He loves to see things zoom into the sky!	$9.31
2. Mark started with:	$50.37 − 47.29 = $3.08	He likes to travel places with his hands free and a breeze in his face!	$47.29
3. Eva started with:	$14.84 − 3.95 = $10.89	She loves to practice her jumping and exercise at the same time!	$3.95
4. Bill brought:	$61.49 − 52.28 = $9.21	He wants to see the heavens for himself!	$52.28
5. Michelle brought:	$40.29 − 32.51 = $7.78	Fuzzy companions make such great friends!	$32.51
6. Cheryl started with:	$16.80 − 12.49 = $4.31	She loves to hear music that is soft and beautiful!	$12.49
7. Heather arrived with:	$20.48 − 15.29 = $5.19	She loves to put it down on paper for everyone to see!	$15.29

Price tags: $12.49, $9.31, $21.52, $13.45, $15.29, $2.43, $3.95, $52.28, $32.51, $47.29

301

One-Stop Shopping

Stash McCash is shopping. **Add** to find the total cost of the items. Then, **subtract** to find out how much change Stash should receive.

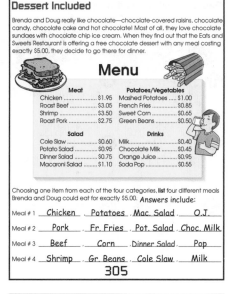

Price tags: $2.68, $3.36, $0.77, $3.15, $3.99, $0.27, $3.61, $1.54, $1.27, $1.49, $0.88, $4.25, $1.94, $2.55, $2.49

Example:

Stash has $5.00. He buys:	Stash has $8.50. He buys:	Stash has $7.04. He buys:	Stash has $9.00. He buys:
$0.88 + 0.77 + 1.54 = $3.19	$1.27 + 3.99 + 2.68 = $7.94	$1.49 + 3.15 + .27 = $4.91	$3.15 + 3.61 + .88 = $7.64
$5.00 − 3.19 = $1.81 Change	$8.50 − 7.94 = $ .56 Change	$7.04 − 4.91 = $2.13 Change	$9.00 − 7.64 = $1.36 Change

Stash has $10.95. He buys:	Stash has $10.00. He buys:	Stash has $9.24. He buys:	Stash has $8.09. He buys:
$3.36 + 2.49 + 4.25 = $10.10	$2.55 + 3.61 + 1.94 = $8.10	$4.25 + 1.27 + 1.54 = $7.06	$2.49 + 2.68 + 1.94 = $7.11
$10.95 − 10.10 = $ .85 Change	$10.00 − 8.10 = $1.90 Change	$9.24 − 7.06 = $2.18 Change	$8.09 − 7.11 = $ .98 Change

302

Match the Sale

Which item did each child purchase? **Calculate** the amount. **Write** each purchase price below.

Jessica:	Tammy:	Heather:	Mark:	Eva:
$17.43 − 8.29 = $9.14	$43.21 − 8.35 = $34.86	$10.06 − 8.42 = $1.64	$52.46 − 38.29 = $14.17	$65.04 − 28.10 = $36.94
pants	shirt	CD	rocket	helmet

Monica:	Katelyn:	David:	Curt:	Michele:
$6.99 − 3.43 = $3.56	$9.06 − 3.82 = $5.24	$15.25 − 8.43 = $6.82	$63.45 − 17.29 = $46.16	$32.45 − 18.95 = $13.50
cereal	drink	telescope	shovel	skateboard

Gwen:	Thomas:
$19.24 − 12.86 = $6.38	$9.43 − 3.84 = $5.59
soccer ball	brush

Price tags: $8.29, $28.10, $38.29, $17.29, $8.43, $8.42, $8.35, $3.84, $3.82, $3.43, $18.95, $12.86

303

What a Great Catch!

Solve these problems.

Fish prices: A $2.47, B $1.69, C $2.18, D $2.36, E $3.29, F $3.62, G $1.77, H $2.54, I $4.39, J $3.76

You buy fish A, C and H. Total cost: $2.47 + 2.18 + 2.54 = $7.19	You have $4.00. You buy fish D. How much money is left? $4.00 − 2.36 = $1.64	You have $10.00. You buy fish E and J. How much money is left? $3.29 + 3.76 = $7.05; $10.00 − 7.05 = $2.95
You buy 4 of fish I. $4.39 × 4 = $17.56. Total cost: $17.56	You have $5.75. You buy fish G and C. How much money is left? $1.77 + 2.18 = $3.95; $5.75 − 3.95 = $1.80	You buy fish D, F, J and B. $2.36 + 3.62 + 3.76 + 1.69. Total cost: $11.43
You buy 6 of fish E. $3.29 × 6. Total cost: $19.74	You buy 3 of fish J and 6 of fish D. $3.76 × 3 = $11.28; $2.36 × 6 = $14.16; $14.16 + 11.28. Total cost: $25.44	You have $10.76. You buy 3 of fish A. How much money is left? $2.47 × 3 = $7.41; $10.76 − 7.41 = $3.35

304

Dessert Included

Brenda and Doug really like chocolate—chocolate-covered raisins, chocolate candy, chocolate cake and hot chocolate! Most of all, they love chocolate sundaes with chocolate chip ice cream. When they find out that the Eats and Sweets Restaurant is offering a free chocolate dessert with any meal costing exactly $5.00, they decide to go there for dinner.

Menu

Meat		Potatoes/Vegetables	
Chicken	$1.95	Mashed Potatoes	$1.00
Roast Beef	$3.05	French Fries	$0.85
Shrimp	$3.50	Sweet Corn	$0.65
Roast Pork	$2.75	Green Beans	$0.50
Salad		**Drinks**	
Cole Slaw	$0.60	Milk	$0.40
Potato Salad	$0.95	Chocolate Milk	$0.45
Dinner Salad	$0.75	Orange Juice	$0.95
Macaroni Salad	$1.10	Soda Pop	$0.55

Choosing one item from each of the four categories, **list** four different meals Brenda and Doug could eat for exactly $5.00. Answers include:

Meal # 1 Chicken, Potatoes, Mac. Salad, O.J.
Meal # 2 Pork, Fr. Fries, Pot. Salad, Choc. Milk.
Meal # 3 Beef, Corn, Dinner Salad, Pop
Meal # 4 Shrimp, Gr. Beans, Cole Slaw, Milk

305

What's for Lunch?

Answers may vary.

Solve these problems.

Lunch Menu			
Salad	$2.25	**Beverages**	
Hot Dog	$1.10	Milk	$0.50
Grilled cheese	$1.00	Orange Juice	$0.60
Pizza	$0.90	Soda	$0.75
Dessert			
Pudding	$0.90		
Ice Cream	$0.85		

1. Craig, Thomas and Laura stopped for lunch on their long trip. Craig had a late breakfast and only wanted some milk to drink. Thomas was feeling a little carsick, so he simply wanted a soda. Laura was very hungry. They spent a total of $4.25. What could Laura have had for lunch?
   Salad and soda
2. Beth and Michelle stopped for lunch during their busy day of shopping. They had worked up quite an appetite after all their bargain hunting! Beth exclaimed, "I'll buy you lunch today, Michelle. After all, you've helped me carry these packages all day!" "Thank you," Michelle replied. Beth reached into her pocket to be sure of the amount of money she had left. "Oh, no!" Beth cried, "I must have lost some money! I only have $3.50 left!" What could they have eaten for lunch?
   Grilled cheese and soda
3. Diane spent $1.60 on lunch. She was too full to get dessert. What could she have had for lunch?
   Hot dog and milk
4. The twins had too much pizza for dinner last night and certainly did not want it today. They each had the same meal, including pudding for dessert. They spent $5.50. What could they have eaten for lunch?
   Hot dogs, sodas and pudding
5. Sue is a vegetarian and she's allergic to milk. Bob ate two slices of pizza and a soda. Together, their lunch cost them $5.40. What did Sue have for lunch?
   Salad and O.J.

306

Multiplying Money

Money is multiplied in the same way other numbers are. The only difference is a dollar sign and a decimal point are added to the final product.

Steps:

1. Multiply by ones.
   1. 4 x 8 = 32 (Carry the 3.)
   2. 4 x 2 = 8 + 3 = 11 (Carry the 1.)
   3. 4 x 4 = 16 + 1 = 17

   $4.28 × 34 → 1712
2. 1. Cross out the carried digits.
   2. Add the zero.

   $4.28 × 34 → 1712, 0
3. Multiply by tens.
   1. 3 x 8 = 24 (Carry the 2.)
   2. 3 x 2 = 6 + 2 = 8
   3. 3 x 4 = 12

   $4.28 × 34 → 1712, 12840
4. Add.
   1,712 + 12,840 = 14,552

   $4.28 × 34 → 1712 + 12840 = 14,552
5. Add the dollar sign and the decimal point.

   $4.28 × 34 → 1712 + 12840 = $145.52

Multiply.

$3.42 × 25 = $85.50	$5.42 × 61 = $330.62
$3.81 × 46 = $175.26	$8.20 × 55 = $451.00
$9.42 × 31 = $292.02	$4.23 × 96 = $406.08

307

Foxy Felix's Shop

Solve these problems.

SALE
10% off
50% off on all CDs

1. Mighty Man comics cost $0.13 at Foxy Felix's. You buy 4 of these comics. How much should you pay? $0.13 × 4 = $ .52
2. Your best friend bought 9 marbles at Foxy Felix's. Each marble cost $0.19. How much money did he spend? $0.19 × 9 = $1.71
3. Baseball cards are $0.11 each at Foxy Felix's. How much will it cost you for 8 cards? $0.11 × 8 = $ .88
4. Your sister decides to buy 2 CDs of the latest hit single by the Bird Brains. Each CD costs $0.89. How much will she pay? $ .89 × 2 = $1.78
5. Crazy stickers cost $0.21 each at Foxy Felix's. You buy 7 of them. How much should you pay? $0.21 × 7 = $1.47
6. Stinky Stickers have a skunk odor. Your best friend bought 7 Stinky Stickers which cost $0.18 each. How much did he spend? $0.18 × 7 = $1.26

308

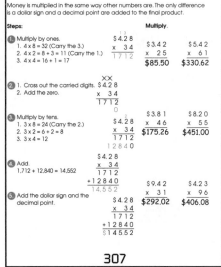

Money Math

Solve these problems. Remember the decimal point and dollar sign in your answers.

$3.42 x 27 $92.34	$2.45 x 34 $83.30	$6.42 x 56 $359.52	$8.43 x 30 $252.90
$0.49 x 56 $27.44	$2.53 x 41 $103.73	$8.21 x 37 $303.77	$4.21 x 36 $151.56
$5.41 x 42 $227.22	$0.21 x 84 $17.64	$0.89 x 32 $28.48	$4.25 x 31 $131.75

309

Science Trip

The science class is planning a field trip to Chicago to visit the Museum of Science and Industry. There are 18 students in the class and each student needs $40.00 to cover the expenses. The class decided to sell candy to raise money.

Answer the questions using the chart below.

Weekly Class Sales				
	Week One	Week Two	Week Three	Week Four
Amount Raised	$282.00	$176.00	$202.00	$150.00

1. What is the weekly average of money raised during 4 weeks of candy sales?

$202.50

3. Did the class meet its goal of $40.00 per child?

Yes

2. What is the average amount of dollars raised per child during 4 weeks of candy sales?

$45.00

4. How much above or beneath their goal per child did the class earn?

$5.00

310

Too Much Information

Cross out the information not needed and solve the problems.

1. All 20 of the students from Sandy's class went to the movies. Tickets cost $3.50 each. Drinks cost $0.95 each. How much altogether did the students spend on tickets? $70.00

2. Five students had ice cream, 12 others had candy. Ice cream cost $0.75 per cup. How much did the students spend on ice cream? $3.75

3. Seven of the 20 students did not like the movie. Three of the 20 students had seen the movie before. How many students had not seen the movie before? 17 students

4. Six of the students spent a total of $16.50 for refreshments and $21.00 for their tickets. How much did each spend for refreshments? $2.75

5. Of the students, 11 were girls and 9 were boys. At $1.50 per ticket, how much did the boys' tickets cost altogether? $13.50

6. Mary paid $0.95 for an orange drink and $0.65 for a candy bar. Sarah paid $2.50 for popcorn. How much did Mary's refreshments cost her? $1.60

7. Ten of the students went back to see the movie again the next day. Each student paid $3.50 for a ticket, $2.50 for popcorn and $0.95 for a soft drink. How much did each student pay? $6.95

311

Sam Sillicook's Donut Shop

Solve these problems.

1. Your mom bought 32 Jam-filled Cream Puffs. They cost $0.89 each. How much did your mom spend?

$28.48

2. Harry D. Hulk bought 14 Banana Cream Donuts for his breakfast at $0.65 each. How much did they cost Harry?

$9.10

3. Your best friend bought 12 Cinnamon Twists at $0.29 each. How much did he spend?

$3.48

4. You love Jam-filled Cream Puffs. Your mother buys 17 for your birthday party at $0.89 each. How much do they cost?

$15.13

5. Your dad decided to take the whole family out. He bought 24 Super Duper Jelly Donuts at $0.49 each. What was the total cost?

$11.76

6. You took 40 Banana Cream Donuts to school. They cost $0.65 each. What was the total?

$26.00

312

Perplexing Problems

Solve these problems.

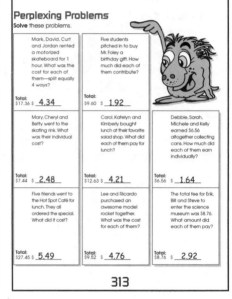

Mark, David, Curt and Jordan rented a motorized skateboard for 1 hour. What was the cost for each of them—split equally 4 ways?
Total: $17.36 $ 4.34

Five students pitched in to buy Mr. Foley a birthday gift. How much did each of them contribute?
Total: $9.60 $ 1.92

Mary, Cheryl and Betty went to the skating rink. What was their individual cost?
Total: $7.44 $ 2.48

Carol, Katelyn and Kimberly bought lunch at their favorite salad shop. What did each of them pay for lunch?
Total: $12.63 $ 4.21

Debbie, Sarah, Michele and Kelly earned $6.56 altogether collecting cans. How much did each of them earn individually?
Total: $6.56 $ 1.64

Five friends went to the Hot Spot Café for lunch. They all ordered the special. What did it cost?
Total: $27.45 $ 5.49

Lee and Ricardo purchased an awesome model rocket together. What was the cost for each of them?
Total: $9.52 $ 4.76

The total fee for Erik, Bill and Steve to enter the science museum was $8.76. What amount did each of them pay?
Total: $8.76 $ 2.92

313

Let's Take a Trip!

You will plan a car trip to calculate approximately how much the trip will cost. You will calculate distances between locations and the amount of gasoline needed based upon miles per gallon of the car. Then, you will estimate the cost of the gasoline, hotel, food and entertainment.

Directions: Using graph paper, plot out your trip starting and ending at "point A." The trip should have five points of travel, including point A. Each square on the graph paper represents 10 miles. Calculate the mileage between points.

Use a copy of the **Expense Chart** on page 143 to keep track of your calculations. Use newspapers, travel brochures and menus to help you estimate the cost of food, gas, hotels, entertainment, etc. You will also want to use a calculator. When you have completed the **Expense Chart**, answer the questions below.

Sample answers given.

1. If two people go on this trip, how will the cost change? _it will increase_
2. If a family of four goes on the trip, how will the cost change? _up to 4 x amount_
3. Would the cost of gas change? _No_
   Why or why not? _going in one car, same distance_
4. What else could change the cost of the trip? _car repairs_
5. Why is this just an estimate? _must take actual trip to find exact cost_

314

Expense Chart Sample answers given.

Distance to travel
Miles from Point A to Point B: _100_
Miles from Point B to Point C: _65_
Miles from Point C to Point D: _50_
Miles from Point D to Point E: _75_
Miles from Point E to Point A: _190_
Total miles to travel: _480_

Your car gets 22 miles per gallon of gas.
Total gas needed: _22 gal._
Gas costs $1.19 per gallon.
Total amount needed for gas: _$26.18_

You will stay at a hotel/motel for four nights at $79.00 per night.
Total cost for four nights: _$316_

Estimated food cost per day (5 days)
breakfast—$2.50
lunch—$4.75
dinner—$9.25
Total per day: _$16.50_
Total for 5 days: _$82.50_

Estimated entertainment expenses
Admission to movies: _$25_
Admission to museums: _$40_
Admission to theme parks: _$100_
Admission to sports events: _$125_

Add all the entries to get a total estimate for the cost of the trip.
Total estimated cost of the trip: _$714.68_

315

Mind-Bogglers

Solve these problems. Then, explain your strategies.

1. Marta receives an allowance of $2.25 a week. This week, her mom pays her in nickels, dimes and quarters. She received more dimes than quarters.
   What coins did her mom use to pay her? _12 dimes, 4 quarters, 1 nickel_
   Strategy I used: _trial and error_

2. Mr. Whitman takes his family on a trip to the amusement park. He brings $75 with him to buy the entrance tickets, food and souvenirs for the family. The tickets to get into the amusement park are $12.75 for adults and $8.45 for children. How much money will Mr. Whitman have for food and souvenirs after he buys entrance tickets for himself, Mrs. Whitman and their two children?
   Amount of money? _$32.60_
   Strategy I used: _figured total entrance cost by multiplying, then used subtraction_

3. There are four children who worked at the car wash. Kelly worked 4 hours. Jack worked 3 hours. Matt and Tammy worked 2 hours. They made $110. How much of that did Kelly earn? _$40_
   Jack? _$30_ Matt and Tammy? _$40_
   Strategy I used: _found amount per hour first_

4. Mrs. Downs gives her three children a weekly allowance. She pays them in dollar bills. Lauren is the first to get paid. She receives half the number of dollar bills her mom has. Don gets his allowance second. He receives half of the remaining dollar bills plus one. Mrs. Downs now has $2 left, which is Edith's allowance. How much allowance do Lauren and Don receive?
   Lauren _$6_ Don _$4_
   Strategy I used: _worked backwards, trial and error_

316
